THE RACKET

THE RACKET

HOW ABORTION BECAME LEGAL IN AUSTRALIA

GIDEON HAIGH

MELBOURNE
UNIVERSITY
PRESS

MELBOURNE UNIVERSITY PRESS
An imprint of Melbourne University Publishing Limited
187 Grattan Street, Carlton, Victoria 3053, Australia
mup-info@unimelb.edu.au
http://www.mup.com.au

First published 2008

Text design by Peter Long
Typeset by Midland Typesetters, Australia
Printed by Griffin Press, South Australia

National Library of Australia Cataloguing-in-Publication entry:

Haigh, Gideon.

The racket / Gideon Haigh.

9780522855784 (pbk.)

Includes index.
Bibliography.

Abortion—Australia—History.
Abortion—Law and legislation—Australia.
Women—Crimes against—Australia.
Women—Australia—Social conditions.

363.460994

For Charlotte

Contents

Prologue

It wouldn't be pleasant, but it had to be done—and, surely, people did it all the time. He knew someone. There need be no fuss. Mum mustn't know; it would break her heart. And Dad, he was so sad lately; he wouldn't understand. But, if they were careful, nobody ever had to find out.

~

Carolyn Jamieson was an attractive woman, attractive enough to turn heads in a room, with blonde hair and a curvy figure that lent her a faint resemblance to Marilyn Monroe. She was twenty-one, but seemed younger, warm and ingenuous. One day, a man had walked into the city pharmacy where she worked as a cosmetician and had asked for French letters. She had smiled: French what? Into her favourite romance novels, such details seldom intruded. Oh, Carolyn wanted children: lots, even. But she fancied working a while yet. She liked her job, enjoyed her independence.

In March 1967, she met a boy at the Bendigo Trots. Johnny Glide was a farmhand working on a property at Doreen, 32 kilometres north of Melbourne. He was soon sweet on her. They visited the pix together, the theatre, parties. She was keenest, though, for him to teach her to drive in his pink and white 1960 Holden sedan. She wanted to simplify commuting between her parents, who had parted some years earlier, and to whom she paid courteously even-handed attention: mother Molly, now in a flat in Preston, and father Norman, who lived in a house in Northcote.

And that was how it happened. One night Johnny visited Carolyn while Norman was working the nightshift as a typesetter at *The Age*... and, after the first furtive grapplings, it was easy. Too easy. Because before too long, Carolyn was complaining of feeling unwell. Her health had never been robust. She was anaemic and had inherited bronchial asthma from her father. But this was different. She was dizzy, nauseous ... then her period, vigilantly monitored, did not come.

There were, her sister counselled, tablets for this sort of thing. Carolyn went to a pharmacy with instructions to ask for 'Green Label Pills', the aloes and iron in which were reputed to bring on menstruation. The bottle bore the legend 'Must Not Be Taken During Pregnancy'—a warning or an enticement, depending on one's position. Feeling a little more confident, she joined her friend Loretta at the trots on the night of 16 December 1967, even showing off a new dress. 'You look a million dollars tonight', smiled Johnny. Carolyn, he recalled, beamed back: 'She was proud of herself for looking a million dollars'.

She wasn't so proud of what else she had to do. At her first attempt to tell Johnny she might be pregnant, Carolyn tried to make light of the situation. Johnny grimaced. 'You're kidding', he said. Carolyn laughed, still hoping the pills would work their magic—no more was said. But the pills merely made Carolyn feel worse. As each day passed, she struggled with her conscience. Molly was Catholic; not a censorious or proselytising one, but Carolyn couldn't bear the thought of disappointing her. And her father—Norman had once said he would shoot any young man who so much as laid hands on her. He spoke that way: a taciturn man, coarsened by three and a half years of war service, who lived alone with his dog, Honey. How could she explain this to *him*? She was anxious; constipated too. From her pharmacy she obtained a sedative, amylobarbitone, and a laxative, coloxyl, although she was too embarrassed to buy a pregnancy test.

On Christmas Eve, Carolyn and Johnny were at the Preston drive-in, neither of them quite able to concentrate on missionary couple Max von Sydow and Julie Andrews converting the heathen in *Hawaii*. Carolyn could wait no longer. 'Johnny,' she said finally, 'I think I'm pregnant'. Johnny had been brooding on the possibility. Through his estate agent brother, he had recently bought a house on Eight Mile Lane near Donnybrook. It was small—58 hectares—but it was a start. Johnny wanted to do the right thing; they would get married.

Carolyn squirmed: 'Not this way'. She wanted marriage and children, but not now: she was young; she wasn't ready. They would have to do something. But first, she had to know for sure if she was pregnant. When they met again on Boxing Day at her mother's flat, Carolyn had written on a piece of paper the name of a drug that would act as a pregnancy test; Johnny would have to get it. He made an appointment with Dr Hoban, whose surgery was just up the road from his farm, and who lent a sympathetic ear. He made out the script, and advised that if it came to *that* to 'get the best'. In fact, Johnny had an idea he knew where to go. When the test confirmed Carolyn's apprehensions, Johnny renewed an old acquaintance.

Dr Billy Flynn was seventy, an old-fashioned but well-established consulting physician who had graduated from Melbourne University in 1922. He still practised from rooms in respectable Alcaston House at Collins Street's so-called 'Paris End', still with a fresh carnation in his buttonhole every day. He was an old friend of the Glides; in fact, he had delivered Johnny. Word was also that he knew what to do in such situations. And when Johnny called unannounced at his surgery at 6.30 p.m. on Thursday 4 January 1968, Flynn was at once reassuring. 'Long time no see', he said. 'How are you my boy?' Then, sensing the young man's apprehension: 'You can speak freely to me. Is it a girl in trouble?' Johnny confirmed it was. 'Do you love her?' asked Flynn. Johnny confirmed he did. Flynn cut straight to the invoice: 'It will cost $300 and be no trouble and no risk'.

Johnny wasn't expecting it to be so matter-of-fact. His mind was suddenly blank of the questions he'd stewed over, save one. 'Will she be able to have babies after the operation?' he asked. 'Oh, yes', Flynn nodded: people were *so* superstitious. He wanted to close the deal. 'What about the money?' he asked. Johnny's mind was racing. 'It will be all right', he said presently. 'I haven't got it on me at the moment but I'll send Carol in with $200.' Flynn was comfortable with instalments. 'Bring the other $100 in after the operation', he said. 'Then you can tell me if she's all right.'

Flynn's practicality impressed Johnny. And, indeed, Flynn was a veteran of Melbourne's illegal abortion rackets: a Catholic who put patients, and money, ahead of his coreligionists' objections to the practice. What Johnny wasn't to know was that Flynn was slipping—an old man losing his touch. For one thing, he had grown enormously fat, and somewhat clumsy. Pete Steedman, editor of Melbourne University's *Farrago*, knew Flynn as a family friend, but would never have sought his professional services: 'These were delicate things, and I never thought of Billy as particularly delicate. For one thing, he was so large I couldn't see how he'd get close enough to the table to do the operation'. Johnny Glide's question about the physical impact of abortion was unconsciously apposite. A few years earlier, Flynn had, at great expense, aborted the 15-year-old daughter of a wealthy Melbourne family, and botched the procedure so badly as to necessitate a total hysterectomy. But news of the mishap circulated only among colleagues; neither Johnny nor Carolyn had any means of knowing.

When Carolyn kept her appointment late the next day, Flynn was distracted, disorganised, tired. He thought his patient 'a smart sort of girl'—'too smart for Glide', in fact—but found her too nervous for a physical examination: 'She tightened up. They crawl up the wall sometimes'. Never mind, Flynn thought; he knew the ropes. Abortion was not so straightforward as it had been. In the early 1960s there had been plenty of money for everyone, with the police disposed to look the other way. Lately, that had changed. The pill was in increasingly widespread use. Those two young doctors in East Melbourne, Bayliss and Sizeland, had gone on trial; veteran William Fenton Bowen had been charged, charming Ken Davidson raided. But Flynn's old friend John Heath, whose rooms were in the next block, had seldom been busier, and Flynn took no chances with raids these days; he used his lock-up premises at 72 Jolimont Street, with their inconspicuous frontage and silent number, for anything on the law's edge. It was at this address, a stone's throw from the Melbourne Cricket Ground, that Carolyn was advised to present on Tuesday morning.

At the weekend, Carolyn told her mother she was planning to go away for a few days, and had booked herself into a Dandenong motel. She was wearing one of her prettiest dresses, yellow with pink stripes, when Johnny collected her at 7.30 p.m. on Monday evening. Molly smiled down from her window; Carolyn, white suitcase in one hand, waved with the other. After a slow drive through Warrandyte, Carolyn rang Molly from her hotel room at about 9 p.m. 'I've got a nice room, mum', she said. 'It's nice here. I'll write you a letter tomorrow and tell you about it.' They never spoke again.

~

The irony of the last death during an illegal abortion in Victoria is that the abortion didn't take place. Carolyn arrived at 8.45 a.m. on Tuesday, to be greeted by Flynn's buxom assistant, June Horak. Flynn arrived an hour later, delayed by a procedure at Allendale Private Hospital, and having been unable to secure an anaesthetist's services. In his haste, he largely ignored Carolyn's medical history, so had no knowledge of her asthma, and no idea of the medication she had been taking. What happened then happened so quickly. No sooner had Flynn administered 7.5cc of pentothal and 10cc of water than Carolyn gave a little cough, shuddered and stopped breathing. Flynn had an oxygen cylinder but it was empty; he had to rely on mouth-to-mouth resuscitation and an old-fashioned air viva, but even an injection of adrenaline had no impact. Panic set in. Flynn told his nurse to ring other doctors who might be able to help, including Heath, but nobody could—and it soon became clear Carolyn was not responding.

What did one do? At least, Flynn consoled himself, he had not even started on the abortion; he could claim he had been intending a routine vaginal examination, perhaps for colitis, even though a general anaesthetic for a two-minute examination would hardly convince anyone medically competent. But he wasn't thinking straight, couldn't even imagine what to do with the body. Finally, he rang coroner Harry Pascoe, but Pascoe was away. A senior constable at the Coroner's Court counselled him to call the East Melbourne police. Constable Frederick Seymour arrived to find Flynn prowling around his operating theatre, explaining that Carolyn had been 'highly strung' and 'very nervous'. Carolyn's body lay undisturbed, feet turned out, head to one side, petticoat incongruously round her middle. When Seymour peered furtively at her vagina, Flynn tried sounding firm: 'You need not think anything like that happened because it didn't'.

Searching Carolyn's yellow handbag yielded more dividends: police found her sedative, her laxative and addresses. The scenario was familiar enough for routine deductions: this would be the boy, this the mother, this the father. And, under section 65 of Victoria's *Crimes Act*, all were potential conspirators in the felony of 'procuring a miscarriage'. Just after 2 p.m., uniformed police fanned out over the Northlands shopping precinct, where Molly Jamieson worked; in fact, they walked straight into her shop asking for 'Mary James'. The boss turned them away, but Molly had been baptised Mary and ran after them, catching them up outside Sportsgirl. 'Excuse me', she panted. 'What name are you looking for?'

'What's your name?' one asked.

'Mary Jamieson', she answered.

'No', said the policeman. 'I'm looking for a Mary James.'

Checks were evidently made because two Homicide Squad detectives walked into Molly's shop an hour later. They were in plain clothes, but unmistakable: there was something about the way they carried themselves, like they owned the place, and the way they briskly approached the only man in the shop, as though this could only be discussed with another male. They conversed in the lunch room at the rear of the premises, from which the boss presently emerged to ask Molly in. She could sense an impending tragedy: the death of a friend, a relative, maybe even Norm, whose brother had committed suicide the previous year. The shock was worse for her feeling prepared yet never suspecting it might be her daughter.

'Your name Mary Adelaide Jamieson?' one of the detectives asked brusquely.

'Yes.'

'You got a daughter Carolyn Mary Jamieson?'

'Well, she's dead.'

Molly Jamieson was not a woman who panicked. She'd had the nerve to leave an unhappy marriage, the nerve to resume work; she disapproved of needless hysterics. So somehow she held herself together, and remained standing with these two grim-faced strangers in the lunch room. 'Oh,' conjectured a detective, 'you knew she was going to have an abortion'.

'What? Look, oh honestly... an abortion?'

'Go on. Of course you knew... you know Dr William Flynn.'

It was too much. Molly burst from the lunch room, screaming: 'Carolyn's dead! Carolyn's dead!'. The detectives announced that they would be taking her to Russell Street CIB, and Molly found herself being frogmarched through Myer, a detective at each shoulder, like she had been caught pilfering or playing up. As she was squeezed into the squad car, she felt an overpowering need to urinate, and begged to use the toilet. She was told she could wait.

Interrogation there lasted four hours. Unbeknownst to Molly, her husband and Johnny Glide were being questioned in other rooms in order to triangulate their stories. In the hiatuses between questions, a senior sergeant took pity on her. He had recently lost his brother, he explained; there was nothing worse than losing one's own flesh and blood. They found themselves comforting one another. Just then, the door burst open and a senior detective stood in the doorway, arms akimbo. 'Come on, get on with it!' he growled. 'Of course you know all about it.'

Molly looked at the floor, trying to take stock of the situation. 'I can't believe it', she said. 'I can't believe it.' The senior detective's mood was black. 'All right, come on', he sneered. 'We'll take you down to the morgue and you can have a look at her…' The senior sergeant paused, not knowing if this was an order or merely a threat. Fortunately, the detective stormed out. Finally, Molly was brought a cup of tea. In the way the stimulated mind has of retaining minor detail, she would always recall the cup, old, stained and cracked, hinting at the tens of thousands of mouths that had drained it.

As Molly was emerging from her interview room after completing her statement, she ran into Johnny Glide. He burst into tears and hugged her. Then she saw her husband. Norm was a cold man, sullen and uncommunicative, a heavy, solitary drinker. Now, she thought, he looked pathetic, bedraggled, shrunken. But they had never lied to one another. 'Did you know about it?' Norm said quietly. 'No', said Molly. It was never mentioned again. After that, their exchanges were practical: she accepted the offer of a lift to her brother's home. Norm headed for an empty house, and Honey's company. Molly felt a pang of pity. Her husband looked so alone.

~

The evidence was unambiguous. The parents might have been ignorant, but Johnny Glide was clearly a conspirator, and an indemnity from prosecution would almost certainly persuade him to testify against Flynn. When four detectives and a constable descended on Alcaston House at 2.35 p.m. on 10 January, Flynn stuck to his colitis story but without much conviction. Senior Detective Kevin Carton, investigator in the celebrated Tait case, was one of Homicide's most relentless officers; his offsider, Senior Detective Noel Murphy, had been intimately involved in Homicide's abortion crackdown. Like their boss, Inspector Frank Holland, they were both Catholics. They could sense Flynn's confusion and vulnerability as he fretted: 'Everything went wrong. What the hell. She had been taking pills. You do not really know with these kids'. Asked to describe his resuscitation procedure, Flynn sounded less like a doctor of half a century's experience than a disoriented and agitated old man.

Flynn: I knew she was gone.
Question: Did you consider calling in another doctor?
Flynn: Yes but I couldn't think of where to get one.
Question: Did you try?
Flynn: Yes I did.
Question: Who did you try?
Flynn: We rang up…I'm not sure of his name. June rang someone, I think it was a friend of someone who works with Dr Heath. I think she tried Dr Heath too. I couldn't tell you where.
Question: You know the Royal Melbourne Hospital has an emergency staff for this sort of problem?
Flynn: Yes I thought of that, but it was too late. She was gone. I got a bit rattled.
Question: Yes, but you had Mrs Horak there…
Flynn: Yes, but you still get rattled.

By the end of the interview, Flynn had been rattled into unintelligibility, murmuring to himself rather than responding to questions.

Flynn: I'm not going to do any rough stuff anymore. The pill has upset doing curettages. I think that's it.
Question: What do you call the rough stuff?
Flynn: [unintelligible] rough stuff.
Question: You said you're not doing it? Is that correct?
Flynn: I haven't been doing them and I haven't done any.
Question: What do you call the rough stuff?
Flynn: Cleaning up after others. There's always some [unintelligible] cleaning up.
Question: Well, this girl was, Doctor, there for the purpose of an abortion. You gave her a needle in order to commit a felony and she died. That, according to the law, is manslaughter.
Flynn: Yes.
Question: Well, it is my duty and intention to charge you with manslaughter. It is my duty to warn you that you are not obliged to say anything or make any statement, but anything you do say will

be taken down in writing and may be given in evidence. Do you wish to say anything?

Flynn: No.

Before Flynn faced his trial, the Jamiesons faced their own. There was the funeral, grimly edged with silence. There was the inquest, where it was revealed that Carolyn had been eight weeks' pregnant, and the anaesthetics director at Royal Melbourne Hospital disagreed with Flynn's counsel that the anaesthetic was minor: 'No local anaesthetic is minor. People die under local anaesthetics...I do not think there are minor anaesthetics; there might be anaesthetics for minor procedures'. There was also, inevitably, media coverage, although not in the strait-laced metropolitan dailies. There it was in the scandal sheet *Truth*, home of screaming headlines and arbitrary capitalisation: 'A beautiful 21-year-old blonde has been FOUND DEAD in an old house. Police say she died during an illegal OPERATION'.

Molly coped; her husband became still more withdrawn, leaving his job, and drinking a bottle of whisky a day in addition to three or four bottles of beer. A lightly built man, he seemed in danger of fading away entirely. Perhaps he even wished he could, for he began to hint to Molly of suicidal designs. Then, on 14 December 1968, Norm's friend George Stanfield passed by the Gladstone Avenue house and found the door open. On the table of the sparsely furnished kitchen were three empty beer bottles, a copy of the afternoon *Herald* and a brief note in a crabbed cursive script:

George,

Have taken the easy way out, don't go down the yard, it won't be a pretty sight, I know, ring the police, and let them carry on, would you find a home for Honey.

Stanfield knew instinctively what this meant. In the backyard was a huge and heavy wooden chest, 2.4 metres by 1 metre wide and weighing about 45 kilograms. Like his brother the year before, Norm had painstakingly held it open with a stick, placed his neck on the edge, and then, as he stared at the bottom, let the lid descend like a guillotine, inflicting a lethal midline fracture of the larynx. At the inquest on 21 May 1969, coroner Pascoe found that 58-year-old Norman Jamieson had died from 'injuries and asphyxiation when he caused the heavy lid of a wooden box to fall on his neck', the investigating policeman having testified that he was ‘very upset over his daughter dying in an illegal operation’.

~

The next day, in another court, in another case, another judge began to read a ruling. By the time he had finished, the operation during which Carolyn Jamieson had died had ceased to be illegal.

'The girl is killed and I will be hanged'

After some weeks of deliberation had elapsed, I in continual fear that my altered shape would be noticed, my master gave me a medicine in a phial, which he desired me to take, telling me, without any circumlocution, for what purpose it was designed. I burst into tears, I thought it was killing myself—yet was such a self as I worth preserving?
Maria or the Wrongs of Women (1798), Mary Wollstonecraft

For much of Australia's history it has been easier to obtain an abortion than to use the word in print. Women compelled to cope with unsought and inopportune pregnancies have found myriad means of circumventing its legal prohibition. Yet anyone reading published accounts of police investigations and court hearings soon adjusts to their delicately coded language. The woman involved was in 'a certain condition' as a result of 'keeping company' with a man. Resolving on 'a certain course', she submitted to an 'illegal operation' during which a 'certain instrument' was used. The law itself has generally refrained from directly referring to 'abortion', preferring to define the felony as 'procuring a miscarriage' by the application of 'any instrument' or 'any poison or noxious thing'. It was the second Vatican Council that classified abortion an 'unspeakable crime', and in public discourse so it has been—not just unutterable but invisible, the stuff of innuendo, euphemism and sordid anecdote. This has wrapped the procedure in mystery, sealing it off especially from men—a peculiar circumstance given that it has been mainly male conclaves whose decisions have determined its availability.

This is not a book about the ethics of abortion, except insofar as individuals making decisions confront their own convictions and conventions. It concerns, rather, the law, and the effect of the prohibition of a sought-after procedure. It is a big story: abortion is a raw subject, precisely because it turns what society celebrates as life's most fulfilling experience into a problem at best, a crisis at worst. Yet its telling is better suited by a small scale, of personal choice, individual experience and local law. That being so, this book concentrates on the state of Victoria, where the principles permitting abortion were first laid down that all Australia would follow, and on the tight-knit groups who, with all manner of motivations, were prepared to operate at the nexus of legality and illegality. It is a tale of cavernous silences and conspicuous absences—history it was in nobody's interests to record, statistics it was in no-one's power to keep, and events few willingly relive.

~

At the time of white settlement, childbirth was a grinding, gruelling, life-threatening experience. Yet birth control was mainly limited to faith in withdrawal, and to superstitions such as that one could not conceive while lactating. As a means of dealing with untimely conception, then, abortion had the field virtually to itself. As historian Janet McCalman explains, it was 'the one form of fertility control that *was* widely broadcast and within the reach of even the poorest'. *And* it was illegal—indeed, for a time it was potentially a capital crime. Australian law was British law, where the earliest relevant statute was *Lord Ellenborough's Act* of 1803, which made death the punishment for 'intent' to abort a 'quickened' foetus—'quickening' being the stage at which 'the infant is able to stir in the mother's womb' at about the fourteenth week of pregnancy. Lord Ellenborough, a Tory chief justice, liked a busy gallows. The death penalty and consideration of maternal sensations disappeared in the *Offences Against the Person Act* of 1834, while the 1861 emendations of that Act established the upper limit of sentence at fifteen years. But the offence now bracketed 'the woman with child with intent to procure her own miscarriage' with 'whosoever with intent to procure the miscarriage of any women whether she is or is not with child'. Abortion, then, tainted everyone touched. 'Whosoever' and 'whether she is or is not with child' gave prosecutors a wide remit.

Who this affected was ambiguous. Few doctors were seriously interested in the pregnant female body. Obstetrics, or care of the pregnant, was regarded as the province of midwives. Gynaecology, the treatment of female reproductive diseases, was in its pioneering stages, and unlikely to conduce to anyone's professional advancement. Doctors dealing with women in their confinements could be callous, even criminally indifferent. In one infamous case at Williamstown in 1860, two doctors treated a 16-year-old pregnant girl suffering convulsions by administering fifteen leeches, mustard packs, calomel and tartar emetic; finally, they abused the husband for importunacy. After the girl's death, a full-term female infant attached by the umbilicus was found in the bed. Most doctors, moreover, would have found the idea of interfering in the natural course of a pregnancy personally distasteful.

This was instead the abortifacient era. In the cliché of the self-administered abortion, the sharp instrument is always the method of choice: the skewer, the knitting needle, the hat pin. Readier still were potions, purgatives, enemas, emetics and uterine douches prepared at home from the likes of oil of savine, oil of tansy, ergot of rye, pennyroyal, aloes and myrrh, or ready-mixed by amateur apothecaries glorying in aliases like Professor Hautmont, Madam Siedel and Madam Kurtz. Indeed, perhaps the era's most prolific medically qualified abortionist hardly needed to see a patient.

Dr Louis Lawrence Smith had an early career fright. A teenager studying medicine in Paris, he fought in the revolutions of 1848, and was twice rescued by republican comrades. But this was not the fright: that came ten years later when, having established a thriving Bourke Street practice, he was arrested for having aborted a young woman. *The Argus* thought Elizabeth Smith's evidence 'quite unfit for publication'—and published it anyway. She had sought Dr Smith's advice as to whether she was pregnant, in order to inform 'a gentleman she knew'; her treatment with 'instruments and medicine' induced a miscarriage. Acquitted rather fortunately, Dr Smith dedicated himself instead to selling patent remedies by mail order: among the most popular were his abortifacient 'vegetable pills', which 'as a female pill stand unrivalled'. Inheriting promotional flair from his father, the impresario on whose land Covent Garden was built, he adorned his city mansion with giant billboards, and made a byword of *Smith's Medical Almanac*: it was a lower-risk strategy than dealing directly with pregnant women.

Demand was ceaseless. Gold drew to Victoria the young, the eager and the fecund. The population's headlong growth from fewer than 100 000 in 1850 to more than a million in 1875 was in advance of many people's ability to provide for it—steps would then be needed. One day in June 1860, Geelong shoemaker John Whitehall noticed that his servant and mistress Annie Rock had grown too stout for her 'stays'. Anxious she was 'in the family way', he laced her so tightly that she fainted. When Rock came to, Whitehall told her he had 'some dark-coloured very bitter stuff' which would 'make her all right', instructing her to lie on her back and commencing to 'rub her stomach very hard with his hands'. She wound up hospitalised, then homeless: 'I wanted to get out of the place because he said I was as guilty as he was. He said many a better girl than I was on the streets and why should I not go as well as them?'

With social mores favouring large families and contraception rudimentary, the choice for married women in years of peak fertility was usually between a state of near-permanent pregnancy or abstinence, although sex in marriage was not lightly refused: Louisa Lawson would call the bedroom a 'chamber of horrors' where frail women were 'expected to endure nightly this horrid ordeal'. But where the expectant married could at least anticipate solicitous interest, the pregnant unmarried faced even bleaker choices. One could marry in haste, then perhaps repent at leisure. One could seek the concealment of live-in employment, then deliver in one of the growing number of refuges for 'fallen' women, originally devised with the rehabilitation of prostitutes in mind, but increasingly dedicated to reclaiming single mothers 'from their evil courses'. Those in desperate straits might turn to abandonment, or infanticide: as many as thirty unidentified infant corpses were found annually in Melbourne throughout the nineteenth century, usually in secluded spots like drains and lanes, sometimes inciting a brief moral panic, as in December 1870 when *The Argus* declared that Victoria sheltered 'a very army of murderesses within our midst'. From the 1880s, there was a vogue for 'babyfarms' where infants could be 'lodged' at commercial rates, albeit that the practice fell into disrepute with the March 1893 trial of Macdonaldtown couple John and Sarah Makin, who had buried thirteen of their charges. Little wonder that a procedure with an end to it looked preferable to years of anxiety. Girls in service or at work were particularly vulnerable—girls like Mary Lewis.

Twenty-year-old Lewis had borne two illegitimate children to the publican of St Kilda's Terminus Hotel, where she was barmaid. In December 1865, she attended Dr WB Rankin, a local GP, complaining of menstrual irregularities: in fact, periods since her second confinement had been accompanied by 'a very disagreeable smell'. She left with oil of savine—a purgative in common use for 'bringing on the menses', but of doubtful efficacy. As Rankin himself admitted: 'Savine is used among the ignorant in large doses to procure abortion; it is a very uncertain remedy'. Evidently so; ten weeks later she followed the road of rumour to Dr Smith—only to find him a paragon of virtue:

> She asked me to determine whether she was in the family way or not. To the best of my belief she was. I examined her partially. She appeared to be three months gone... She asked me if I could procure abortion for her. I told her I could not. I saw her subsequently about a week after. She came to persuade me to reconsider my judgement. I dissuaded her from it.

Not for long, because she shortly visited Dr James Beaney. 'Champagne Jimmy' was a celebrity medico known for the diamond rings he scorned to remove while operating, and the invitations he issued to friends to watch his surgical legerdemain. Beaney, it would be alleged, performed an abortion 'with a recklessness seldom met with even in cases of this sort'. Beaney would protest that he had simply diagnosed 'disease of the womb consequent on... sub-involution of that organ'—that is, the womb's failure to return to normal size after childbirth.

> Her lips were very dark coloured, face dusky and expressive of great anxiety, the hands and feet were of a bluish colour, and the extremities were cold; there were sores around the teeth; the breath was very offensive; pulse rapid and feeble, scarcely perceptible; there was pain of a bearing down character which caused protrusion of the vagina, the lining membrane of which was a deep purple colour; the discharge was so foetid as to lead me to suppose that sloughing was going on in some part of the internal generative organs.

Lewis died on 15 March 1866 in terror-stricken agony, pleading that she would 'give the world for sleep'. And *R v Beaney* quickly became a cause célèbre, not only because the womb was found empty, implying abortion, but because the ovaries went missing after the autopsy, implying theft. It wasn't unknown for colonial doctors to purloin medical specimens from the dead. Caught in the act of stealing a hanged criminal's brain, Melbourne University's surgery lecturer imperiously bid his accuser never again to enter his office wearing a hat.

For three weeks, Victoria's finest medical minds were tossed and gored by Beaney's counsel: Butler Aspinall, defender of the Eureka insurrectionaries, peppered one expert with no fewer than 700 questions. 'But for his good fortune in having secured the services of Mr Aspinall,' *The Lancet* noted, 'Mr Beaney must almost certainly have been executed by mistake!' Aspinall's coup was asking jurors to consider the implications of a guilty verdict.

> Dr Beaney, who never knew this woman before she came to him, is to be held answerable for all the chief acts of her life—for her vices and her pregnancies. If a doctor were to be subjected to this responsibility it would justify any doctor in the future—when a poor girl came to him with the pangs of expected labour, or with sub involution, or any other disease, and asked him for God's sake to attend on her—if he had a wife and family dependent upon him saying to her: 'Charity dictates that I should attend to you but while doctors have such minds I do not dare do so.'

The jury flinched; who knew when one might have one's own embarrassment? They failed to reach a verdict and were discharged, and the jury at Beaney's retrial acquitted after fifteen minutes, causing a popular celebration which police and tipstaves could not quell. 'I never saw anything so disgraceful', thundered the judge. 'I think it a stigma and a stain upon the colony.'

What stands out to modern eyes about the case is that Mary Lewis did not merely recede to nothing; she never *was* anything. For months, doctors and lawyers argued back and forth over her ravaged remains as though discussing a fraud or embezzlement. Such humanity as she was afforded came in her father's testimony: 'She was always a strong, wholesome girl. I was at the Terminus Hotel the Saturday before her death. I was there about two and a half hours; she was standing in the bar. I never thought she was in the family way…I never knew she had children'. Beaney dedicated much of the rest of his life to reliving his ordeal, publishing two editions of a self-justifying pamphlet in the belief that 'never was there in the history of Great Britain a more flagitious case'. The graves of doctor and patient in Melbourne General Cemetery tell a tale: Beaney's is a lofty cenotaph; Lewis's is unmarked.

In the end, a 'not guilty' verdict impacted little differently to a 'guilty'. Beaney's complaints that he would never again attend a woman without consulting a colleague persuaded doctors in general that there were easier ways to make money. Those who remained were the wilful and obdurate, like Williamstown's Dr Edward Figg. Making a speculum examination in 1876, Figg left a 32-year-old mother of nine like 'a bleeding pig'; she 'virtually rotted away' of septicaemia. By the early 1880s, the *Australian Medical Journal* could claim that abortion was 'utterly scouted by the majority of the profession', something which removed 'any necessity for dilating on the evils that flow from so foul a practice, which tends to destroy the fear of open shame which is unfortunately necessary in a great number of people for the preservation of morality'.

The breach was filled, increasingly, by midwives: their constant and intimate involvement in reproductive health made them regard abortion as part of the continuum of conventional procedures. Historians Shurlee Swain and Renata Howe have painstakingly estimated that there were twelve midwives regularly performing abortions in Melbourne between 1885 and 1915; of five doctors, only one worked alone. 'There are several institutions devoted entirely to procuring abortions', commented coroner Dr Richard Youl in 1890. 'It is a demoralising thing. Murder is a fine art, and persons who get used to it do not stop.' Nonetheless, he saw advantages to the development: 'There are several institutions kept by women and, if I was a woman and wanted to have an abortion procured, I should go to one of them, because they have more care'. Options were increased by the development of dilatation and curettage, a routine surgical procedure used after miscarriage involving the scraping of the endometrium as a precaution against septicaemia. Faced with a request for abortion, the midwife could use whatever methods at her disposal to procure a miscarriage, then leave curettage to a doctor without exposing him to illegality. The effect on the Royal Women's Hospital was profound:

> The cunning digitally dilated the cervix slowly over a number of days so that they could not be accused of anything more heinous, until the woman began to bleed, whereupon she presented herself at a doctor's surgery or a hospital to be curetted. They came in droves to the Women's Hospital with threatened or incomplete abortions; the hospital suspected the worst, but the women would rarely tell.

The effect was also to widen the risk spectrum, because of the hazards women willingly ran in order to qualify for this legal procedure. On 18 October 1882, 34-year-old housekeeper Mary McPhail died from 'a large rent with ragged edges' in the uterus, having thrown herself down the stairs several times while pregnant. The jury accepted Dr Edward Barker's deadpan defence that 'he had told her to take exercise but not exercise of that sort'. Many midwives, too, operated in dismally dirty conditions, and patients with foul-smelling infections arriving in hospitals tended to bring curious police in their train. But the midwives never lacked clientele, and brazened out scrutiny. Elizabeth Taylor, who operated from Waxman's Cottages in Richmond's Bridge Road, was brought to court on six occasions between 1885 and 1891 before being convicted, and had no sooner served her time than returned to work. A few, too, were notably sophisticated, digesting new literature on birth control popularised by the so-called 'Freethought' movement, like Charles Knowlton's *The Fruits of Philosophy*, and George Drysdale's *Elements of Social Science*, the circulation of which was publicised by police raids and obscenity prosecutions. For some years, Melbourne's leading midwife was a Freethought disciple and proponent of women's suffrage. Brettena Smyth, widowed after five well-spaced children, supported herself by running a drapery and chemist shop from 51 Errol Street, North Melbourne. There she stocked 'the best female French, English, German and American contraceptives, French preventatives (male), enemas and syringes'. She also sold copies of her *The Limitation of Offspring*, a sober enumeration of the best methods of contraception—and the worst. Cervical cap? Serviceable. Pessaries of quinine and cocoa butter? Beware.

Of course, quite how many exploitative quacks and well-meaning incompetents were operating will never be known. Even Smyth had her eccentricities, believing that holding the scrotum to prevent ejaculation caused impotence, and championing 'medical electricity' for 'all nervous affectations'. The brief vogue for electricity also featured in its genre's most macabre story: publicly infamous, privately hapless 'Madame Olga Radalyski'.

~

Elizabeth Elburn was daughter of the licensee at Essendon's National Hotel. Her husband, Charles Boswell, a career criminal, was put away shortly after their marriage for receiving stolen goods. After his release, they went to Launceston in August 1894, and set up as a 'masseur and medical electrician', 'Carlo Adolph de la Lebedur' and 'Olga Radalyski': in fact, he was an abortionist and she his nurse. Later, they moved to Dunedin in the same capacity, where he ran off with a music teacher.

Olga Radalyski and daughter Mary returned to Melbourne in December 1896, indigent and indebted. Unable to find room at home, she rented premises to practice palmistry, fortune telling and card cutting, but soon was flitting from address to address a step ahead of rent collectors, finally sharing digs in Prahran's Osborne Street with a teenage maid cum prostitute, Thekla Dubberke. And she might never have attempted to emulate her former husband but for a chance meeting.

Osborne Street's estate agent was a good-natured 20-year-old, Travis Tod, who had a reputation for 'honesty, sobriety, civility, attention to business', and a problem: 17-year-old prostitute Mabel Ambrose was bearing his child. 'Madame Olga' volunteered assistance. Ambrose moved in to Osborne Street where, daily for three weeks, she was treated with electric shocks from a galvanic battery through two cords, one held in the hand, one placed 'up the girl's womb'. 'She used to cry', Dubberke would recall. 'I heard her crying while she was upstairs. This occurred every day while she was being treated.' Alas for Madame Olga, tears were Ambrose's only secretion; she began to doubt the girl was pregnant, and sent her to a Collins Street physician, Dr William Gaze.

Gaze actually *was* an abortionist. Among official case records is an unflattering description from police in Westport, New Zealand: 'He kept several women at various times and had the reputation of immoral relations with others. He also has the reputation of having practised abortion while following his profession'. Now advertisements ran for his 'Polypathic Clinic' in daily newspapers. But Gaze was too shrewd to treat Ambrose himself: as Dubberke described it, he contented himself with examining her, confirming pregnancy, and issuing advice.

> Madame said: 'I cannot make out why the battery has not acted'. Dr Gaze said: 'I cannot make it out either; but inject a little Condy's Fluid into the girl's womb. It will bring it on for certain, but it will give a great shock to the system as it is instant death to the foetus' ... Madame said to Mabel: 'I am going to use stronger measures than ever in the morning.' Mabel said: 'I will be glad when it is over.'

Condy's Fluid, a disinfectant, was indeed a 'strong measure', and the 'great shock' when it was injected through a metal nozzle from an India rubber bulb was instantaneous. Rushing to investigate two muffled screams, Dubberke found Ambrose unconscious and Madame Olga ashen. 'The girl is killed and I will be hanged', she lamented. Dubberke hastened to the surgery of Gaze, who recommended brandy. It was too late for anything. Madame, maid and client now had a body on their hands.

Boys rowing the Yarra River soon after spied what they fancied to be a treasure chest. In fact, it was a yellow boot trunk, from which one boy saw something protruding: 'I saw the foot of a human being. It was a green colour'. The body within was three months' pregnant, but otherwise free of identifying marks: it had been stripped and shaved before being bent to the contours of its container. Further indignities awaited: police displayed its severed head pickled in a jar at their headquarters, soliciting clues to its identity from members of the public. *The Argus* deplored the ghoulishness of the exercise: 'There exists a large number of people in Melbourne who see nothing reprehensible in dragging children of tender years to view the revolting relics of humanity in the morgue'. But it worked: Mabel Ambrose's mother recognised her daughter from a scar on the forehead and a pock mark beneath the left eye. Dubberke was then betrayed by a gentleman lover, and the police moved in on everyone, including Gaze, who spluttered indignantly: 'All I have had to do with this has been honourable!' The great Australian journalist Montagu Grover, later founder of Melbourne's *Sun News-Pictorial*, thrilled to the chase:

> The news had spread already. When I reached the cottage there was a crowd of fifty people in the street. I found [Detective] Carter and

the woman in the front room. Madame was cool and friendly. She gave me a cigarette and we conversed as well as her deafness permitted...

Next morning I contrived to get an interview with Thekla Dubberke. Thekla was a girl of twenty, good looking at a distance but coarse when close at hand. She was well-spoken and refined in her manner. Her parents were very decent German people and she had been engaged to be married when she first fell from grace. The cool manner in which she gave her evidence at the inquest and the trial led the public to regard her as a monster of callousness, but I don't think this was the case. She was simply driven into a corner.

Another sensational trial ensued, this time enlivened by Dubberke's risqué reminiscences of the wages of sin ('Three men were giving me money. I don't know if each knew there were two other men. Other men had intercourse with me besides the three') and money for modelling ('I posed to young men in the nude, so did Madame... Some of my friends urged me to get a younger woman than Madame. They said she was too old and ugly'). Fortunately, perhaps, Madame saw little more than she heard: in addition to being nearly deaf, it transpired, she was also going blind.

Again, jurors deferred to men of science: Gaze, defended by future High Court judge Frank Gavan Duffy, was acquitted. But they could do no other than find Madame Olga and Tod guilty, whereupon both were sentenced to death. A letter from the former to her father dated 28 February 1899 shows that she felt the disgrace:

I may never see you again in life. Better had it been I had died last year than I should have lived through this disgrace and sorrow. You know all my past struggles and can guess how I was led into such company simply for a home... Ah, if I had only had a corner of your home I would not have been there but there was no room and it could not be.

God comfort you my father and pray for your unfortunate heartbroken girl and forgive me—death makes all things right and I am writing as one already dead for I have very little hope if any of anything else and as the time gets nearer I shall be less composed for writing so I send this.

Also surviving, on parchment in a superb copperplate hand, is a petition for gubernatorial mercy signed by the Elburns, including Mary, 'her dear little daughter'. This blamed their benighted relative's travails on 'her unscrupulous husband, proved and convicted as a scoundrel' and 'a being named Dubberke, a creature young in years comparatively but old in crime'. At length the sentences were commuted: Madame Olga's to life, Tod's to six years.

Madame Olga's tale is perhaps too vivid to be considered representative: she seems more in the nature of a hostage given up by abortion to maintain the pretence of community decorum and rigorous prohibition. Victorian police did not compile crime statistics until 1963, so prosecutions for abortion are difficult to quantify. But given that abortion still bore the brunt of the need for fertility control, successful prosecutions seem underrepresented in judicial proceedings of the time; indeed, *The Age* conceded that the repression of abortion 'by legislative enactments, however skilfully these may be drawn up, must always remain a matter of extreme difficulty'. On paper, the law was powerful and sweeping; in court, it occasioned personal squeamishness, and even a knowing nod. In 'Biddable Selina', a *Bulletin* short story of April 1906 by 'A. W.', a maid seduced by a dastardly boarder meets her end at the hands of a doctor and midwife who nonetheless go free.

> At the subsequent inquiry the doctor did not appear. He had been called away on 'urgent private business'. Nurse Black, immaculate in starched uniform and spotless collar, professed ignorance as to the cause of death, but vouched for the care she had lavished on the patient. The bench winked at her, so to speak, and in the face of much medical testimony discharged her without a stain on her character, only she had better not do it again.

Abortionists, then, settled into a twilight world, visible enough to be accessible, not so visible as to invite interference. Distinguished medico Dr Herbert Moran described his neighbourhood practitioner in 1910 as a kind of local landmark.

> Just down the road an old abortionist practised flagrantly, though she made some pretence of doing midwifery. Such self-named nurses were then to be found in every suburb so hard was it to get a conviction against them. The monetary reward was high, so they were

> ready and willing to take any risk. Sometimes one of the less reputable chemists would act as an agent...The local abortionist near me was a hard-visaged, big angular mare of a woman given to frequent bouts of alcohol. Her personal habits were filthy, yet she carried on for years under the nose of the police. It was only when a woman died that any real action was ever taken, and even then it was rare to establish a proof that an illegal operation had been performed. The dead cannot bear witness and the evidence of the dying is hobbled with legal difficulties. Furthermore, some of the jury feel sympathy for a woman who is trying to help another out of trouble.

The squeamishness of juries had two dimensions—one related to composition, one related to power. Juries at the time, of course, were exclusively male—and would be in Victoria until 1970. Defence counsel in abortion matters would learn to exploit this: the two commandments of jury selection were always to choose young men, and to challenge anyone with an Irish name. You would usually be guaranteed at least a few jurors with personal experience of girls 'in trouble'; you would also have minimised your Catholics. In other words, juries were tailored to bring to their deliberations a vested interest in abortion's continued availability.

The other factor related to the sheer extremity of punishment. Abortionists seldom came before the courts on the charge merely of procuring miscarriages. Usually a death was involved, making theirs a capital offence. Two other midwife abortionists were sentenced to death before World War I: Isabella Downey, convicted in June 1910 of the murder of 21-year-old Isabella McCullum, and Louisa Rooke, convicted a year later of the murder of 23-year-old Ella Wilson. The circumstances are instructive. Both were condemned by the so-called 'lightning judge', Joseph Hood, famous for an alacrity bordering on haste, and also an Irish Catholic. He meted out justice in both cases with a notable astringency. During the Rooke case, he directed jurors sternly:

> Murder means the slaying of a human being with malice aforethought. It is a common error to think that this means intention to kill. It means a great deal more than that. If a man fires at one person and kills another that is murder. If a woman performs an illegal operation which causes death that is murder. If the girl had

done the operation herself with the accused's connivance then the latter would be guilty of murder.

Yet juries *were* drawing a distinction, for it took a very particular idée fixe not to; ultimately, the sentences on Downey and Rooke were commuted. In May 1912, *The Argus* pondered the paltry number of abortion convictions: 'It is hardly conceivable that in every instance the person so acquitted is innocent'. Urging a rethink, it hypothesised that punishments were simply too harsh: 'Sentences that are too severe defeat the deterrent aim of the criminal law, since they lessen the probability of the guilty persons having to endure punishment'. Juries, then, shrank not just from potentially restricting abortion's availability, but quailed at their discretion. Abortion was becoming not merely the unspeakable crime but, hovering between public disapproval and private tolerance, the unenforceable law.

'I won't be alive in the morning'

There Fay lay, white-faced and fearful. She was trembling so violently as to shake the bed. 'I thought you were never coming… Oh Justine, am I going to die?'
'No, don't be a fool.' Curtly. 'Be quiet. Do you think you're in for a picnic? You've got to put up with it and be quiet.'

Riven (1929), Jean Devanny

Abortionists and their clients a century ago ran gauntlets other than the law. The Church's influence was broad and deep. And while Anglican opposition to birth control would erode, Roman Catholic opposition was hardening. In October 1869, Pope Pius IX declared abortion a mortal crime, saying that the foetus was human from conception. And Leo XIII's encyclical of February 1880 on Christian marriage marginalised even those few theologians prepared to argue for abortion in the event of medical emergency, like fallopian pregnancy or uterine cancer. To fortify against moral degradation, the Church began conglomerating abortion, contraception and infanticide as 'violations of the sanctity of human life': it made the Church a formidable social and political force.

Melbourne's Catholic archbishop, Thomas Carr, was particularly sulphurous in his denunciations. In the matter of *Buckley v Buckley* on 15 November 1899, Justice Williams extemporaneously deplored the divorce law he was compelled to administer. The complainant was a husband suing for desertion on the grounds that his wife, having borne eight children, could face no more. Williams publicly regretted granting a decree nisi under the circumstances: 'If the law says it is desertion for a woman to refuse to go on bearing children after having already brought nine or ten into the world then the law is an ass'. Carr decried this 'singularly dangerous' judgment as attempting 'to frustrate the principal purpose for which the almighty instituted matrimony, and to bring down the marriage state to a condition little elevated above concubinage'.

Opening the war against depravity on another front, Carr complained to parliament and police about a circular soliciting investor interest in a small company to manufacture contraceptives—probably condoms. Carr's complaints that this was 'the most disgraceful thing that ever occurred in Melbourne and indicates a return to pagan rituals' did the trick: shareholders dissolved the company. Nor was this the Church's last impact on such investment: a few years later, Melbourne rubber giant Dunlop ceased manufacturing condoms on the say-so of its Catholic chairman, Nicholas Fitzgerald. Ansell family lore is that Eric Ansell, having helped dismantle the machine, made an offer for it, and started the business in Richmond that now dominates the world market.

An emboldened Carr then tackled abortion in a pamphlet, scorning those who would find exceptions for it: 'No censure can be too strong for those who hold a medical justification'. And in the marriage vow 'for better or worse, for richer or poorer', his emphasis fell on the worse and poorer:

> Risks and dangers are incidental to the married just as they are to several other states. They are no greater…than the dangers of the battlefield, the mine, the factory and the forest, which are the lot of men. The woman was warned of old, 'I will multiply thy sorrows and thy conceptions; in sorrow shalt thou bring forth children.' If she is not willing to run the risks, or suffer the sorrows of married life, let her remain single.

The effusions of Carr and other Catholic clergymen were not only for coreligionists. Fin-de-siècle decadence also worried the medical profession. In his annual review for 1896, the British Medical Association's local president, Dr Michael O'Sullivan, ruminated on the 'ever-increasing invalidism which would seem to have become the heritage of civilised women'. Social developments, he felt, had upset the natural order. Higher education, sewing with machines, bicycling: these had alienated the fairer sex from their proper function. 'Remembering the close kinship existing between the brain and the generative organs,' he argued, 'the almost inevitable result must be increased instability of nerve power and derangement of the uterine function'. Worse still was criminal abortion, which, 'performed generally by illiterate and unclean charlatans of either sex, claims numberless victims'.

Although O'Sullivan was Catholic, this was the voice of a new force in reproductive thought. 'Pro-natalism' was partly a response to the heresies of Freethought and partly an index of anxiety in a young country with a thinly dispersed, slow-growing population. Reasons for the decline in Victoria's birthrate were actually not far to seek, the gluttonous 1880s having become the gaunt 1890s. Not that sex ceased by any means: it is estimated that Melbourne's streets hosted as many as 10 000 prostitutes. But procreational sex seemed almost in abeyance. The *Australasian Medical Gazette* worried that women might be exerting control over their fertility, deploring that women 'erroneously regarded the taking of drugs to procure abortion as safe and perfectly legal', and contending that 'many married women know how to pass an instrument into their own wombs and they teach one another their dangerous tricks'.

Pro-natalism's triumph came in June 1903 when the New South Wales government statistician Timothy Coghlan published *The Decline in the Birth-Rate*, ascribing the phenomenon to 'precautions taken against the birth of children'. The alarm was sufficient to prompt a Royal Commission led by former Board of Health president Dr Charles Mackellar. An Australian political truism is that no government constitutes a Royal Commission without knowing the outcome in advance, and it might even have been inspired by this commission: Mackellar had long bemoaned his countrymen's heedless pursuit of comfort while issuing jeremiads about Asian fertility. His commissioners painstakingly steered their four fat volumes towards premeditated conclusions, deciding that the decline of the birthrate was induced by women's 'love of luxury', 'selfishness and pleasure-seeking' after a 'wave of popular feeling across the civilised world to control size of families'; women, it reported, were asking chemists for abortifacients 'as openly and indifferently as they would ask for a toothbrush'.

Evidence was adduced to shock tender sensibilities: a policeman claimed to know of thirty-six abortionists in his district and estimated more than 100 in Sydney; a doctor reported that city hospitals saw evidence of 400 abortions a year; a surgeon calculated that almost a third of pregnancies ended in miscarriage, consistent with an induced abortion rate of more than one in five pregnancies. Yet much else was simple assertion, such as: 'Bad as are the consequences or prevention of conception, still worse is the destruction of health and life which follows the procuring of miscarriage'. The commission's arguments budged nobody: pioneer feminist Rose Scott dismissed the 'whirlwind of talk and superficial comment', which, 'like Adam of old, wound up very contentedly with assuring the public that everything was the fault of the woman thou gavest to be with me'.

Most of the commission's chief recommendations were implemented. The new *Private Hospitals Act* required the licensing of such institutions; the *Police Offences (Amendments) Act* deemed the advertisement of contraceptives or abortion services 'indecent' and 'obscene'. But apart from forcing midwives a little further underground, its effects were nugatory—which drove one of its number to distraction.

In contribution to the birthrate, Tasmanian piano manufacturer Octavius Beale, one of eight children and father of thirteen, could not be faulted. He had also become a votary of eugenics, especially theories of 'race suicide'—that faster-growing black and Asiatic masses would steadily submerge the world's white populations. While the other commissioners faded from view, Beale ever more noisily condemned the 'secret drugs' and 'interferences with the sexual function' which were 'ruining the moral fibre of the nation'. Finally, his friend Alfred Deakin appointed Beale to inquire into 'secret drugs, cures and foods'—a report shorter on fact than anecdote:

> A city merchant in Australia said: I met one of the tenants in our building and observing that the man was pale and nervous, even trembling, asked him what was the matter. 'My wife has made up her mind that she will have no more children. She and her sister who is also a married woman, have come to that decision together, and I cannot keep them apart. A few days ago I was called home from business, and there was this sister, and a nurse who had operated on my wife, and she was dangerously ill... What am I to do with my two poor little children?'

When his report was mainly ignored due to an improving Australian birthrate, a chagrined Beale self-published *Racial Decay*, a 425-page scrapbook of his travels, permeated with impending doom in headings like 'Sexual Perversion in Ancient Rome Identical With that Of Our Day' and 'The Corrupt Tree and Its Corrupt Fruit'. It sold 365 copies. Meanwhile, pro-natalism would shortly be outmatched by a countermovement—albeit one with which it shared key characteristics.

~

World War I is sometimes considered a watershed in Australian birth control, many soldiers receiving their induction in contraception when issued condoms to counteract the spread of venereal disease. Yet no evidence suggests slackening of the abortion trade. The practice among midwives of inducing miscarriages, then leaving hospitals to scrape the scraps, was so common that Melbourne's Women's Hospital devoted a whole floor to post-abortal sepsis when it opened its new infirmary wing in 1912. Within five years, sepsis cases had multiplied six-fold, constituting two in five admissions, and the floor had become infamous for its odour: the acrid reek of decaying flesh; once smelt, never forgotten. The soundscape of moans, snores, whispering and weeping, a survivor recalled, was broken only by the occasional delirium.

> Well, the girl in the bed opposite, she woke up one morning and said: 'Oh I'm winning, I'm winning, I'm winning, I'm winning, I'm in front, I'm in front, I'm winning, I'm winning, I'm winning. Ah! I've won I've won I've won!' And she fell back dead. True as I'm sitting here. That must have been her last thought, that she was winning.

The application of pounds of cure, of course, was the inevitable cost of unallocated ounces of prevention. Working in hospitals before and after the war, aspiring gynaecologist Norman Haire was staggered by the unwisdom of many pregnancies.

> Every day I saw babies born of diseased or enfeebled or defective parents; babies born into families which were already too large for the economic resources available; mothers whose health had been damaged often irreparably by excessive or overfrequent child-bearing. I saw, too, large numbers of women admitted suffering from the effects of abortion, sometimes induced by themselves, sometimes by

> others in the desperate endeavour to avoid the birth of an unwanted child. Some of these women recovered; some of them died; many of them suffered long periods of illness before recovering sufficiently to be discharged but remained permanently damaged as a result of the abortion.

Haire acknowledged himself an 'unwanted child'. Eleventh in an already overtaxed family, he claimed firsthand knowledge of 'the disadvantages which may arise when the number of children is excessive'. But when he proposed advising patients about precautions against unwanted pregnancy, his suggestions were 'very coldly received'. He shortly left for London, becoming the very model of a modern sexologist, a protégé of Havelock Ellis. For a *succès de scandale* was in the offing: Marie Stopes's *Married Love* and *Wise Parenthood*, with their preachings of sexual pleasure, were devoured by disciples of Free-thought, and inspired a new feminist generation.

Modern birth control's pioneer saw herself primarily as a scientist: 'An impersonal and scientific knowledge of our bodies is the surest safeguard against prurient curiosity and lascivious gloating'. Ironically, Stopes's revolution also had a eugenics content: where the pro-natalists had been obsessed with the quantity of the white race, Stopes's apostles were preoccupied with quality, mixing messages of female empowerment through sex education with calls to sterilise the mentally deficient and racially mixed. It was the so-called Racial Hygiene Association of New South Wales that opened Sydney's first birth control centre in December 1933.

In Melbourne, contraception's cause was championed by Dr Victor Wallace, a passionate believer in the diaphragm, just back from a stint as a government medical officer in Papua. Although recently a father, Wallace understood that not everyone enjoyed his advantages: 'Children do not ask to come into this world of conflict and ceaseless struggle'. In October 1934, choosing premises in working-class Fitzroy where he fancied it would make the most difference, he opened what he called, to deflect 'strong opposition in certain quarters', the 'Mothers' Welfare Clinic'. Wallace also steadily came under the influence of eugenics, becoming the one and only secretary of the Eugenics Society of Victoria in October 1936—he was still there when it expired twenty-five years later.

For a woman in quest of a termination, of course, eugenics was irrelevant. As for contraception—well, one had to know to ask, and levels of sexual ignorance remained high. Conveyed a midwife's advice that she was pregnant, South Melbourne girl Lois Nicholls was indignant: 'How do you get pregnant? Did she tell you that?' Husband Gordon was shamefaced: 'I think it's what they call "sex", Lois'. Lois was adamant: 'Well, you'd better make it last because you're not getting too much more of that'. Advice about birth control and sex education was also far from uniform. In *Safe Marriage*, Ettie Rout scorned condoms: 'Sheaths impose an impermeable medium between husband and wife, destroy contact and may thereby prevent the joy of sexual intercourse. In some cases both the husband and wife become nervous wrecks'. In *Tell Them!*, Marion Piddington argued for trousers without pockets to thwart masturbation, which led to 'dysgenic' or 'haphazard' matings. Kylie Tennant recalled a 1920s meeting of Melbourne Freethinkers where a youthful firebrand asserted that birth control had changed 'the whole economic scene'.

> 'Show me one fool-proof method of birth control,' I demanded.
>
> He blushed as red as his hair. 'Well, I understand there are—er—ways,' he mumbled.
>
> 'Tell me one.'
>
> He couldn't.

If anything, the Stopes revolution was probably responsible for more abortions, because more married women resolved to continue having sex and also to space their births, while single women became more venturesome—thus the ribald rhyme: 'Sister Susie built her hopes/On the book of Marie Stopes/But I fear from her condition/She must have read the wrong edition'. By revealing sex and its consequences to have options, however, it also broadened narrow horizons.

~

Among Melbourne's circle of midwives after World War I were two doctors with a strong grasp of abortion's social context. Richmond's Dr Daniel MacGillicuddy was relied on by generations of Little Lonsdale Street prostitutes; Prahran's Dr Albert Bretherton was as close as the suburb had to a hero. Like Haire, Bretherton had been conditioned by his upbringing, being the fourth of thirteen children to a rural police constable's wife: by then a medical student, he never forgot his mother's desperation during her final pregnancy. When he opened for business after the war, the trauma of childbirth hit even closer to home: his wife died of influenza a week after the arrival of son Rodney. To his father, Rodney recalled, abortion was never simply a medical procedure:

> There was one case. The husband was a returned man and he had bad tuberculosis. He came home from the sanatorium and got his wife pregnant. She came round very distressed. Albert said: 'Your husband's got only a matter of weeks to live. You can't have this baby. It wouldn't have a hope in the world.' He aborted the woman and not only did he do that, he sent her to another holiday place and he had that house cleaned and supplied with food for her to come back to.

Even after Bretherton remarried, his household was rugged, rigid and rather austere: a disciple of physical culture, he built a home boxing ring so disputes could be settled in manly fashion. He also exercised a puritan's discrimination—he aborted single girls for free, but never more than once; yet where married women were concerned, especially those with service connections, he was unfailingly open-handed, while his pastoral initiatives included distributing unsold food from Prahran market among the disadvantaged. According to his son, he also enjoyed some judicial protection: 'Prahran court was nothing to Albert. It was almost part of his daily routine'. Despite attending 'hundred of times', and facing at least two sets of murder charges, he was never convicted.

Police were finding convictions ever more elusive. Probably the best guide to abortion prosecutions in Melbourne in its time was the multi-volume index of *The Argus*, which grouped them under the rubric 'Illegal Operations'. *The Argus* ran about an article a week between 1910 and 1929, naming about 240 people, including seventy women who died from the effects of induced abortion, and 130 individuals charged as perpetrators or accessories. The littleness of the effect is striking. Putting the ratio of prosecutions to convictions at 'less than twenty to one', the paper complained in May 1926:

> The law has virtually become a dead letter and the public contemplates its paralysis unmoved...It is a real menace to the integrity of the community. In order to protect itself against primitive

> and destructive impulses, society erects barriers in the form of laws. In every community there are enemies of society whose conduct necessitates the maintenance of such barriers. They would break through them; they would allow the surge of those passions which, if left unchecked, would soon become a flood of anarchy and lawlessness and submerge the whole social structure.

Some operators worked with remarkable impunity. Hannah Mitchell ran a lucrative abortion practice from a two-storey townhouse in Burnley Street, Richmond; so lucrative that she also owned houses in St Kilda and Carlton. She was unusual in that after inducing contractions with a catheter, she suffered patients to remain on her premises until they had finally miscarried. The house's three downstairs bedrooms were seldom other than full with sore and stupefied girls, three and four to a bed, recovering from Mitchell's ministrations. Married thrice amid many amours, Mitchell lived with an abandon suggestive of great confidence in her resourcefulness—or her connections. For one of her lovers was Percy Ridgeway, Melbourne's top criminal barrister, who lived in splendour in Brighton and defended her with chivalrous zeal.

Not that 'Nurse' Mitchell did not run risks—notably in the case of 27-year-old Bertha Coughlan from Honnomunjie, near Omeo. Coughlan and her father, John, arrived in Melbourne for a sojourn on 6 November 1922. Unbeknownst to him, she was pregnant, apparently by a married farmer, and desperate for an abortion. Burnley Street was humming when she arrived. Mitchell's nurse, Maggie Milward, and her two children were on the premises; likewise ex-husband Frank Bonfiglio, with whom she had just enjoyed a £600 windfall from the Caulfield Cup, and their daughter. Then it all went wrong.

Bonfiglio was idling in the sitting room when Mitchell burst in. 'I have a girl taken bad', she announced. 'Take your coat off and help carry her to the bathroom.' He and Milward hefted a semiconscious Coughlan from her blood-soaked sheets onto a bathroom table, whereupon Mitchell commenced scraping, syringing and soaping, pausing only to reassure Coughlan that she was 'a good girl'. But the blood and uterine debris flowed unabated, as Coughlan weakened by the minute. 'I am very tired', Mitchell finally admitted. 'I cannot do any more. I think she is gone.' She left Milward in charge. 'You are kind', said Coughlan quietly. 'You are so good to me.' Milward soothed her:

'Never mind dear...You will have a nice breakfast in the morning'. Coughlan sensed otherwise: 'I won't be alive in the morning. I'm dying'. She was and did.

The indiscriminate nature of the *Offences Against the Person Act* now impinged on events: if all were conspirators before the law, Mitchell thought, they might as well conspire. 'It's your place to help me!' she hectored Bonfiglio. 'You don't want to see me hanged!' They burned Coughlan's clothes, and interred her body in a leafy gully near Coldstream. But the conspiracy collapsed when Bonfiglio made a clumsy effort at blackmail. With a perfunctory apology—'Frank, I am sorry but I have to do it'—Mitchell shot him four times at close range, then organised for Coughlan's body to be moved.

Bonfiglio awoke in St Vincent's Hospital attended by two note-taking detectives. A fortnight later, police dragged a corn sack containing human remains, a toothless human skull and a slimy length of brown hair from the Yarra near the Anderson Street bridge. From the presence of insects and leaves it was inferred that the body had first been buried, and John Coughlan's identification of his daughter illuminated a trail back to Mitchell. But again, despite seemingly damning testimony from Bonfiglio and Milward, no charges were laid. Nor did Mitchell become noticeably more circumspect. She was charged in October 1923 with aborting mother-of-four Mabel Hodgkinson, who subsequently died from infection: Mitchell was acquitted in February 1924. She was charged again in September 1924 with aborting spinster Beryl Moreno: the Crown decided against filing a presentiment two months later. She was charged in February 1925 with aborting Eva Pitt: the Crown relinquished the charges the following month. And so forth. Not for nothing does the caricature of Ridgeway in the biographical dictionary *500 Victorians* show him pursuing his favoured trout fishing with the caption: 'The Ridgeway is the best way to get you out of deep water!'

Mitchell's celebrity was secured by the case of Inez Martin, who arrived at Burnley Street on the night of her wedding to draper George Rosser. Inez was pregnant, although not to George; rather, it seems, to the chief petty officer of *HMAS Sydney*. When next the newlyweds met, the bride was recovering from the effects of a termination, and to the groom 'did not look too good'; soon after, she disappeared. Having plagued Mitchell for days, Rosser finally proposed: 'If I go to the police and tell them the truth, will you get out of this trouble?...You have been in trouble before and have got out of it'. Mitchell muttered: 'There was a lot of blackmail about that'. She faced crowds at her Richmond Court trial with characteristic insouciance. 'Mrs Mitchell wore a frock of biscuit-coloured *crepe de chine* with a smart grey fur and a small hat trimmed in oriental colours', noted *Richmond Weekly*. 'Her daughter Queenie and another female relative were in cool white tussore with black hats.' When police dragged the Yarra fruitlessly and Rosser's evidence was deemed that of an accomplice, Mitchell was discharged in November 1928.

Evidence against abortionists was not merely difficult to collect because, like Mitchell, they buried their mistakes. Women after World War I developed an omerta, partly from fear of charges, but partly out of solidarity. In May 1921, for example, Justice Schutt jailed Olive Lock for declining to testify against Dr James Teague, who had aborted her. When she nonetheless maintained her silence, Schutt directed the jury to acquit: 'She has been punished to a certain extent already. She has not changed her mind and so far as I can tell will not do so'. Women's Hospital staff took a similar attitude. Officially, they were to alert police to signs of illegal interference. Unofficially, admitted a medical superintendent, they 'didn't use to let the police know until the last minute, and by then...the women were so moribund that the police couldn't do anything'. Even when police made it in time, admissions were rare. When dying septicaemia victim Margaret Priest was interviewed at Royal Women's on 12 August 1923, she yielded nothing to Detective John Madin save the state of her marriage.

Madin: What is the cause of your illness?
Priest: I have used a crochet needle on myself to bring on a miscarriage.
Madin: I do not believe that. Someone has operated on you.
Priest: No, I have told you the truth.
Madin: How long were you pregnant?
Priest: About two months.
Madin: How many children do you have?
Priest: Five. I could not have any more children on account of my husband who is a terrible drunkard and is very cruel to me. I have led a terrible life. With him I would not have any more children even if I have to die.

Six months later, 18-year-old Olive Babaud was probably admitted by the midwife who had lethally lacerated her cervix in the act of aborting her. But to Detective Daniel Mulfahey she proved inscrutable.

> Mulfahey: What is your age?
> Babaud: Eighteen years.
> Mulfahey: When did you come from Portland to Melbourne?
> Babaud: On 29th March last.
> Mulfahey: Who was the cause of your trouble?
> Babaud: I was walking on the beach with some other girls and I had a fall.
> Mulfahey: It is alleged that an illegal operation has been performed on you by some person.
> Babaud: I am too ill. I will say nothing.

A harrowing toll was paid for the uncompromised availability of abortion services, there being no fewer than thirty-one deaths from puerperal sepsis at the Women's Hospital in 1927–28. But such deathbed silences were a continuation of the stoic practicality women adopted for the procedure itself. When abortion began featuring in women's fiction between the world wars, it was a challenge tackled with determination and collegiality. In Jean Devanny's *Dawn Beloved,* Rose rejoices at success:

> I searched among the blood clots... but nothing in the shape of what she bade me look for turned up. The afternoon wore on. The discharge ceased. Determined, her face ablaze with anger, Rose got off the bed with the intention of taking the remainder of the mixture—and when she stood up the tiny embryo, not more than an inch long and dead white, fell to the floor. At the sight of it I vomited, then fell into uncontrollable weeping.
>
> Rose, however, bubbled over with exultation; she became prodigiously energetic. Everything was bundled up, first in a cambric petticoat, then layers of paper, and lastly in an oiled cloth dragged from her small dining table. 'As soon as it's dark,' she said joyfully, 'we'll carry it up to the bridge and drop it in the creek. The tide will carry it out.'

Abortion is a gender hazard in Kylie Tennant's *Tiburon*, whose Mrs Mulvey refers breezily to 'me operation'; in Eleanor Dark's *Waterway,* where Aggie Trugg counts herself as a mother of six, 'not counting odds and ends'; and in Dymphna Cusack's *Jungfrau,* in which free-spirited Marc Roberts describes the procedure as 'messy but no different to having your appendix out'. So it was in life. Elderly women from Port Melbourne and South Melbourne who were interviewed for 1984's Time and Tide oral history project recalled their experiences with brutal frankness. Jean Brett's husband was particularly oblivious to her ordeal.

> I'm telling you, it's damned agony. You'd have no anaesthetic or nothing, all they would do is clean out your womb and you would be conscious. At any stage they would do it. They weren't doctors, they were midwives. They were supposed to be midwives. I can't remember how much you'd pay...but I do remember my husband was waiting for me in the car when I came out. I was half damn dead, I might tell you. He said: 'Christ I'm sick and tired of bloody waiting, I was nearly going to go home.'
>
> How can they possibly...how can he...because I had no idea either, I don't know what I expected. But you do think they're going to do something...something gentle, don't you? No they don't. They just scrape it out as though it's a...scraping up mud out of a gutter. That's the truth. They had no feelings whatsoever. You paid whatever sum it was, it was far more than a man's weekly wage would be. Some women couldn't have any more kids after that. As I said they just scraped you out, like scraping out the inside of a marrow.

To obtain convictions amid so many gritted teeth and tight lips, police went to extremes. In January 1934, for example, they staked out a house on Elwood's Esplanade. Inside was part-time abortionist and full-time sailor Ronald Hill, his wife Rose, dental mechanic Cecil Taylor (handling the ether), unconscious Elizabeth Ritchie, her labourer husband John, and three others. Police demolished the door, arrested everyone and confiscated everything, even the operating table. Hill was a fantasist: his barrister explained unconvincingly that he was a kind of 'amateur doctor', having 'been associated with a medical institute'. Yet Justice Wasley gave Hill and Taylor only a few months' jail while releasing the rest, and added with regret: 'I wish I could see it consistent with my duty to release the prisoners on a bond but I do not think I can do so'. As a prosecution it hardly justified the effort.

~

For all the Hannah Mitchells and Ron Hills of the 1920s and 1930s, the bulk of abortions were probably still self-procured. Those doing so out of shame, fear or thrift could choose from a host of folk remedies: castor oil, baking soda, eating matches, drinking turpentine, pills from lead-plaster, liquor in which copper coins had been boiled, riding bicycles, reclining in hot mustard baths, jumping off high places, driving on bumpy roads. Three infection deaths before the coroner on 22 April 1929 had little in common. Twenty-three-year-old Kathleen Hudson had used 'a large number of pills and repeated doses of Epsom salts'; 30-year-old Alice Dicker had ridden repeatedly on Luna Park's Big Dipper before employing a crochet needle; 32-year-old Elizabeth Bren had used a trusty piece of elmbark kept in a jar on the mantelpiece—inserted in the cervix, elmbark tended to swell from the moisture until it precipitated contractions. Bren, a friend revealed, was a serial offender: 'I said she was a foolish woman to do it. She said: "What else could I do with four hungry children around me? I could not possibly bring any more into the world." She did happen to mention she had done it eighteen times previously in the last four years'.

As depression pushed Australia's birthrates to their lowest levels in history, abortion-related admissions to the Women's Hospital soared. Of the more than 3000 women admitted in 1933 and 1934, 22 per cent were infected, and not quite 2 per cent died: fifty women, suffering mainly clostridial myonecrosis. So common became what was colloquially called 'gas gangrene' that it made an international authority of hospital superintendent Arthur 'Bung' Hill. The culprit was probably the era's most widespread abortion instrument.

The Higginson's syringe—a nozzle, rubber reservoir and pump devised in the 1850s—was so popular that the Women's Hospital sold them for douches and enemas at cost price. It was also widely rumoured that solutions of Lysol, a Reckitt & Colman disinfectant, or Lifebuoy, a Lever Brothers soap, induced miscarriages. Yet indiscriminate use of the syringe was fraught with peril: its rubber perished, its connections were a haven for dirt and bacteria, and there was always the risk of an air embolism from a stray bubble. A neighbour heard Alberta Neal whistling as she swept her backyard in Geelong's Fyans Street on 25 August 1943. Half an hour later she was dead, a four-and-a-half-month-old foetus in her uterus, bubbles in her vena cava. In a bowl nearby bobbed a well-worn Higginson's syringe.

Although inquests by definition concern mishaps, they also suggest that the syringe was favoured for relative speed. Thirty-three-year-old Doris Sanderson died after syringing a three-month pregnancy with Lifebuoy on 17 August 1946 while her husband was at the football and her sister listened to the radio in the kitchen. Thirty-three-year-old Janie Harrington suffered a fatal embolism on 16 January 1948 using Lysol, having told a friend over morning tea: 'I think I will fix myself up before the boys come home'. It was popular long afterwards too, recalls veteran feminist writer Beatrice Faust.

> I was instructed in the use of the Higginson's Syringe by a grandmother whom I met during vacation employment in 1958. She was appalled to find that I was getting married without knowing how to 'bring on a period'. She had syringed herself thirty-two times and only had septicaemia twice. Although she had nearly died on each occasion, she still taught her daughters to use this method.

It's probable that this old contraption, put to a use that would have scandalised its inventor, ended more pregnancies than any professional procurer of miscarriages in the country, qualified or unqualified. In hindsight, Archbishop Carr had denounced the wrong appliance.

'Not a fit subject for debate'

'You've no idea what the place was like.
No lights anywhere—spooky like a morgue.'
'Was she a nurse, this woman—a trained nurse, I mean?' I asked.
'No, just a dirty old hag with filthy fingernails.'
'Why didn't you walk out when you saw she wasn't clean?'
'Huh! It was too late then—she already had my dough.'
The Autobiography of a Sydney barmaid (1953), 'Caddie'

They called her 'Milly', although this was not her real name. She was fourteen years and nine months old, lived south of the Thames and had just begun work for a well-known firm. Of her no more is known, except that she unwittingly changed the course of medico-legal history. Because on the evening of 27 April 1938, having gone to watch the Horse Guards parade at Whitehall, Milly was invited into the stables to see 'a horse with a green tail', and sadistically raped over a period of hours by multiple guardsmen. Three were arrested. Each received four years' jail.

Milly's ordeal left her 'agitated and overwrought', as policewoman Lilian Wyles put it politely. She was also pregnant. The male doctor under whom she was admitted to St Thomas' Hospital discountenanced abortion on grounds that the child 'may be the future prime minister of England', and 'that anyhow, girls always lead men on'. The female doctor to whose attention she came, Joan Malleson, was active in the British birth control movement, and begged to differ. And if there is a hinge-point in the history of abortion where it passed mainly into the hands of doctors, it is when Malleson contacted Aleck Bourne, a consulting gynaecologist at St Mary's Hospital in Paddington. Three years earlier, Bourne had aborted a 15-year-old girl at another doctor's request, and been irked when the two Catholics on the theatre staff, including his house-surgeon, walked out in protest. Bourne had resolved that if another such case came his way, he would take the job and then turn himself in so that the law might be clarified. Milly's plight seemed to him 'a God-given opportunity' in that 'she had suffered the extremity of cruelty and horror and was, withal, an innocent child'. He wrote Malleson: 'I have done this before and have not the slightest hesitation in doing it again'.

The celebrated matter of *R v Bourne* almost didn't happen. A few days before Milly was admitted to St Mary's, her father asked Bourne that the operation be kept secret. To this day, nobody knows who wrote Wyles at Scotland Yard advising her of the operation to take place that day, 14 June 1938. 'That letter was descriptive', recalled Wyles, 'and left nothing to the imagination'. Whatever the case, it wasn't only Bourne who faced trial at the Central Criminal Court on 18 and 19 July: a 77-year-old law faced *its* accusers.

R v Bourne didn't provide birth control reformers with exactly what they wanted: affirmation of abortion as a humane act. Roland Oliver KC, a consummate criminal barrister with a flair for murder trials, was intent on dazzling the court with the quality of his expert opinion that continuation of the pregnancy would have jeopardised Milly's physical and mental health: medical witnesses included Lord Horder, physician to five consecutive British monarchs. But this may have been wise: Justice Macnaghten was not a notably lenient judge where abortion was concerned, and had jailed an unqualified female abortionist in the same session of the court. By contrast, he was impressed by Bourne, 'a man of the highest skill' who worked 'in one of our great hospitals'. And he homed in on the construction of section 58 of the *Offences Against the Person Act* where it specified that any person who 'unlawfully' used an instrument with intent to procure miscarriage was guilty of felony: 'In my opinion the word "unlawfully" is not, in that section, a meaningless word'. He referred the jury to section 1(1) of a more recent statute: the *Infant Life (Preservation) Act* of 1929. This Act had smoothed a quaint wrinkle in the law whereby a baby killed in the process of birth could not be said to have been murdered while any part of its body remained in the mother. The offence of 'child destruction', he advised jurors, specifically excluded medical operations carried out 'in good faith for the purpose only of preserving the life of the mother'.

> In this case... my direction to you in law is this—that the burden rests on the Crown to satisfy you beyond reasonable doubt that the defendant did not procure the miscarriage of the girl in good faith for

> the purpose only of preserving her life. If the Crown fails to satisfy you of that, the defendant is entitled by the law of this land to a verdict of acquittal.

What did he mean by 'preserving the life'? Macnaghten had an answer for that too:

> If the doctor is of the opinion on reasonable grounds and with adequate knowledge that the probable consequences of the continuance of the pregnancy will be to make the woman a physical and mental wreck, the jury is quite entitled to take the view that the doctor, who, under the circumstances and in that honest belief, operates, is operating for the purpose of preserving the life of the mother.

Bourne found the experience a trial in every sense, even its favourable conclusion. Wyles recalled him as a 'mass of nervous anticipation' who 'left the dock older by many years', and found the forty minutes in which the jury deliberated to be 'exquisite torture'. Macnaghten's ruling, too, was immediately subject to well-merited criticism. Was the use of the statutory proviso in the *Infant Life (Preservation) Act* legitimate? After all, the threat to a woman's health in childbirth is a great deal more immediate than that involved in abortion. And how was 'mental wreck' to be defined? No system of determination was offered; no threshold level of proof.

One of Macnaghten's most perceptive critics was a rising star of the Victorian bar, Jack Barry. A lapsed Catholic of liberal leanings, Barry had been examining the clauses of the *Offences Against the Person Act* concerned with abortion since they had been subsumed in Victoria's 10-year-old *Crimes Act*. Like Macnaghten, he had concluded that the designation of some abortions as 'unlawful' connoted necessarily 'that there were some forms of abortion which were lawful'. He also felt that any exception to the rights of the unborn child threw the 'whole principle overboard'. He told the proceedings of Victoria's Medico-Legal Society in February 1933: 'If the medical profession found that the termination of the pregnancy was at times necessary in the interests of the mother's health, then it seems just as reasonable that it should be because economic circumstances are unfavourable or for other sufficient reasons'. Thus his disappointment with *R v Bourne*. In a provocative and prescient address to the society in November 1938, he proposed a more robust defence of abortion drawing on the legal principle of necessity: classically defined as the excusing of a crime committed 'in order to avoid consequences which could not otherwise have been avoided' and which would otherwise lead to 'inevitable and irreparable evil'. Doctors, he opined adventurously, might even one day be felt to have a 'duty' to perform abortions. In one assertion, Barry was adamant: the matter of abortion was better left to the judiciary than the legislature, because 'on a subject such as this the reaction of the average person...is not intellectual but emotional', and it was therefore 'not a fit subject for debate in popular assemblies or in the Parliaments we have', the 'quality' of representatives having 'deteriorated'. If this sounds like the voice of brazen legal elitism, he had some evidence for his conclusion.

War is often a pretext for the extension of state powers and persecution of internal enemies, and, with the outbreak of World War II, some knew where to look. Catholic hegemony in Labor circles was at the time deeply embedded: the proportion of Catholics among Labor parliamentarians grew from less than a quarter before 1914 to about half between the world wars, heading towards a 1954 peak of 60 per cent. Abortion vexed them sorely, especially Arthur Calwell, MHR (Member of the House of Representatives) for Melbourne from September 1940, who was staunchly opposed to the 'hedonistic doctrine now being popularised...that woman has the sole right over her own body, and can alone decide on an abortion for some reason, or no reason'. Calwell turned a debate the following year about the need for fit men in the Army into a lecture on moral depravity, flourishing a range of figures of mysterious provenance: there were, he claimed, 5000 terminations in Melbourne a year, 2000 self-induced, a quarter of them involving single women. 'I have also been informed', he stated, 'that at least five per cent and it may even be ten per cent of the medical profession in Melbourne engage in criminal abortions'. He recommended:

> 1/ All abortionists—and they are well-known—should be interned forthwith. No fifth columnist or pedlar of subversive literature is half so dangerous to society as these destroyers of young Australian lives.
>
> 2/ The law against abortion should be strengthened as it was in Germany and Italy. The National Health Act could be used effectively to this end.

Adoption of the policies of nations with which Australia was at war was too surreal an idea to catch on. No federal politician would be more steadfast against abortion, and the tide of permissiveness in general, than Calwell. 'Every nation in history that has practised infanticide… has been destroyed, and deserved to be destroyed', he insisted. 'God is not mocked. Race suicide does not pay. Those who advocate abortion on demand should not be tolerated in any civilised society.' But his crusades tended to be solitary affairs, and the priority of this one steadily waned by comparison with others.

One initiative of the Curtin government was to set the new National Health and Medical Research Council on the old vexed question of the birthrate—still below its pre-Depression level. Unlike Dr Mackellar's earlier Royal Commission, the NHMRC was prepared to entertain sociological explanations rather than simply to infer moral decline. The report tabled in November 1944 includes testimony solicited from women who had 'deliberately resolved not to have children or to limit their families', some of the 1400 letters received being extremely trenchant.

> I believe you desire the reasons of mothers for only having a limited family. Well, one of them is this: what do we owe Australia? It starved us and our children after the last war and it will do the same after this if we let it. Therefore we have decided that there won't be so many of us to starve this time. It is better to gaze on one or two hungry children than, say, eight or nine, and if one can arrange to have none so much the better. We, the mothers, hold this power in our hands. We have a freemasonry among ourselves that is colossal. If we find out any birth-control hint we pass it on. I myself know of an easy, safe method of abortion, I know of hundreds of other ideas that have been passed on to me by desperate and despairing mothers of hungry children. Things will have to be mighty attractive in the new world before we consider the inconvenience of big families.

The council's conclusions were that 'the economic insecurity of the large family' lay at the heart of the decline.

> There are several important and quite genuine motives influencing this decision. Perhaps the two most important of these are the desire to retain the companionship of the husband and the happiness of

> married life, and the desire to see that the two children are properly equipped for their later life.

'Companionship', of course, was a euphemism for an active sex life, and the desire for this freedom came through strongly in letters expressing apprehension about possible restrictions on the sale of contraceptives. The report was still laced with moral judgements, including on abortion, where the law was said to be 'almost entirely inoperable', and that 'society should punish adequately this violation'. But when it lay mainly unacted on, Barry's wish was effectively granted. Politicians held their hand, leaving the judiciary and police to cope with a law of dubious workability. Two wartime cases show the bench groping for guidance—and in doing so, as in *R v Bourne*, skewing the abortion field towards doctors.

Twenty-three-year-old Edna Freeman of Louvain Street, Coburg had one infant child to husband William, but her second pregnancy was cruelled by pain and heavy discharges. She described her symptoms in a letter to local midwife Florence Trim, and received a solicitous reply:

> Dear Edna,
>
> You had better come up here Monday between 10 and 11 as it must be dead for what came away from you. It is best to see you early as possible and fix you up. It won't do any good to stay as you are. Hoping you are feeling well,
>
> Yours sincerely,
> Mrs Trim.
> PS: I have never failed you before so I will get you right in the end, don't worry.

Freeman died of shock and haemorrhage and Trim went to trial for murder. Defended by the virtuoso criminal silk Jack Cullity, she was found guilty of manslaughter, and two confederates were acquitted. But Cullity was vexed by the judge's summing up, during which he directed the jury that 'to use an instrument... with intent to bring about the emptying of the contents of the womb, even if it were a dead child, would be a felony'. He pressed for clarity, and in April 1943 sought leave to appeal. No such luck: by two to one, his application was dismissed.

Melburnians were fascinated two years later by the case of Vera Wiper, ruled to have died on 14 July 1945 from 'shock resulting from an attempted abortion'. Twenty-three-year-old Aircraftswoman Wiper was found dead by a milk carter on a poorly lit thoroughfare in Auburn still wearing her Women's Auxiliary Australian Air Force overcoat. Unlike most victims of abortion gone wrong, she was buried with full military honours at a funeral conducted by an air force chaplain. The story was pieced together by a shrewd detective, Charles Petty. Wiper, it transpired, had been in camp at Ballarat, and confided in another WAAAF, Alice Pearson, of her condition. Pearson had sought advice from a health inspector she knew, James Loughnan, and been directed to mother and daughter midwives Ruby and Iris Carlos in Myrtle Street, South Yarra. Wiper had left Ballarat on 4 July, staying with Pearson's mother Josephine in Auburn before the operation. All were charged.

The Crown case quickly began fraying. Wiper had died while being prepared for the procedure: representing the conspirators Pearson and Loughnan, Hannah Mitchell's erstwhile lover Percy Ridgeway persuaded jurors that for this his clients were hardly responsible. Ultimately, too, the jury decided that the Carloses could not 'have contemplated that death or grievous bodily harm was likely to result from the use of such means'. But again, it was the judge's directions that left the deepest impression. Echoing Macnaghten's regard for the skill of Bourne, Justice Gavan Duffy distinguished between the use of 'an instrument' by a doctor and a non-doctor: 'It was no business of hers to use it; a doctor may cause a miscarriage in order to save the life of a woman or for some other reason, which would be lawful, but if *she* did, obviously it would not be lawful' (my italics).

This distinction intrigued the representative of the Carloses. Thirty-five-year-old Ray Dunn was the son of a police inspector, Jack, who had advised him to concentrate on gaming offences: there were so many loopholes in gaming law that a clever solicitor could extract a client every time. But Dunn's pal Jack Cullity had aroused his interest in abortion law. Already burly, and on his way to becoming hugely fat, he looked like a man who'd seen a bit of life, missing the tips of three fingers after a grenade explosion in Lae (New Guinea). In time, he would make a reputation as Melbourne's foremost petty sessions solicitor, with a speciality in the next quarter-century of defending police. But nobody would defend more doctors on abortion charges.

~

Between the world wars, aborting doctors remained few and far between. The researches of Swain and Howe turned up only four in Melbourne, amid numerous midwives. Conservative doctors had traditionally been opposed, like the Catholic Dr Herbert Moran:

> I have never known any except the habitually unscrupulous who did not feel a malaise in deliberately scraping away a life. In their hearts they know that this is not the role of a body vowed to the art of healing. Even those who regard morality as something merely concerning the mores of people see in the deliberate destruction of human life the falling away from a high apostolate.

Liberals also found it difficult. Bourne hated doing abortions: 'It's a horrible operation. Everyone in the theatre loathes it and you can feel the gloom'. Norman Haire devoted his practice to birth control, and inscribed on its window the rhyme of the old woman who lived in the shoe 'with so many children she didn't know what to do'. But he ruled out law-breaking:

> I have no moral objections to the interruption of pregnancy *per se*. I think that every case should be judged on its own merits and that a great many cases deserve to be terminated where the present law forbids termination. But in spite of my sympathetic attitude and of my disapproval of the present law, I am unwilling to perform illegal operations. Firstly, by so doing I should lessen any influence which I may hope to exert towards bringing about a change in the law; secondly, I should be risking imprisonment and disqualification and the loss of my livelihood.

Doctors prepared to hazard prosecution, however, had built sizeable practices, and been much loved. When Albert Bretherton died on 2 February 1937, Prahran's High Street was gridlocked by 3000 mourners, rows of stationary trams stretching in each direction. And although nobody aspired to be 'the Bourne of Australia', *R v Bourne* attracted a good deal of attention in the local medical profession, while

R v Trim and *R v Carlos* consolidated the status of the doctor over the midwife in bearing the brunt of desperate women's needs. The security of doctors was then further enhanced by changes in policing philosophies.

Victoria's tempestuous chief commissioner in the 1920s and 1930s, Thomas Blamey, had loathed abortionists: rumours swirled that he had lost a girlfriend to Albert Bretherton. For all that, the police's efforts to curtail abortion were mainly pointless and thankless—an outcome of the law, as we have seen, but also a symptom of a force demoralised by bad management, poor recruitment and constant industrial unrest. Blamey's urbane successor, Alexander Duncan, a former chief inspector at Scotland Yard and member of its famous 'Flying Squad', favoured policing methods less pointlessly punitive. *Tenez le Droit*, or 'Uphold the Right', was the motto introduced in his watch, an echo of the catchcry of the Royal Canadian Mounted Police, *Maintiens le Droit*, and a commitment to duties more evolved than waiting for crime and then barging in to break it up. Duncan thought police should be visible, mobile and integrated with the community. He put uniformed men on bicycles, rallied detectives by radio, and encouraged members of the force to join the National Fitness Council as a means of bringing police and public, especially youths, into closer contact. As the *Police Journal* rhyme put it: 'Give them a place for innocent sport/Give them a place for fun/Better a playground plot than court/And a jail when the harm is done'.

The force Duncan inherited was the most undermanned and poorest paid in Australia, and under him briefly worsened: force strength fell from 2333 to 2131 during the war. All the more reason to concentrate resources in areas, like gun crime, that posed serious public danger, and illegal gambling, rampant since the arrival of baccarat in the 1920s. In *The Argus* index, there were no entries under the heading 'Illegal Operations' in the second halves of 1939, 1941 and 1942, whereupon the practice of designating abortion as a special category of crime ceased.

From 1943, the Victorian Police's Criminal Investigation Branch was reorganised. The Special Branch founded by Blamey was disbanded; in its place were established 'squads' headquartered at the handsome new ten-storey building at the corner of Russell and La Trobe Streets, topped by its 45-metre radio mast. Some squad names still resonate: Armed Robbery, Vice, Gaming, Arson, Fraud. A few acquired reputations for esprit de corps bordering on the cultish, like the Breaking Squad, aka 'the Breakers'. But first in prestige always was Homicide.

Constabulary duty was then a way of life rather than a job: the *Police Manual* still required a policeman to obtain his superior officer's permission before marrying. Homicide took this to a degree without parallel. It was the only squad entered purely by invitation: a detective doing well at divisional level would receive a tap on the shoulder—and nobody ever said no. It was the only squad whose office door at Russell Street was bare: the word 'homicide' was thought a little confronting to visitors. *The Herald*'s legendary police roundsman, Alan Dower, revelled in calling their quarters 'the Room Without A Name', and described its warm and clubby atmosphere.

> That Homicide Squad probably was the most democratic and united group in any police force of the world. There were no screens and little privacy. The detective-inspector—an august rank in those days—shared the conditions of his lower ranks, ate the same sandwiches or pies from the milk bar in MacKenzie Street and drank the same doubtful tea from the nearby urn.

Under Superintendent Bill Donelly, its head for twelve years, Homicide solved all but five of the 272 murders it investigated, including some of Victoria's most famous. It tracked down Edward Leonski, the Brownout Killer; it found Tony Agostini, murderer of the Pyjama Girl; it put away high and low alike, from the uxoricidal celebrity disc jockey John Brian Kerr to the cop killer William John O'Meally; it sent Jean Lee to the gallows, the last woman hanged in Victoria. Members arrived on crime scenes like deus ex machina: tough, aloof, sure of their stature, jealous of their jurisdiction, deaf to those who disparaged them as 'the silk suit brigade' and scoffed at their 'wog shoes'. Some were even famous for their dandified airs: William Wall Warner 'Wagon Wheels' Mooney affected a bowler and cravat; Frederick Wenzel 'Big Fred' Russell was known for his silk socks. Nobody doubted their implacability. When Donelly relinquished command in favour of Charles Petty in October 1955, he honoured their legend with a *Police Life* column chronicling their exploits: 'Homicide Squad Scrapbook' continued until his retirement in January 1963.

How demeaning that Homicide should have ended up with carriage of abortion; it would *never* be fit for 'Homicide Squad Scrapbook'. Not surprisingly, abortionists assumed secondary significance in their surveillances. Like Trajan and the Christians, CIB Superintendent Hugh Valentine Clugston disapproved but did not persecute. 'Old Smokey', as he was known for the cork-tipped Craven A cigarettes laid up in his office in cartons of 500, took a pragmatic approach. Detectives were told to garner intelligence, but not to storm surgeries unless a death was involved or a serious allegation had been levelled. Police files from the decade after World War II show officers taking a distant, even paternal attitude to abortion, such as in the case of Mary May Victoria Duffy: 'Police asked for magistrate not to proceed. Girl (17) said she self aborted. Police thought could charge girl but no good purpose—quite respectable intends to marry, mar her chance of future happiness'.

These developments reversed the American experience. In the 1920s and 1930s, American police and hospital administrators had taken a relatively lenient view of abortion, but the postwar regime involved tighter enforcement and harsher punishment. In two significant trials, doctors were jailed: Dr George Timanus in Baltimore and Dr Edgar Keemer in Detroit. Historian Leslie Reagan has theorised that this 'promotion of maternity' was an 'assault on female independence': an attempt to roll back the advances women had made towards equality during the Depression and World War II. Women aspiring to work were caught in 'a double bind', observes Reagan: 'required to control their reproduction and forbidden the means of doing so'. Women in Melbourne after the war lost some citadels they had seized during it, when they had worked in banks, conducted trams and driven taxis. But, if they had but known it, they were probably at less risk of prosecution than at any stage in the state's history. Being illegal, of course, abortion remained a frightening and furtive experience, with the potential for morbidity if one blundered into an unscrupulous or incompetent practitioner. But abortion's age of discretion had begun—and with it doctors made a snug fit.

‘That old bastard, he knew’

‘Is [the doctor] safe?’ Joe asked, a little suspiciously…
‘That doesn’t matter,’ Rennie said quickly.
The End of the Road (1958), John Barth

When *The Sydney Morning Herald* awarded Ruth Park its inaugural fiction prize in 1948 for *The Harp in the South*, it was unprepared for the outraged reaction. The novel places heroine Roie on the path to a Surry Hills abortionist, egged on by thoughts of the proud working-class women she knows: ‘Didn’t old Mrs Campion next door openly boast of her fifteen misses? She took something…’ Clawed at by her Catholicism, Roie baulks at the last moment, only to be beaten by marauding sailors. But her mother has already experienced a shock ‘which was never altogether to leave her’—and the same applied to the readership. Cascades of correspondence ensued. ‘The book was immoral, filthy in fact, though no specific filth was ever mentioned’, Park recalled. ‘Some letters were well-intentioned and written by people who gave their names and addresses. The filth-protestors mostly signed their letters *Yours Prayerfully, A Christian, or Catholic Mother,* and gave no addresses.’

Yet by the late 1940s, the face of abortion was changing. Doctors were suddenly perceiving its attractions. Many were dealing with the impact of penicillin, which made treatments simpler, but also shorter, and thus cheaper. To move into abortion was to go with the flow: to take advantage of the power of antibiotics to curb infection, which had been the procedure’s gravest risk. The chief beneficiaries of the illegality of abortion would henceforward be doctors, able to extract super profits from medicine becoming increasingly exoteric.

Chief among them in Melbourne would be Dr John Heath. Nobody meeting the upstanding Heath would have guessed his tawdry upbringing. John Read William Allan was born in Northcote on 10 April 1902. His father was 22-year-old journalist James Alexander

Allan, his mother 16-year-old Ignez Louise nee Heath. Theirs had been a rush to the altar in October 1901, followed by a brief marriage that ended when James cast Ignez out, and she fell back on her builder father Bill. Then, when John was not quite two, his mother died of typhoid; his earliest memory would be of people crying at Heidelberg Cemetery as what he took to be a box was carried past.

John was uneasily incorporated into his grandfather's family, taking their name, and treating Bill's children as siblings. Enrolled first at Alexandra College, a small Northcote school, he was then grudged a couple of years at Geelong College before being pressed into a real estate apprenticeship he disliked intensely. It was on taking a lowly job with a chemist that he resolved to bootstrap himself up in the world by tackling medicine at Melbourne University. His self-propelling upward mobility paid off. On 25 July 1928, after spells as a resident medical officer at the Alfred Hospital and a GP in Mooroopna, he married Olive Baird, daughter of a family wealthy from the grain trade: he borrowed £200 from his new father-in-law to open rooms in Rathdowne Street, Carlton.

Abortion came to Heath rather than the other way round. With the benefit of a year at Edinburgh Infirmary, he started work as a gynaecologist at Burlington Chambers, 94 Collins Street. Like Sir Hugh Devine, the much-admired founder of the Royal Australasian College of Surgeons, who operated nearby, Heath equipped an operating theatre on the premises. Then, around 1940, his uncle/brother Bill Jnr, now a pilot, approached him. He had a girl in trouble. John was a doctor: couldn't something be done? In fact, Heath found he had an aptitude for abortion, not to mention some personal insight into inopportune pregnancies.

'I am a strict disciplinarian', Heath said of himself, 'and insist on efficiency in every way'. He was strict not least with himself, keeping a tight lid on his background. Silvering, moustachioed and dapper, Heath oozed rectitude. He became a major in the Army Medical Corps and a Justice of the Peace, joined the Naval and Military Club, and helped found the White Ensign Club, providing comfortable lodgings for visiting naval personnel. He was a dedicated supporter of the Newsboys Club, the charity for underprivileged youth run by Edith Onians. He belonged to the 'Pups', a group of wealthy businessmen, doctors and lawyers who held an annual lunch to pool money for good works. He could afford to be a generous benefactor, because in abortion he had the sleekest of cash cows. And whatever his charitable instincts, charity for Heath began at home—or, to be more exact, homes. For from 1951, he was leading a curious double life.

Heath's marriage was never happy. Olive had a sister in a mental institution, and punished her husband for inattention with brooding and rage; daughter Patricia was moody and intractable. Corinne Blackwell, a former hostess with Australian National Airways, joined his practice as a receptionist; pretty, shrewd and strong-willed, she became his partner in every respect but marriage. He already owned 'Mowbray', a two-storey Toorak mansion in cream rendered brick with a U-shaped driveway and tennis court, and 'Los Angeles', a teeming St Kilda boarding house. Now he acquired Burlington Chambers, Collins Street's only remaining single-storey building, a nearby Alfred Place nightclub called 'The Delphic', and a bluestone retreat off Camp Road in Campbellfield called 'The Manor House'. Abandoning Olive to rattle around in 'Mowbray', Heath spent most of his time at the last with Corinne.

On the 4 hectares of 'The Manor House', they began an adjunct to their business. Girls whose pregnancies were too advanced for termination could live in as domestics until they reached full term, when Heath would deliver them at Coburg Hospital. As many as six at a time were billeted, their occupancy highly ritualised. On Sunday mornings, Heath would take them to church; after serving the Sunday lunch, they would give a concert in the rumpus room, into which Heath joined with recitations from Banjo Paterson, Henry Lawson and Adam Lindsay Gordon. A personal favourite was 'The Sick Stockrider':

> I've had my share of pastime, and I've done my share of toil
> And life is short—the longest life a span;
> I care not now to tarry for the corn or for the oil,
> Or for the wine that maketh glad the heart of man.
> For good undone and gifts misspent and resolutions vain,
> 'Tis somewhat late to trouble. This I know—
> I should live the same life over, if I had to live again;
> And the chances are I go where most men go.

The offspring would then be placed with wealthy Catholic families through the St Vincent's Hospital matron. The scenes as the girls gave up their babies were often heart-rending, but, Corinne recalls: 'It had to be done'.

~

Abortion suited the avaricious. Money was largely tax-free: cash hesitantly offered in envelopes was not the kind that required receipts or double-entry book-keeping. Fee scales, moreover, were entirely unregulated. Heath sometimes charged on the basis of the patient's car: the better the marque, the more they could afford. Of course, nobody shopped around: poor patients might seek special consideration, but rich ones tended not to haggle, while fees for perceived premium service were astronomical. In Barbara Baird's oral history of abortion in South Australia, Dr Bill Smith related a story from his country practice in 1956:

> Mother insisted on telling me every detail, to get it off her mind I think. She told me how she had enquired from sources in Adelaide who was the most skilled abortionist in Australia, because she and her husband—who had plenty of money and their most precious possession was their daughter—so they were going to get an abortion whatever it cost. They wanted the best—they didn't want any problems.
>
> So they were given the address of this well-known Melbourne gynaecologist and they took their daughter to Melbourne and they saw the gynaecologist and, in brief, he aborted her in his rooms under general anaesthesia and he did it, obviously, in a very skilled and professional way because later that afternoon of the day of the abortion, the daughter was able to walk to the car...The fee was £800...about $20,000 now.

Abortion was also easy money for doctors who didn't fancy working so hard. Examples in Heath's generation included Billy Flynn, another member of the Pups, and Lewis Phillips, an indolent man devoted to music and the punt: he operated with a lit cigarette at his lips singing snatches of Gilbert and Sullivan; his desk drawers were full of peanut shells and old copies of *Sporting Globe*. It was Phillips who in 1940 initiated 35-year-old gynaecologist William Fenton Bowen in the trade. They had the formative experience of being prosecuted together:

charges against them of procuring a miscarriage were dismissed in a petty sessions court in September 1941. It did not make them noticeably more cautious. Phillips's surgery in Bourke Street's Bank of New South Wales was two blocks from police headquarters; Fenton Bowen hung his shingle at 456 Lonsdale Street, across the road from the Supreme Court and next door to the Australian Broadcasting Commission.

After World War II, a younger medical generation arose, which included at least one with a powerful sense of calling. Albert Bretherton's son Rodney had intended studying engineering but could not resist the siren song of medicine. Discharged from the Army Medical Corps in May 1947 as an honorary captain, he took over his father's old premises, intending to be like the old man whose virtues he extolled even in verse.

> My father was a doctor and he practised there in Prahran,
> A rebel always siding with the ordinary man.
> And when the slump descended with the storm clouds overhead,
> He had to pay when illness put a hardworking man to bed.
> Doctor paying patient? 'For the urgent drugs,' he said,
> 'A worker can't afford them when the industry is dead.'

Tall, rangy, with a 96-centimetre chest and green-blue eyes, Bretherton was perhaps the most complex of all the abortionists, a man passionate in his pursuits and violent in his breaks. His closest friend was Cedric Ralph, aka 'Ced the Red', a Marxist lawyer of obsessive purity who had defended the Communist Party of Australia in the Lowe Royal Commission. But even to Ralph, Bretherton was single-minded: 'He had a way of getting onto a subject and in a solo way discussing it on and on. He would not be diverted. I would try anything I could think of to change the subject but Rod would answer any interjection and return to his subject'. Bretherton's daughter Dianne remembers a childhood in which apparently close family friends would suddenly and inexplicably disappear after quarrels, never to be seen again.

Bretherton understood that abortion was a divisive issue for the community because it was a divisive issue in his own life. Wife Shirley disapproved, believing he had wasted opportunities to pursue more conventional careers; he kept everything from his children. The bearing of a child he also knew to be fraught with unimagined stresses: it had, of course, killed his mother; it then undermined his marriage when his first son Christopher died of what would later be called Sudden Infant Death Syndrome. The death rocked the household, aggravating in Shirley an incipient schizophrenia, worsening in Rodney a tendency to seek solace in alcohol. An attractive young housekeeper, Thelma Butcher, came to help hold the household together, inevitably became Bretherton's mistress, and helped have Shirley involuntarily committed.

To spread the load, Bretherton took a partner. Suave Jim Troup, who had graduated from Melbourne University a year after Bretherton, was also following family footsteps: his father was also a surgeon, and a ladies' man, destined to have seven children by three wives. Unlike Bretherton, Troup was not pursuing an ideal so much as a lifestyle, exhibited in his affectations: David Niven moustache, Saville Row suits, two-tone shoes, floral bow ties, Jaguar XK120. The partnership lasted two and half years before the inevitable personality clash.

Bretherton was not his father. For all his avowals, he liked living well almost as much as Troup. With his half-brother, Bruce Bretherton, a wartime fighter ace, he indulged a lifelong love of skiing by investing in the Hotham Chalet, the Bulla chairlifts and an Armadale skiing school that taught the Vaydln technique; he would sometimes interrupt a monologue by jumping to his feet to demonstrate a tricky turn. He professed approval of radical causes, but never beyond the point where they might endanger his comfort. His views of women, too, were surprisingly naive. 'My father and his generation had very old-fashioned attitudes to women', says Dianne Bretherton. 'It was all very World War II, all very heroic: in Bruce, we even had a heroic airman in the family. They saw themselves as saving women. They weren't so keen on women saving themselves.'

After a period with his father, Troup partnered another doctor, Arnold Finks, who had just bought out the practice of Phillips. Finks had earlier operated with Troup's university contemporaries Alan Burman and Harold Grinblat from well-equipped rooms in Stanhill, a Queens Road apartment block. He and Troup made a rather odder couple: Finks was as decorous as Troup was gregarious. But it did not seem to matter—and little did. In a period of plenty, respectable doctor abortionists operated with comparative openness. What Dr Fenton Bowen might be up to was even the subject of rather heavy-handed legal ribaldry across the road. An apocryphal story concerned an elderly judge in whose courtroom a witness collapsed, whereupon it was suggested that Fenton Bowen be sent for. 'I'm not sure that's quite his line', his Honour is reported to have said. Barrister Brian Bourke recalls a case in Fifth Court when Fenton Bowen was asked to deal with a juror who had fainted. Crown Prosecutor Len Flanagan snickered: 'Do you think I should tell Fenton Bowen that it's a man?'

Police files show routine checks without much zeal. Visits are recorded, for instance, on Bretherton in March 1953...

> Not much evidence to proceed. Info talking to woman in Belgrave Café...B denied—said silly, no party to abortion. Apart from a strong suspicion that he is an abortionist there is practically no evidence against him at all to date.

... and on Finks and Burman in November 1955.

> Reports of abortion via anonymous letter to chief commissioner posted Met 29/8/55...Detectives made inquiries. No suspicious circumstances...Highly qualified specialists of high repute. Manager very police-minded citizen.

Clugston's CIB doctrine of 'no investigation without a complaint' was observed even for public figures. Dr Leslie Edmunds was an institution in working-class Coburg, Essendon and Moonee Ponds, holding one-day clinics in different local houses, painting abortion in hues of vivid normality:

> Mothers abort their daughters, sisters abort one another. I had one street where they handed the same piece of wood over the fence for twenty-six houses. Only two got a temperature of 105 degrees and had to go to the Royal Women's Hospital. The rest aborted satisfactorily...The law is regarded as archaic and obsolete except insofar as it applies to charlatans...I never failed to give £10 to the lady of the house because she had a considerable family and rearing them well [sic]. As for the other £30—well, it went back to them or to charity or the Newsboys or the state school.

Edmunds's popularity was reflected in his election to Coburg council as a Labor member; in August 1958, with Labor and independents each holding six seats on council, he was elected mayor on the draw from a hat. John Heath was the richest of his tribe, but not even he parlayed abortion into electoral success.

~

The predominance of doctors after World War II put a patina of respectability on the abortion market, but was far from an unmixed blessing. For one thing, the doctors were often not particularly good, the recklessness needed to operate in a legal twilight being reflected in their work. It was a failure of the prohibition on abortion, Norman Haire observed, that laws purporting to make the public safer had therefore opposite effects.

> If a woman is really determined not to go on with her pregnancy, she usually finds some way to end it, even if she makes herself seriously ill, or meets her death, in the attempt. Competent medical practitioners who can make an honest living without breaking the law are unwilling to undertake the illegal interruption of pregnancy which would expose them to the danger of imprisonment and to the additional penalty of having their names removed from the medical register and being deprived to the right to earn their livelihood… The result is that for the most part abortionists are either medical practitioners who for some reason—often incompetence or drunkenness—have been unsuccessful in building up a good practice, or else non-medical persons, sometimes nurses or midwives, or sometimes completely uninstructed lay persons.

The doctor abortionists were heavy drinkers almost to a man, and often careless with money—Heath stood out for being neither. They were also usually indifferent technicians with, to use the standard surgical phrase of disapprobation, 'no respect for tissue'. Max Sizeland, a Queen Victoria Hospital resident, particularly recalls the execrable handiwork of Edmunds.

> I was in charge of the septic abortion ward for a while. It had twenty-eight beds and was full non-stop with botched terminations. The mayor of Coburg, he used to half-fill that ward. You know, he'd go into these homes in Brunswick with a bag of instruments, pour boiling water into the sink and sterilise that way, then do it on the kitchen table. They were horrible to see when they came to us.

Nor did doctors have any notion of preparing the patient for the psychological impact of their pregnancy's end. Corinne Blackwell would discuss options for their predicament with patients at 94 Collins Street, but abortion elsewhere was a two-dimensional experience: extraction of foetal tissue and extraction of the patient's money. Nicola Black found the experience of treatment terse and practical.

> You went in and went out. There was no 'hello'. No 'how are you?' No 'do you know what you're doing?' No 'are you sure you want to go through with this?' They didn't even use the word 'abortion'. They might have used the word 'termination' once. You get more instruction at the hairdresser. The only thing they stressed was that if the police talked to me, I wasn't to mention anything.

This suited those many women averse to reflecting too deeply on their experience. Rosemary Breen was told something about contraception after her abortion, but didn't hear it: 'Look, I know she [the nurse] was talking about it but I just wanted to leave. In fact—well, I wasn't rude, but I wasn't listening, I just wanted to go'. And to use the word 'abortion' in the context of seeking one was regarded as very bad form. Gwen Harston recalls a visit to Collins Street where she committed the solecism.

> The doctor said: 'You're a university student, aren't you? What are you studying?' I said: 'French and English literature.' He said: 'Well someone like yourself should be able to express yourself more fluently. What you should say is: "Doctor, I am having some problems with my period".'

Doctors did not feel so constrained by proprieties. Adelaide girl Anne Cooper, collected from the corner of Collins and Russell Streets for an abortion 'somewhere in the suburbs', was stunned by the crudity of the procedure and practitioners.

> I undressed and climbed onto the table, noticing with horror a plastic bucket on the floor near my legs. Suddenly the reality of what was happening hit me...I did not know at the time there were other cheaper options—and I am glad I didn't because I worry even today about what I might have done. As I started to go under the anaesthetic, I heard the two men discussing my body; they were speculating about what I would look like in a bikini.

When Cooper began haemorrhaging, she needed aftercare from a doctor bearing a marked resemblance to Billy Flynn.

> He was a horrible old man with a fat belly and heavy breathing that suggested catarrh. I felt inexplicably nervous about being alone with him... He gave me some tablets that he said would stop the bleeding. He also told me he would pay me a commission if I sent other Adelaide girls to him. As I was leaving he grabbed me and tried to kiss me.

Worse, he was incompetent: 'I needed to go into hospital for a dilatation and curettage. No wonder, I thought, shaking with rage, no wonder the Collins Street doctor was trying to buy me off. He knew. That old bastard, he knew'. Yet she felt better off than some in hospital: 'Her abortion had been done by her boyfriend. He had punched her in the jaw to knock her unconscious then used a coathanger'.

Nobody advertised, of course, but referral networks of GPs and chemists expanded in the doctors' service. To such high-turnover, low-margin operators, commissions on abortion referrals came in handy. A standard set of instructions was for the patient to ring the surgery from a nearby phone box and say that they were already bleeding and needed help—abortion could then be deemed a response to medical emergency rather than a premeditated treatment. By these and other means, stress on the possibility of police intervention was played up—mainly to justify high fees. Sue Ingleton remembers being terrorised for her trouble.

> Graham [her boyfriend] knew about the place. Boys knew about these things, and the cost I can remember was £150. I said: 'Well, I'm not paying. I can't afford that. Anyway, I'm the one who's got to go through with it.' So he sold his mother's film projector. Over the next few years, his mother would occasionally say: 'Graham, where's my film projector?' And we'd just look at each other.
>
> I felt so unsafe. Not because of the place so much but because the nurse absolutely put the fear of God into me. She sat me down and read me the Riot Act. She was saying: 'If you get arrested when you walk out, you don't have to tell the police anything. They can't force you to admit to anything.' On and on and on. So when I went to meet Graham, who was waiting under a tree, I was just terrified. I was vomiting, from what I later learned was far too much anaesthetic, but

> I was saying: 'Come on, come on, we've got to get away!' I was expecting a policeman's hand on my shoulder any second and to be taken away in a paddywagon.

For all their pretensions to respectability, too, medical practitioners involved in abortion were strongly interpenetrated with the lower end of the market: the remaining midwives, the unqualified operators, crosses between the two. Inquests and anecdotal evidence suggest that 'backyard abortionists' faded as a force after World War II. But a few notable examples survived, with the full approval of doctors, who referred to them those patients whom they could not see because they were busy, would not see because they didn't have the cash, or would not treat because they were too advanced: to abort a pregnancy beyond twelve weeks was felt rather infra dig among medical practitioners—at least, if an exorbitant fee could not be obtained.

Fenton Bowen referred to Edwin Daggard, a male nurse with Canadian qualifications who worked at Dingley Hospital, and to 'Nurse Mussert', the alias of midwife Gwendoline Bailey. Phillips farmed out to 'Nurse Schaefer', alter ego of midwife Mary Moulder, and 'Nurse Cholet', the notorious Ivy Matthews. Matthews guarded her privacy jealously: her real name was Irene Sutton nee Dolan; her police file, listing charges dating back to 1933 of abortion, receiving, unlawful possession and insulting words, identifies her variously as Irene Cholet, Irene F Sholet, Irene Smith, Florence Mackie and Nurse Mack. Her vocation was only part of the reason. It had been on her evidence that Colin Ross had gone to the gallows in 1922 for the infamous Gun Alley Murder—a denunciation earning her £437 in rewards from the state government and *The Herald*, but which on more recent analysis may have fingered an innocent man.

Doctors did not refer, of course, for charitable reasons: they received commissions, usually of 30–40 per cent on fees of between £30 and £100. But there was some discrimination. Most everyone steered patients to the remarkable Jean Field. Born Jean Shaw at Lavington on the Victorian border with New South Wales, she was part of a family deeply involved in the abortion trade: sisters Annie and Bessie and brother Donald all dabbled to greater and lesser degrees. Having qualified as a nursing sister in 1927 and trained at Prince Henry's, Jean married insurance superintendent Hugh Field in November 1935, but for them parenthood was an unmitigated tragedy.

Their firstborn, David, was stricken with gargoylism: acute deformity of the skull and progressive mental retardation. The pneumonia that killed him aged three also claimed the Fields' infant daughter Sandra.

Field resumed nursing for a Middle Park general practitioner, Ray Hart, one of the very first GPs to systematically arrange referrals for abortion, and focus of one of the period's few major raids. Storming a South Camberwell house in May 1951, police found Jean Field's sister Bessie and friend Lillian Paisley wearing white rubber aprons in a kitchen 'fitted out like a hospital'. Hart was alleged to be their procurer, but the charges were dropped when the magistrate decided that while 'there is no doubt that instruments were used by someone', he could not say by whom. Field herself became so accomplished that Hart gave her the run of his small Brunswick private hospital, on condition that no unqualified people worked there. She also began working three days a week for Heath. He would insert a rudimentary version of the modern laminaria tent—a cervical dilator that expands from absorbing fluid. When contractions began within a couple of days, Field would handle the miscarriage, then direct the patient back to Heath for a curette. Field later accepted patients from Fenton Bowen, Bretherton and Burman, with the result that all individually claimed her as a protégé, and she boasted of never needing to advertise. 'I would not accept the patient unless I knew the sender', she said proudly.

When Field fell out with Hart over Daggard's involvement at the hospital, she joined her friend Belle Moran nee Lewis in a mobile abortory. Belle was the mother, while married to Des Moran Snr, of the hardcore criminal duo Lewis and Desmond (Tuppence) Moran. In the Moran family station wagon, Jean and Belle drove from safehouse to safehouse with their steriliser, disinfectant, suitcases of surgical instruments and collapsible laminex operating table. Once the steriliser was on and a linoleum square had been laid on the kitchen floor, Moran would fetch patients from prearranged rendezvous points at street corners and tram stops. Beatrice Faust was a Field patient for the first of her three abortions, being whisked through the backstreets from Brunswick's Sarah Sands Hotel to a house in Coburg, and impressed to find that every other patient had used Field before. Twilight sleep gas in a simple vaporiser kept her awake but comfortable through the procedure: 'I found the sound of curettes clinking on dilators and the shoving sensation of the curettage more distressing than any pain that might have occurred but still tolerable'.

In time, Field became a woman of means, claiming to have saved £62 000 from her work from 1950 to 1958. She was also called upon to teach others, her instruction manual containing such fruits of experience as:

> Don't give receipts
> Don't ask them to bring pads & c—it makes good prosecution evidence
> Don't ask patients to call own doctor if complications arise
> Be careful of patients who ask too many questions
> Remember, civil witnesses are the most dangerous

One Field student, 25-year-old architectural draftsman John Brookes, had first dabbled in abortion in June 1955 as a driver for 'Nurse Schaefer', who operated from houses in Mitcham and Hawthorn. When his car was in for servicing, he had his commercial traveller brother James help—until a complaint had them all rounded up. James Brookes wisely did a bunk for Canada, because his brother and Schaefer were convicted. But silver-tongued Jack Cullity persuaded Justice Norris to take pity on the former, who celebrated his release on probation in September 1957 by locating Field to obtain instruction in the abortion arts for himself.

Brookes knew of Field through Bretherton, with whom he had struck up a friendship based on their mutual love of flying: he had persuaded Bretherton to invest in a flying school where he kept a Tiger Moth. Bretherton in turn had taken a solicitous interest in Brookes's trial, persuading Fenton Bowen to kick in £1000 for his defence. When Field imparted her knowledge, Bretherton consented to Brookes operating from his premises in High Street, Prahran at weekends. He was soon probably the busiest unqualified abortionist in Melbourne.

There were still horror stories, some unqualified abortionists being reluctant to use anaesthesia at all in case of interruption, and here and there remained an outright crank. Court records turn up the likes of Aspendale's Frederick Claude Adams, a spiritualist who regarded himself as a faith healer, and Peter John Cawardine, a former St Paul's Cathedral bellringer who gave away free abortifacients. Even his defence counsel described Cawardine as a 'very secretive person': 'He has no friends and is withdrawn from society. These acts...satisfied his yearning to win respect and made him feel important in his own eyes'. But unqualified abortionists were now most often found among the most deprived, such as Melbourne's new migrant communities. Juliana Hasses, formerly a masseuse at St Joseph's Hospital in Sterkade, West Germany, looked after Hungarian women from her St Kilda boarding house. Henry Bierzynski, a skilful gynaecologist whose qualifications in prewar Cracow were insufficient for him to practise legally, was used by Polish women. Outside the metropolitan area, there remained stalwarts like Ballarat's Florence Donovan, first charged in September 1934 and finally given a custodial sentence on her sixth conviction in December 1964, aged seventy-four. In the country, too, with the shortage of conventional medical care, customs of self-induced abortion lingered long. Admitted to Wangaratta Base Hospital in October 1956, 35-year-old Benalla waitress Muriel Swindle admitted to attempting to abort herself with Dettol. Her apparatus: a bike pump hidden in the cabinet of an old wireless set. The valve, sealed in a plastic pocket, is still in her inquest file at Victoria's Public Records Office.

Relations between doctors and the unqualified in the abortion trade were decidedly ambivalent. Doctors were, of course, apt to condemn the 'backyard abortionist' out of hand. But as bogey men, such figures showed them in a favourable light. In doing business with unqualified operators, however, doctors kept unappetising company. Garrulous Brookes was a relaxing influence on the Bretherton household; Rod could be a severe, unforgiving father. Elsewhere, Brookes was a crooked businessman, a violent husband and an increasingly careless unqualified practitioner. His wife Irene would describe him as 'a peculiar man, a perverted man who took some sort of sensual or sexual pleasure in performing abortions'.

Irene Brookes also recalled a night-time visit to the home of Homicide detective Gordon Timmins, when Brookes was anxious to obtain an adjournment in his trial. While Irene waited in the car, Brookes and Timmins conversed at length in the street. Then, when Brookes was arrested again, he drove to a deserted stretch of unmade road in Noble Park where another car was parked. Having pulled out a big roll of notes and surreptitiously placed a miniphone wire recorder in his breast pocket, he sat conversing in the other car for five minutes.

Then he drove off at speed, pausing only to play back a little of the tape: his wife heard a voice she would identify as Timmins's. In doing so, she became probably the first outsider to sniff the abortion racket's dirtiest secret.

'It's not what you say; it's what *we say* you say'

Well, a gentleman knows where he is if the police own the brothels.
'Return of the Native' (1979), Gwen Harwood

For how long abortionists nurtured corrupt relations with police will never be definitively known: it is not the stuff of telltale documents or disinterested testimony. The likelihood is that they always did. The licence Hannah Mitchell enjoyed certainly savours of favours, and protection money was then de rigueur among city brothel owners, whose cartel, 'The Combine', crossed police palms and excluded the uncooperative. In Sydney, the society gynaecologist and sly grog tsar Reginald Stuart-Jones had run an abortion protection racket from the 1930s, with the approval of the city's top cop, Ray Kelly, and his protégé, Don Fergusson. So it is scarcely unthinkable that Victorian police had for some time been financially encouraged to look away when mishaps occurred. Mitchell would hardly have been alone among abortionists in finding herself encumbered with the occasional body: from time to time, rumours circulated of cadavers dumped in Port Philip Bay or interred in Sherbrooke Forest.

It makes sense, too, that the broadening and deepening of corruption in Victoria's abortion trade should have coincided with the rise as service providers of doctors—rich, naive and protective of their reputations. Police, by contrast, even detectives, were wretchedly paid; worse, as the force's historian Bob Haldane notes, they were 'expected to live as one class while paid to live as another'. The force's improving postwar prestige, Haldane says, had invidious side effects: 'Police had to live in a nice home, with a nice wife and send their nice kids to nice schools. But they were paid labourers' wages'. In the fifteen years from 1955, police constables lost pay relativity by 28 per cent, until they earned a fifth below average weekly wages. There were no incentives, bonuses or overaward payments. Nor were police permitted to supplement their incomes in their spare time: Chief Commissioner Selwyn Porter believed that officers 'must always be on call in case of emergency', avoiding pursuits that might 'lower their status in the eyes of the community'.

Little wonder that some began supplementing their incomes on the job—chiefly in the 1940s and 1950s through off-course 'Starting Price' bookmaking, an industry that turned over £250 million annually. Punting was a favoured recreation among police; for some, it was a way of life. Officers were involved in every layer of the SP industry: as customers, agents, protectors and proprietors. At 1958's Royal Commission into SP Betting, counsel assisting AE Woodward suggested that 60 per cent of police charged with administering gaming laws were corrupt, 20 per cent were apathetic, and only 20 per cent did their jobs properly. Inspector MJ Healey, leader of the Licensing, Gaming and Vice Squads, counterestimated 50 per cent honest, 30 per cent dishonest, 20 per cent inept—as if this was much better. Police, as was their wont, instinctively closed ranks. The Police Association raised hell; Porter conceded laziness and inefficiency, but no corruption; premier Henry Bolte's chief secretary, Arthur Rylah, declared that further investigation 'would not only be futile but uncalled for'. Reform proceeded more circuitously through the instigation of the legal off-course betting apparatus of the Totalisator Agency Board, which from March 1961 began putting SP racketeers out of business—and cutting underpaid police off from their chief form of graft.

Some police continued doing well. The Breaking Squad did flourishing trade in stolen goods: future chief commissioner Kel Glare would tell a story of a 'Breaker' arriving at a burgled menswear store, stripping noiselessly to his underwear, then fastidiously making himself over from the racks. Yet as Homicide detectives were apt to complain, there was little money in murder. The prestige of the Room Without A Name didn't pay the bills. In hindsight, it seems almost inevitable that they should have cast covetous eyes on the illegal industry forming part of their bailiwick that had grown so lucrative.

~

Detection was not then a subtle activity. Criminology, ballistics and forensic pathology were in their infancy. Police remained overwhelmingly dependent on confessions, which they pursued relentlessly; before Legal Aid, when the majority of defendants were unrepresented, confession virtually guaranteed conviction. The convention of a solicitor's presence during interrogation was honoured more often in the breach, and because the tape recording of interviews was unknown, police notes were accepted in court as gospel. Techniques of intimidating a suspect into a statement, known as 'verballing', inspired the immortal Homicide saying: 'Remember, it's not what you say; it's what *we say* you say'.

Perhaps ablest of all in these dark arts was the shambling, ursine figure of Detective-Sergeant Frederick 'Bluey' Adam, a Tasmanian timber cutter and underground miner who became one of the force's most decorated manhunters; not to mention an individual who, as the great criminal barrister Frank Galbally described it, 'saw little harm in distorting the truth if he thought that the accused deserved to be convicted for one reason or another'. Some criminals nicknamed him 'Thumper', for reasons needless to elaborate; he called it administering 'a touch of the public benefit'. Future chief commissioner Mick Miller recalled a razor-wielding felon melting in horror at the very sight of him: 'Gawd—it's Bluey Adam himself!' Police informer Brian Latch remembered one career criminal showing him the weeping ulcer on his shin, the result of a two-hour session in which Adam had repeatedly kicked him with the toe of his boot in order to have him sign a statement.

It is a short step from a culture where guilt can be fixed by force to one where innocence is sold for money, especially in a society retaining a deep-grained deference to uniformed authority. That deference, indeed, was one of policework's more enjoyable aspects, consolation for poor pay and interminable hours. One day, Adam was walking with an acquaintance along Bourke Street when he came upon an Indian man whose complaint had vexed him. He hurled the man through the Myer Emporium's front window. The message was not lost on the acquaintance. Her name was Peggy Berman.

~

Corruption can only be partly explained by sociological forces; its origins almost always lie in personal characteristics, needs and vulnerabilities. And in the case of abortion, much of the story is wrapped up in the combative, contradictory character of an illegitimate, working-class, Irish-Catholic girl born in Geelong on 17 March 1923 as Margaret Dorothy Costello, but always known as Peggy. She never knew her parents and was raised for a lifetime of menial labour by her boarding house-manager aunt and retired-railwayman uncle, being left barely literate by her Sisters of Mercy education. From age twelve, she had spells as a factory hand at a rope works, salesgirl in a department store, stacker in a cannery, labourer in a glass factory and assembly line worker at Ford. In Sydney she was for eighteen months a pantrymaid at Crown Street Women's Hospital, studying 'droves of single women constantly coming and going, suffering agonies in deciding whether or not to keep their babies'. Yet her own motherhood was probably the more formative experience. Compelled to marry at sixteen when she fell pregnant to real estate clerk Harold Berman, she bore a deaf and blind daughter, Helen. When Harold enlisted, it became her lot to spend three and a half years watching Helen die at the Royal Children's Hospital.

In April 1945, Peggy Berman bore a son, Peter. Investing in the idea that a sound education would lift his life's station, she threw herself into sending him to Xavier College. The pivotal point of her own life would also come at an educational institution. After her marriage failed, she took work in Melbourne University's sandwich bar, where she met Norval Morris, the New Zealand-born founder of the university's pioneering criminology department, not yet thirty but on the brink of a professorship. Berman's recollections are not always incontestable, but the strong inference of her autobiography is that they became lovers and she pregnant; it was Morris who guided her to Lew Phillips's Bourke Street surgery in December 1953. For Berman, abortion proved a salvation, for she also left with the offer of £25 a week to scrub the doctor's floors, do his laundry and ironing, and eventually to act as his receptionist—something for which she soon showed aptitude. 'There was nothing that the patients could tell of in the way of troubles that I had not experienced personally', she recalled.

Phillips was then in the process of selling his practice to Arnold Finks. And being an abortionist's receptionist, Berman discovered, required rather more than a sympathetic ear. There shortly barged in a familiar figure: 'Bluey' Adam. Coincidentally, they had met in Geelong during Berman's gadabout adolescence, when he had given her a book, *A Message from Garcia*—an inspirational homily by Elbert Hubbard published in 1899 about a soldier of unswerving obedience. Adam soon asked Berman to come for a drink with him across the road at the down-at-heel Carlton Hotel. 'Have you still got that little book I gave you in Geelong?' he asked. Berman confirmed she did. Niceties over, he moved on to business: 'If Finks wants to go on working, he's got to pay £50 a month'. Berman would become the bag lady, darting across the road to the hotel with the money inside a magazine whenever Adam called and identified himself as 'Garcia'. 'If you tell a soul I will learn of it', Adam warned. 'I hear everything.'

If Berman's account of the establishment of the relationship has a ring of truth, one element is worth noting, seeing as it became a template for future arrangements. The implication is that Adam had previously stood over the principal, Phillips; in this deal, he chose to bully an agent, Berman. Berman does not explain what Finks thought of the arrangement, why he let Berman manage it, and even why Berman was willing to do so. Where the last is concerned, the inference must be that Berman managed it because she wished to; indeed, in the final analysis, the arrangement was one that delivered her a degree of power. Corrupt inducements never flow entirely one way: the extorted obtains influence too, through knowledge of the extortionist's legally compromised position. It would have been as much influence as a former factory hand and pantrymaid had ever enjoyed, and wakened a talent: Berman would develop a flair for placing herself at junctions of power and acting as a broker.

Exercise of power was a subject of which Berman became a connoisseur. After the Labor Party split, she joined the ALP's Yarra branch, where in September 1955 young Jim Cairns was anointed to challenge anti-communist incumbent Standish Keon. At the behest of Cairns's campaign manager, Clyde Holding, Berman formed a women's organising committee, and relished a bitter campaign replete with mutual disinformation, with its moonlit forays to sabotage opponents' leaflet drops and to scrawl on walls: she might even have perpetrated the anti-Keon graffito at the corner of Tanner and Margaret Streets that acquired National Trust heritage listing. On 10 December, polling day, when fists flew outside St Stephen's Anglican Church, Berman was busily ferrying voters to booths in her Rover: a vital contribution to Cairns's victory by fewer than 800 votes.

Whatever the case, Adam's menaces do not seem to have bothered Berman overmuch, and his monthly ransom, even when later doubled, rather pales by comparison with Berman's estimate of the practice's weekly turnover of £2000. Nor was she so alarmed about his threat that he 'heard everything' not to confide details in Norval Morris, solicitor Ray Dunn, and local Communist Party president Ken Miller. For Berman, this was a heady period. After a year, Finks relocated the practice to a terrace house at 1087 Hoddle Street, East Melbourne. It had a waiting room and doctor's surgery on the ground floor, an operating theatre with three recovery cubicles on the first floor, and a phone room beneath the stairs that Berman stationed: for this she took home about £35–40 a week, enough to rent a flat in Burnley Street, then in September 1958 to acquire the pretty villa at 11 George Street, separated from the surgery by a cobblestone lane. The acquisition formed part of an arrangement bringing Rod Bretherton's erstwhile partner Jim Troup into the practice. Troup paid Berman a year's rent in advance to run the front of the premises as his own rooms.

Berman enjoyed her new lodgings by entertaining broadly and bibulously: at her salons, Labor comrades and trade unionists rubbed shoulders with academics, doctors and scientists, as well as the odd former criminal, including Norman 'The Chaffeur' Bradshaw, a renowned killer to whose handicapped child Berman was godmother. When her relationship with Morris ended with his appointment as Adelaide University's dean of law, she added to her string of lovers, whom she showed a notable propensity for keeping as friends. One paramour, Barney Marrows, who rose to be second-in-charge of the Postmaster-General's Department, rang her every day for the rest of his life. Another, motor mechanic Ray Warren, became her husband—albeit for ten days. They remained close: when Berman was arrested a decade later, Warren raised her bail.

Adam's presence loomed. He lodged at nearby Victoria House, sometimes taking delivery of his graft there. But he *was* as good as his word. While Troup was acting as locum, the practice was the subject of an unexpected inquiry: a girl being questioned about her appearance in pornographic photos distracted police by revealing a recent abortion. Adam suggested Troup undergo the formal interrogation denying everything, and was displeased when the doctor initially took John Brookes's advice to avoid the practice. 'I've had to send the car around the block three times to delay the bloody raid', Adam complained. The practice had to pay £300 each to Adam and Brookes. Adam rang to thank Troup for the '300 cases of oranges', Brookes to advise Troup against smoking during interrogations: he shook too much. It proved an embarrassment rather than a serious problem—and there was shortly a reminder that problems could become serious indeed.

On 13 September 1958, Lew Phillips, who had continued dabbling in abortion after selling out, was consulted by a 39-year-old pregnant Englishwoman with seven children who simply 'did not want another child'. He gave her an address in Nott Street, East Malvern, home of 63-year-old nurse Melinda Woolcott. The woman arrived there at 8.15 a.m. next day, and was 'laid on the operating table' by Woolcott, whereupon Phillips arrived in his street clothes—closely followed by police, at the disgruntled husband's behest. Leading the raid was a zealous Irish-Catholic detective, Noel Murphy, who was unusual in his determination to punish abortionists. He had the backing of the shrewd Irish-Catholic Homicide chief Charles Petty, and hearing the case was a stern Irish-Catholic judge, Justice Robert Monahan. Ray Dunn successfully obtained Woolcott's acquittal, but, on 25 June 1959, Monahan dished out eighteen months' jail to Phillips on one count, and fifteen months on another.

Nobody could remember a doctor receiving such a serious custodial sentence for abortion: since the days of James Beaney and William Gaze, doctors had enjoyed protected status in the eyes of the law. Phillips languished in Pentridge nursing a worsening ulcer while his appeal was prepared, a report on his health by a colleague finally judging him 'seriously ill', whereupon the full bench accepted an argument based on *R v Trim* that the law was principally concerned with unqualified abortionists. 'A prison term for a man in Phillips' condition would amount to torture, something banned for a hundred years', said Justice Starke. The conviction, nonetheless, had already instilled in Berman a sense of grievance against the policemen concerned. 'She did not like Mr Murphy. She was annoyed when Mr Murphy charged Mr Phillips. She said he should not have charged him. He was hard'—and the speaker was in a position to know. His name was Jack Ford.

~

Promotion in the Victorian police was a convoluted ritual preluded by a period away from Russell Street. And there were other less formal but no less rigid rules, top positions being divided up and alternated between Catholics and Protestants. This was no longer so much sectarianism as tradition: as Bob Haldane recalls, 'neither' was the only wrong answer to the question of what one was.

> After I was in the force a few years, I decided to run for the Police Association. I got a phone call from a Masonic Lodge saying: 'We haven't seen you on our rolls.' Then my chief inspector called me in, and he said: 'I see you're running for Police Association. We haven't seen you at any of our meetings.' You had to be either a mick or a mason, nothing else.

So when mick Petty moved out of Homicide in November 1959 in order to move up, he was succeeded by mason Jack Matthews, which raised in the pecking order his right-hand mason Jack Ford. They would eventually be Victoria's most notorious policemen. At the time they were two of the most talented—if an absolute study in contrasts.

Matthews, born in Brisbane in July 1910 to well-to-do parents from Birmingham and educated on a scholarship at Royal Worcester Grammar, had an unusual background for the force. He had donned the uniform in 1933 after eight years as an optician, and was fond of old-world courtesies like addressing all women as 'my dear'. Not that there was anything effete about him. Instructed by trainer 'Dodger' Ryan in his well-known city gym, he boxed for some years as an amateur. Then in 1945 he was shot in the arm and foot while raiding a Fitzroy house, and carried eighty shotgun pellets in his body for the rest of his life. It was the stuff of law enforcement legend, and he enjoyed almost universal respect, even affection. For where criminals tended to fear 'Bluey' Adam, they were hard-pressed not to like avuncular Jack Matthews, seldom seen without the pipe that lent him an air of Chifleyesque trustworthiness; like Peggy Berman, he counted 'Chaffeur' Bradshaw among his friends.

Nobody much liked Jack Ford: he wouldn't allow it. Once a butcher's boy, he was a hard-boiled, hard-working career cop who had shown phenomenal endurance and absolute fearlessness since joining in February 1940. He was also a deeply untrusting man who let nobody close. He neither smoked nor drank, and picked at his food as though loath to admit liking it, abhorring sauce of all kinds. He drove a different route home every night, eyes on the mirror in case he was being followed. To grim-faced, crew-cut Ford, it was all about being strong. He exuded the high-strung, self-mastering energy of a man waging war on the world as a proxy for the struggle with his own instincts. For just occasionally, the mask of austerity slipped. Ford ravened for sweets, especially pavlova and chocolate. And he gambled—how he gambled, with hopeless instincts and explosive rage. Otherwise, he was a mystery even to his steadfast wife Elsa. They had a son and daughter but, she would later reveal, sexual relations had ceased between them after three years' marriage: 'I was naturally upset but I didn't make a big deal of it because I blamed his job. He worked a lot'. She described him as a 'shy and reserved man', and nobody knew him better; under the heading 'character' on his police service record, the space is blank.

Matthews and Ford. Ford and Matthews. To outsiders they seemed indivisible, but even their hunger for money differed: Matthews wanted it, mainly for his family's comfort; Ford needed it, for a £60 detective's salary was insufficient for someone with his ruinous punting luck. As for their justifications of entitlement, they commingled self-interest and personal philosophy quite distinctly. Matthews regarded graft as compensation for being an overworked, underappreciated policeman; Ford saw it as recompense for enforcing a law he disliked. Some years later, in his only television interview, he expressed a disarmingly nuanced view of the law's proper role: 'No-one having an abortion gets off scot-free—it's a matter between the woman and God. Sometimes women have to have an abortion, but they should be able to have it with dignity and care'.

When Matthews first visited Berman at George Street in December 1960, accompanied by Homicide colleague Gordon Timmins, it was all matter-of-fact. The Hoddle Street practice would be expected to pay £300 a month for advance warning of all raids. 'Things will be done my way, my dear', said Matthews. 'Remember, it's not what you say; it's what *we say* you say.' For illustrative purposes, Matthews went through the motions of investigating a complaint. Four days before Christmas, Matthews acted on word from Dandenong CIB that 15-year-old Helen Taylor, an inmate of Winlaton Youth Training Centre, had told her mother Dorothy of being aborted by Finks. Berman was informed by an unidentified voice looking for the doctor. When she said that Finks was taking a sailing holiday, the voice sneered: 'If you don't get this message to him he'll be on permanent holiday'.

Matthews suggested Berman approach the Taylors about changing their story: if they would swear that the girl had been bleeding on arrival, the case would enter the 'semi-safe legal twilight zone' of medical necessity. It took two long car journeys to the outer suburbs before Dorothy Taylor could be addressed alone, but agreement was reached, and the surgery was squeaky clean when Ford 'raided' Hoddle Street at the appointed time. It was an auspicious meeting: Peggy recognised Ford's as the sneer on the phone, and had a first glimpse of the most important figure in her life for the next decade. Compared to hulking Adam, he was a graceful figure, and apparently trustworthy, for the deal was quickly done. Although Finks was identified in a Russell Street line-up, Matthews honoured the bargain by omitting to note it in the station's Special Occurrences Book, then permanently mislaying the file. The detectives charged £1000 each. Ford called Troup to thank him for the 'thousand cases of oranges'; he also invited himself to George Street, and not merely to ensure his own £300 monthly fee.

So began a relationship, the sex of which Berman would later glory in, and Ford as adamantly deny. Berman would then argue à la Mandy Rice-Davies ('Well, he would, wouldn't he'), causing Ford to retaliate rather more bluntly ('You are the biggest fucking liar of all time'). Whether or not Ford overcame his sexual inhibitions, it was clearly a relationship of acute emotional intensity. Berman would describe his 'wraithlike personality', his fastidiousness 'to the point of fanaticism', his tendency to erupt if thwarted in any way. In March 1961, Troup having become a full partner in the practice, Berman moved into a first-floor flat above Safety Brakes in City Road, and gave Ford a key because of his temper if he had to wait to be admitted. Nonetheless, she was excited by Ford's stern mastery. Taxed later about the seeming improbability of their mutual attraction, Berman would say: 'Oh darl, he seemed like such a *strong* man'. He was, too, a clumsily attentive swain, showering Berman with gifts: Orrefors vases, a hanging clock, a silver candelabra, a champagne bucket.

The relationship between law enforcer and breaker was scarcely improbable: the line between the two was always apt to move. Because of the centrality of the confession in inquiries, police made widespread use of informers, and informers of police, and Jack Matthews could cheerfully say: 'Just because you cause a man's arrest doesn't mean you become bitter enemies'. Crime had not yet been degraded by drugs and child pornography, and some crooks had a quaint glamour. In April 1961, Finks and wife Freida attended a famous Brighton party with a 'roaring twenties' theme. Comedian Jackie Clancy, booked to provide the entertainment, invited not just the Georgettes and singer Elaine McKenna, but 'Chaffeur' Bradshaw as a real-life gangster. Clancy was sacked from *In Melbourne Tonight* for undermining McKenna's innocent image, but it enhanced his saucy reputation that he was a pal of an underworld figure killed six months later in a mysterious light plane crash. Ford's relationship with Berman, then, is a curio of a time when police, wielding absolute authority, interacted with whom they pleased; its implosion embodies the end of that previously unexamined assumption.

It was also a relationship in which power shifted constantly. Berman would later present herself as a helpless victim of Ford and Matthews, but their favour made her a powerful figure by association. In her autobiography, she grumbles often about the doctors she worked with: 'The doctors would only tell me what they wanted me to know, but I would tell them everything'. Her relationship with Ford can be seen as a campaign for redress, a demand to be taken seriously as a partner in the enterprise. Berman suffered constant, nagging insecurities about money: when Jack Ford exalted her as his 'princess', she could briefly put aside her natal and class origins.

Berman was at her best dealing with poor and migrant women, to whom she showed unfeigned compassion: she sided instinctively with outsiders, and believed in keeping fees as low as possible for them. The more economically secure the patient, the less sympathetic she tended to be; she detested educated women. Her chief Hoddle Street helpers were flatmates: Paula Green, who joined in November 1961, and Maureen Young, who followed her in October 1962, both former nurses at Jessie MacPherson Hospital. They found Berman mercurial: warm-hearted one minute, a virago the next. Green described an atmosphere of 'secrecy and door shutting', where staff 'ran around looking harassed'. Young endured the air of intrigue by a simple rule: 'If I was told to listen, I listened. If I wasn't, I didn't'. Green stayed because she liked Finks, but her relationship with Berman soured after Finks sold out to Troup in December 1963. When later she worked for John Heath, she appreciated his calm professionalism.

Sometimes the changes of mood were too much to keep up with. One day, Finks emerged from the office at his new St Kilda general practice after suffering a tirade, and commented ruefully to his secretary, Winifred Telgenkamp, that he would willingly pay £1000 to have Berman run over. Overprotective Telgenkamp rang Berman anonymously to insist that she 'leave him alone'. Berman exploded, and Finks felt the only way to propitiate her was to let Telgenkamp go—whereupon Berman promptly offered Telgenkamp work at Hoddle Street. The shifting alliances of this strangest of markets were shortly to turn into open animosities.

~

'The faceless men' was the epithet Prime Minister Robert Menzies famously bestowed on the Labor Party's executive. The same title might have been settled on members of Melbourne's abortion trade: a clique of rich, powerful, well-connected and secretive individuals controlling a much-in-demand service for which they could essentially charge as they pleased. Yet among them, there was constant jostling for position and market share, as well as apprehension when anovlar became available in 1961 about what such birth control pills might mean. In the end, the net effect may not have been significant. Its availability probably increased recreational intercourse, and thus the scope for mishaps. 'The pill' also attracted a luxury tax, required a prescription, and was unavailable to single women under twenty-one: the segment of society most at risk of inopportune pregnancy. 'I was going out with an architecture student...and to get the pill in those days was really weird', recalls Sue Ingleton. 'Really the only girls who could get it were either going out with medical students, or who had doctors for fathers, or somehow knew someone with access to it.' But if its effect was perhaps more perceived than real, it formed another competitive pressure in a lucrative trade. And insofar as it is possible to tell, there was a shake-out in the abortion trade at the start of the 1960s.

The highest-profile casualty was former Coburg mayor Dr Leslie Edmunds, who, a little over two weeks before he was due to stand as Labor candidate in Essendon in the state election, received a visit from police while holding a day clinic at a Brunswick house owned by 37-year-old Myrtle Troja. 'I have been helping these poor people out', he protested to Senior Detective Perce Cooke. 'This is a political stunt—it all comes about because some New Australian woman goes to Russell Street.' He likened himself improbably to Gladstone, at least in the grand old man's concern with reclaiming prostitutes. 'Quite a nice bloke', remembers his defence counsel, Brian Bourke. 'Just a bit of a nut.'

Hearings attracted such intense local attention as to be held at Brunswick Town Hall, and took a few twists, the first trial being aborted due to jury tampering. Bourke was pleased when the second trial was held before Justice Woinarski, a judge of notably liberal views. 'Woinarski would have put a backyarder away', says Bourke. 'But he was never going to do anything to a doctor.' The jury found Troja guilty, but Woinarski gave her probation, and directed Edmunds's acquittal on grounds of insufficient evidence. But Edmunds's political career was over, and he was promptly arrested again in June 1963, only to suffer a fatal coronary during an adjournment in the trial. Meanwhile, the Stanhill practice went into decline after Burman also died of a heart attack, and a raid and charges discouraged Harold Grinblat.

Among the more successful unqualified abortionists, John Brookes remained in operation, but Jean Field was temporarily out of the industry, and Edwin Daggard died in November 1960. Indeed, by now, the 'backyard abortionist' of infamous memory was nearly a living fossil. Ford himself busted two of the last few, charging Ivy Matthews in December 1963 and John Bell in November 1964. Like Edmunds, Matthews died while awaiting trial; Bell was sentenced to six years' jail after certification of his insanity was revoked. Ford later credited Berman with information causing these arrests, and her denials were unconvincing: there is no doubt that at the time she wasn't simply protecting the Troup practice, but actively involving herself in the affairs of others.

Just before Christmas 1962, Jack Matthews contacted Berman about a complaint against Billy Flynn. Annie Van Loon, the Asian wife of a Dutch husband, was claiming that Flynn had confiscated her handbag in part-payment for an abortion. Matthews said £1000 would fix it. Berman rang Flynn's assistant, June Horak, who passed the message to Flynn, holidaying at Surfers' Paradise. Three weeks later, Van Loon identified Flynn, Horak and nurse Marcia Torey in a line-up. It is unlikely there would have been a prosecution, for the Van Loons shortly returned to the Netherlands, but Flynn was not to know this: he hastened to visit Berman, and tossed a fat roll of notes on the table 'just to get out of the place'. 'He was prepared to pay it', Troup recalled. 'He was quite happy about it.'

Another case brought Berman into contact with Heath. On 19 March 1963, coroner Harry Pascoe SM heard the tragic story of 22-month-old Victor Grimshaw, who had died from cerebral oedema after scoffing tablets laced with quinine and strychnine, which had been given to his mother for post-operative bleeding following a procedure at 94 Collins Street. Rhonda Grimshaw related:

> The tablets were in a paper envelope in my handbag which was on top of an old-fashioned wireless. Alongside of the wireless was a kerosene heater which he must have climbed up on to get the tablets out of my bag. I was in a habit of giving him 'Smarties' from the bag and he had seen me take a tablet earlier in the morning.

Under questioning, Rhonda Grimshaw conceded having been aborted by Heath: 'I am waiting for a divorce to come through and the man I am going to marry is also waiting for one; and if we had had this baby we would never have got our divorce'. Matthews told Berman that £1000 would buy Homicide's neglect. The only known meeting between the two most powerful figures in abortion in Melbourne, Heath and Berman, is subject to conflicting testimony. Berman, vague at first then increasingly precise in her recollections, would insist that Heath paid; Heath would insist otherwise, and Corinne Blackwell recalls interrupting a heated conversation by saying: 'Doctor, you have patients to see'. The role Berman was carving as protection racketeer was entangling her in ever more-complicated arrangements. She claimed later to have handled payments for a host of practitioners: not just Flynn and Heath, but Bretherton and Fenton Bowen, as well as new doctors on the scene in Peter Bayliss, Max Sizeland, Lister Catchlove and Zygmont Epstein. Though some of her claims proved impossible to substantiate, it was a heavy workload. One case demonstrates how fraught and involved the mechanism was becoming.

On 1 September 1963, Mildura Base Hospital nurse Violet Phillips, believing herself eleven weeks' pregnant to boyfriend James Cavallaro, arrived in Melbourne to consult Fenton Bowen. In a brief period of timidity, Fenton Bowen sent her to Catchlove, a general surgeon in Richmond, who aborted her the next day at Hawthorn's Allendale Private Hospital. Soon after, word of Phillips's flight reached her matron, who informed a detective at Mildura CIB, James Barritt. Barritt passed word to Detective-Sergeant Noel Murphy, and Murphy to Jack Matthews—who advised Berman, who advised Catchlove.

Catchlove and nurse Claire Matheson hastened to Allendale, discharged Phillips, and conveyed her to Spencer Street railway station, where Catchlove confided being in 'a spot of bother', and asked her to 'deny everything' if police called. It failed: Barritt cajoled Phillips and Cavallaro into admissions. But when Barritt presented the statements at Russell Street, Matthews reproached him.

> He said he was not satisfied the girl had told the truth. He said he was informed that the girl was on a tram going along Church Street when she started haemorrhaging. He said she was taken off the tram by the conductress and taken to the doctor's rooms. I told Mr Matthews I did not believe that. He asked why and I said in view of what the lass had told me I was satisfied she was telling the truth.

Barritt insisted they consult CIB chief Hugh Clugston, who conciliated by sending two detectives to Mildura to collect further statements. But the file wound up with Matthews anyway and disappeared—likewise £1500 from Catchlove's bank account, passed to Matthews via Berman. Catchlove shortly received a phone call from a male voice: 'Fifteen. Thank you'. At Berman's suggestion, he distributed bottles of whisky among police at Christmas.

Again, on whose behalf Peggy acted in the affair was ambiguous. On Christmas Eve 1963, her commercial relations with Troup were formalised in a partnership document drafted by Ray Dunn, granting her absolute discretion in fee scales and recruitment. The indigent, illegitimate, semiliterate girl with no training now ran a busy and growing medical practice—for which she had to thank her friendship with Matthews, and her mutual obsession with Ford. Indeed, if there is a corruption equivalent of Stockholm Syndrome, Peggy epitomises it, for her resentment at this time was directed less at police than at doctors: 'What puzzled me...was the lack of any appreciation of their situation on the part of the other doctors we helped. With each incident their ingratitude and resentment increased, and so did their underestimation of the police whom they seemed to think could be bought off without any difficulty'. Police, by contrast, were grateful, Matthews especially, then struggling to afford a holiday home at Rye. 'Thank you my dear, I'll never forget you', he told her one day, unaware how true that would prove.

'Boys in a man's world'

Dear Frank,
Whatever happens please don't
blame yourself.
Revolutionary Road (1961), Richard Yates

Thanks to Peggy Berman's relations with Jack Matthews and Jack Ford—'Senior' and 'Junior' as she referred to them—the fortunes of Melbourne's abortion rackets and police were now inextricably linked. The year 1964 was a good one for the former partly because it was an exceptional year for Homicide. Melbourne had been convulsed by a series of shootings at Queen Victoria Market between August 1963 and January 1964, suggesting organised ethnic crime in the city's midst. It became perhaps Homicide's finest hour. Jack Matthews persuaded Arthur Rylah that foreign expertise was needed, obtaining assistance from senior officers of the Rome Police and the US Bureau of Narcotics—to startling effect. A grateful Rylah funded the secondment of a Homicide detective to the FBI to study its countermeasures against organised crime, and Ford was overseas from May to August. Berman met him in Honolulu en route home, where he indulged his love of desserts but volunteered little more of himself than in Melbourne: secrecy, she was learning, was a matter of nature, not occupation.

The squad's fame was paid the ultimate tribute in October: television. When producer Hector Crawford decided that *Homicide* should be clearly set in Melbourne, the effect was a rare verisimilitude: Inspector Jack Connolly, played by Jack Fegan, even resembled his real-life equivalent, Inspector Jack Matthews. The series was the more convincing for being filmed in black and white on a traditional Australian shoestring, outdoor sequences being composed with minimal dialogue because of the pain of dubbing them, and filmed on location rather than in front of sets. 'We were jumping over fences in

Collingwood, Prahran, Port Melbourne', recalled actor Bud Tingwell. It also won praise for dramatising genuine social issues: drugs, suicide, prostitution, euthanasia, domestic violence. Yet it may not be entirely coincidental that not once in its 510 episodes did *Homicide* so much as touch on the subject of abortion, and that the idea of a squad member being corrupt remained entirely taboo: Crawford's police adviser was none other than Matthews's close colleague Gordon Timmins, who appeared as Senior Detective Doug Marshall in two episodes.

Even at this pinnacle of prestige, however, seeds were sown of challenge to Homicide's authority. In September 1964, Justice Sholl caused a furore when he found that two Italians accused of conspiracy to murder a market gardener had been punched, kicked and pistol-whipped in the course of their interrogation at Russell Street; he declared their confessions 'involuntary' and thus inadmissible. Two months later, a painter accused of car stealing alleged that he had been belted with a baton by a Detective First Constable, who told him: 'Bigger men than you have signed statements when I have finished with them'. More cases emerged with a similar theme, some even slightly comical. A court was told that one John Maxwell had confessed to picking up five youths in a stolen car; medical evidence was presented that Maxwell was actually incapable of forming a coherent sentence. Other cases were extremely nasty, like that of Vance Moore, whose confession to charges of burglary was found to have been signed after a detective had put a pistol to his temple, then stuck a wastebasket over his head and struck it with a baton.

Allegations culminated in July 1965 when police informer Brian Latch turned against those who had used him. Latch was a petty crook who had been 'somersaulted'—prosecuted in spite of his police connections—and was bent on revenge. Under circumstances of deepest anonymity, Latch compiled a detailed dossier of police malpractice involving no fewer than twenty-six officers, allegations that included handling stolen goods, swearing false evidence and 'verballing'. Solicitor-general Tony Murray submitted a 6500-word report to Chief Commissioner Rupert Arnold, recommending such measures as the use of tape recorders and the compulsory presence of solicitors for interrogations—recommendations publicly endorsed but very slowly adopted. Under pressure to do something about the allegations of Latch, still known to the world as 'Mr X', Rylah constituted a Police Discipline

Board to investigate possible 'overenthusiasm to get confessions not strictly in accordance with the law'.

The 'Mr X' hearings which began at Richmond courthouse on 2 December 1965 were notable for the legal talent on display—some of it to feature in the abortion story ahead. The board was represented by a silk on his way to the bench, Clifford Menhennitt; the police were defended by Peggy Berman's ubiquitous solicitor, Ray Dunn. Dunn dominated proceedings, intimidating Latch by revealing his identity through a defamation action, then cross-examining him mercilessly. The inquiry was shortly overshadowed by the sensational escapes of Ronald Ryan and Peter John Walker from Pentridge, but among police it permanently gilded Dunn's reputation. 'Ray Dunn became virtually an honorary police person', says Bob Haldane. 'They used to say in those days that if you had the slightest problem as a copper, you needed Ray Dunn.' The relationship had far-reaching consequences, as abortionists were suddenly assailed as never before.

~

On 28 December 1964, Jack Matthews clocked off at Homicide for the last time, destined for sojourns in Swan Hill, Mildura and Shepparton as part of his promotion to superintendent. That meant not just a change of boss at Homicide, but a change of that boss's denomination. Into the role stepped first a familiar figure, William Wall Warner Mooney; when he was promoted to deputy chief of CIB after a few months, a fresh face arrived, 50-year-old Francis Holland. 'Wagon Wheels' was a traditional copper whose father had been Thomas Blamey's deputy, and an old hearty once disciplined for buying a car from a felon he was about to put behind bars. 'The Dutchman' was shrewder, sharing acute political instincts with his father Joseph and brother Kevin, consecutive Labor members for Flemington. Where Mooney's Catholicism was companionable and convivial, Holland's was serious and organised. Educated by Christian Brothers in North Melbourne, he was the long-time secretary of the Order of St Christopher, the club of Catholic policemen that organised an annual breakfast and mass for its members, where senior church figures enjoined them to resist society's moral decay, whether in the form of the 'purely satanic force of communism' or the 'publishing of sexy advertisements'. In November 1957, Holland had also revived the annual CIB dinner, in abeyance since Blamey's time, where Russell Street's brass rubbed shoulders with judges, civic worthies and business heavyweights. Matthews privately disparaged him. 'Don't worry about Holland', he told Berman. 'He's a social butterfly.' Yet Holland was in other respects far savvier. Matthews was happy enough to live comfortably; Holland saw moral campaigns as integral to his role—and his advancement.

For its first target in the anti-abortion campaign, Homicide chose two of Melbourne's most successful younger practitioners. Peter Bayliss and Max Sizeland had graduated together from Melbourne University in 1954 and been medical officers at Prince Henry's before turning to general practice. Theirs was an improbable friendship. Bayliss was a larger-than-life figure with a moustache like Jimmy Edwards and, until he crash-dieted, a girth like Fatty Arbuckle; among his affectations would be a gold bow tie, which he explained as a precaution in case of a quick exit. Sizeland, lent a studious air by his horn-rimmed spectacles, acted as foil. 'It used to be said that I was the only person who could control him', Sizeland recalls. 'He would listen to logic from me.'

Bayliss and Sizeland served their apprenticeships as abortionists with John Heath, then in December 1963 paid £7200 for an unprepossessing terrace house, 'Windsor Place', at 39 Albert Street in East Melbourne, not far from 1087 Hoddle Street—and there, perhaps, made a mistake. For when the practice was raided on 25 May 1965, Sizeland's first thought was that they had been shopped by Peggy Berman: 'She had a go at us, told us we needed to pay protection, and it's possible we should have listened to her. But we said to go to hell, and I think from that day she had it in for us'. Berman was indeed often disgruntled by competition, and dismissive of doctor's efforts to deal with police themselves: 'All thought they had an exclusive relationship with the police but in my view they always came across as boys in a man's world'. She had recently strengthened her police connections by putting two more contacts on her payroll. Having heard Troup's name mentioned by two women in a ladies' toilet, Maureen Twisse visited Hoddle Street for an abortion; like Berman years earlier, she left with the offer of a reception job, for it transpired that her common-law husband, Martin Jacobson, was a Homicide detective. Twisse was paid

$70 a week for her labour and Jacobson $200 a month for his loyalty, joining Matthews, Ford and Adam as recipients of Hoddle Street's largesse. Matthews at the time, moreover, was standing in as acting superintendent of CIB: eliminating a practice not paying graft was also to his advantage.

Whatever the case, the Windsor Place raid was chaos. Police staked out the back and front entrances, then moved in led by Detective-Sergeant Noel Murphy, the policeman who had busted Lew Phillips, with Detective-Sergeants Bill Walters and Kevin Thompson. Murphy flourished a warrant at the practice's nurse, Rita Attwood: they were authorised to search for the medical history of a Jean Mayaid Mitchell. Information about Mitchell, a Hobart nurse twice aborted at Albert Street, had come from Tasmanian police. But Murphy would later admit he had believed that Windsor Place was an abortory for 'two to three years', and Bayliss's reputation preceded him. A couple of years earlier, when Ford had visited 94 Collins Street, Bayliss had thrown himself against a wall and claimed assault. Ford had warned Walters to 'expect anything from Bayliss', for he was 'a man without scruples who would do anything to embarrass an investigator'.

Police fanned out, upending everything they did not confiscate. In execution of their warrant, Walters began rummaging through the patient information cards on Bayliss's desk. 'You have got no right to go through those', Bayliss interjected. 'They are confidential documents.' Just then, cries of triumph wafted from upstairs. Murphy and Thompson had found three groggy women recovering from the effects of operations: 19-year-old hairdresser Robyn Ridings, 20-year-old nurse Anna Ashford and 27-year-old infant school teacher Geraldine Rose. All were from interstate: Ridings had driven overnight from Adelaide with her mother and boyfriend; Ashford and Rose had flown from Tasmania that morning.

Bayliss and Sizeland were young, but grasped what the Nixon White House would call 'plausible deniability'. In preparing patients for procedures, the pretence was maintained that they were being anaesthetised merely for examination. Ashford, consequently, was unclear about her condition. 'You have had an abortion, haven't you?' Murphy told her. Ashford said sleepily that nobody had told her she was pregnant. Bayliss, meanwhile, was spoiling for a fight, loftily demanding to know Walters's superior officer and to speak to solicitor

Cedric Ralph. Then, while on the phone to Ralph, he saw police bringing Ridings downstairs, and demanded that Walters stop: 'She is my patient and under my care'. Walters retorted: 'She is prepared to go with the police and furthermore she is due to go as she is to be picked up'. Bayliss had one trick left: he fell against the wall and crumpled to the floor. 'You assaulted me', he complained. 'Doctor, you were not touched by anybody', replied Walters. 'Your display was an act. You attempted a similar act on Sergeant Ford two years ago when the premises you were in at Collins Street were visited.' Bayliss nonetheless insisted on being examined by police surgeon Dr John Birrell, who found him suffering a 'very minor bump on the head'; Sizeland said he would take responsibility for his colleague.

While Bayliss, Sizeland and Attwood were run into Russell Street, the women were spirited to the Royal Women's Hospital for examination. As registrar John Grove probed their vaginas with a speculum, a police photographer hovered with camera and flashbulb, taking pictures: hugely magnified, they would form a macabrely intimate part of the prosecution brief. 'I asked them to stop and he [Grove] said it was necessary', recalled Ashford. 'The police wished to have the evidence and I just had to bear with it.' She asked for her mother, but Ada Ashford had her own problems. On returning to Albert Street to collect her daughter, she had been taken into custody too. Threatened with conspiracy charges, she had twice tried to leave and been restrained, then left in a dark room to ponder the consequences of uncooperative behaviour. The other mothers had similar experiences.

Preliminary hearings began before WN Thompson SM in a petty sessions court on 1 September 1965. Grove's testimony was that the conditions of Ashford, Ridings and Rose were consistent with abortion. Police had wrung a formidable amount of information from Tasmanian colleagues on the referring doctor in Hobart, also a suspect in a local horse-doping ring. Proceedings were adjourned after a week, and Bayliss and Sizeland resumed business, now more circumspect, with the suspicion that Homicide was watching—as indeed they were. When Holland took up his new responsibilities on 1 November, he wanted Bayliss and Sizeland hemmed in by other charges. On Homicide's behalf, Tasmanian police were scrutinising outbound, short-term flights by young women to Melbourne. On 17 March 1966, they thought they had one in the name of 'Sullivan', and staked Windsor Place out.

It was a mistake. The girl was Kerryn Litherland, a 16-year-old shorthand college student: the airport clerk had misheard her name. And the doctors had been more cautious than usual, Bayliss telling Litherland's mother Iris that she had not been pregnant at all, and needed merely a therapeutic curette. Constables cruising the block thought they had a live one when they picked up Litherland's nervous boyfriend Colin Priest loitering outside. But when Holland arrived to lead the raid at noon with Senior Detective Harry Morrison, he didn't find what he expected. For one thing, there was nobody called 'Sullivan'; for another, Bayliss, who had treated Litherland, wasn't there; Sizeland, moreover, wouldn't cooperate. 'Has she been aborted Doctor?' Morrison asked. Sizeland scoffed: 'Abortion? It's a ridiculous allegation'. Morrison wasn't to be swayed: 'Well, it's not so ridiculous. Her boyfriend is now at Russell Street about this and we find her here. Now the action we propose is to have the girl taken to a public hospital'. He grabbed Sizeland's arm: 'I am now arresting you…on grounds that you have committed a criminal abortion on this girl'. Sizeland asked to speak to Ralph, and while he was on the phone noticed stretcher-bearers scuttling past carrying the still-unconscious Litherland. 'Hey, you have no right to remove that girl!' he barked. 'If you do you'll have to accept full medical responsibility for her.' Holland barked back: 'I'll accept responsibility for her'. Litherland awoke in the Royal Women's Hospital, hovered over by a speculum-wielding registrar. In an effort to buttress their case, Homicide now included the original causa rerum, Mitchell, giving her an indemnity against prosecution. What they could not do was provide her immunity from cross-examination.

~

In Ralph, the doctors had a formidable ally. He had started practice in November 1945 in premises formerly occupied by the Eureka League, the youth branch of the Communist Party, and took only cases he believed in; for 'any offence arising out of left political activity', in fact, he did not charge. He was intimidating in debate even with loved ones. 'Cedric does not argue', his wife said of him. 'He attacks.' For the recommencement of the case before Justice Gordon Just of the County Court, Ralph also wanted an attacking barrister. Jack Lazarus, one of eight children in a remarkable five-generation Ballarat legal family, was just the man. Admitted to the bar in 1957 after selling his solicitor's practice to Clyde Holding, Lazarus had at first been known as the brother of Joan Rosenove, Melbourne's queen of divorce, whose career encompassed an estimated 20 000 matrimonial briefs. He soon acquired a reputation for clinical, almost surgical, cross-examination, and was fresh from saving Peter John Walker from the gallows to which Ronald Ryan would shortly walk. Brian Bourke recalls:

> Jack...didn't engage in pleas. He had an absolute fascination with acquittals. I've never known anyone so persistent in their examination. He never missed a point. He worked and worked and worked. Police would be petrified. And he shunned publicity. You got a guy like [Frank] Galbally, who was so flamboyant. If there was a press photographer round, he'd wonder why there weren't two. Well, I remember coming out of a court with Jack Lazarus once and we saw a journalist coming towards us. Then I looked around and he was gone.

Lazarus found the initial problems to be of his own household. The impulsive Bayliss was the client from hell, a rogue one minute, a recreant the next. Finally, he sought his own representation. Alan Croxford QC was more amenable to Bayliss's suggestions because he wasn't frightfully interested in the case. Recently named incoming chairman of the Melbourne and Metropolitan Board of Works, he spent considerable time at the bar table composing thank-you notes to letters of congratulation. 'A couple of things transpired in the trial where Jack Lazarus cursed Peter', recalls Sizeland. 'He'd do something good, then Croxford would stand up and undo it, so Jack would have to do it again.'

Lazarus was in his element. He picked apart the testimonies of Walters and Morrison, both of whom had undergone close questioning about the 'confessions' they purported to have wrung from Ronald Ryan. He steered John Birrell into praising the practice at Windsor Place as 'first-class' and 'extremely clean and neat'. He painstakingly persuaded Grove to concede that the conditions of the women he had examined were also consistent with curettage following partial abortion. He then conveyed that coming interstate for gynaecological care was not necessarily a telltale sign of abortion.

> Lazarus: I take it Miss Ashford that one of the reasons you decided to come to Melbourne was because Tasmania is a small place?
> Ashford: Yes very small.
> Lazarus: And you believed, did you not, that a curettage was the sort of thing...which could lead to some misconceptions?
> Ashford: Yes it could.

When Lazarus had a witness at his mercy, he stopped at nothing. One day, it is said, a witness passed out from the ordeal. 'Get her a stool and a glass of water', he said. 'I'm having none of this.' Now, on the most potentially dangerous witness, he was characteristically harsh, battering Mitchell's credit on the basis of her pregnancies to two men.

> Lazarus: What I am putting is simply this. Although it is true the jury would be entitled to act on Miss Mitchell's evidence, she falls within that category or class of witness of a girl who, on her own admission, could be described as promiscuous.
> Just: We know she has had two boyfriends...but Mr Lazarus, does the fact a girl is promiscuous affect her credibility in any way?
> Lazarus: In this sort of case it might.
> Just: I would be hesitant to accept that because a girl was promiscuous she was more likely to commit perjury.
> Lazarus: Whether or not that be so, I do not think it really matters ...The prejudicial nature of the evidence greatly outweighs its probative value.

Bayliss and Sizeland suffered their own unpleasantries. Justice Just began his summing up on Friday 3 June, and decided that the doctors could sit out the weekend, then Monday night, in Pentridge. Birrell secured them work in the prison hospital, but the judge ignored Croxford's plea for lenience on the basis of Bayliss's glaucoma: 'I assume ...the hospital authorities at the jail know that the eye drop bottles must be looked after properly'. The experience left its mark on Sizeland too: 'I've never forgotten being manacled as we went to court in the morning and were put in the Black Maria [paddy wagon] with the other prisoners. I remember this other prisoner...saying: "You've got no business being here. You're performing a service for society"'. Nor did Sizeland forget his social ostracism, even after the jury returned with a 'not guilty' verdict: 'After the case, I remember walking down Collins Street. Fellas I'd graduated with, men whose wives and girlfriends I'd treated—they crossed the road to avoid me'.

It was considerably better, of course, than the alternative. Bayliss was exultant, gloating to *Truth* journalist Evan Whitton: 'Never forget this, Whitton: the law exists for the protection of the rich no less than the protection of the poor'. It was the end of the partnership, for Sizeland went to Prahran to work across the street from Rod Bretherton. 'Peter wanted to keep going', he recalls. 'But he wasn't an easy man to work with. Strong man in some ways, emotionally unstable in others.' But both remained in business, and the industry's profits were undisturbed. Holland's determination to secure a conviction was redoubled—and it was on occasion not difficult to see why.

~

In the weeks before and after Christmas 1965, murder was hardly off the newspaper front pages, what with the Ryan/Walker escape, the discovery of Yvonne Hutchinson in a shallow grave in Richmond, and the lethal attack on Maureen Ferrari near Holmesglen train station—any one of which would have kept tabloid journalists busily employed for weeks. Yet one murder was particularly haunting, both for remaining unsolved and for overlapping with Homicide's other area of responsibility. The body of 15-year-old Oakleigh schoolgirl Dominique Kristaly was found just a mile from Ferrari's, but there resemblances ended; for pretty, intelligent, vivacious Kristaly was found strangled in her own bed on 1 January 1966. The crime scene photographs are somehow ghastlier for their humdrum setting and prosaic detail, like the handkerchief folded in the breast pocket of the victim's pyjamas.

The story had started in a surgery seven weeks earlier. On 12 November 1965, Dominique Kristaly kept an appointment at 456 Lonsdale Street, accompanied by a sullen, uncommunicative man in his mid-twenties. William Fenton Bowen's nurse, Glenda Walker, saw them first: Dominique said that she was pregnant, claimed to be seventeen, and asked advice. 'Get married', said Walker. Dominique explained that the father was already married. Walker suggested they go to Dominique's parents and explain the situation. Dominique said they did not know she was pregnant. Fenton Bowen disliked 'the look of the situation' and referred her on—where, he did not remember. He thought it might have been Lister Catchlove. Then he thought it might have been John Heath. He had a dim recollection of Heath on the phone urging him to deny sending the girl on. Because of the reasons for Dominique's reticence, it was a case for which nobody by then wanted responsibility.

Dominique was the first of four children to Peter and Lucy Chorazy. But Dominique's companion at Fenton Bowen's surgery, whom Walker assumed was her 'boyfriend', was in fact her stepfather, 27-year-old Hungarian polythene extruder Joseph Kristaly; it would be alleged that it was to him she was pregnant. Evidence would also be presented of Lucy finding Joseph in a compromising position with her daughter, Dominique explaining that 'Daddy is just teaching me to kiss', Joseph complaining that he could not get the girl 'out of his system'. Dominique's brother Henry would recall frequent bitter exchanges in the house over Dominique's usurpation of her mother, and Joseph's confession that they had had intercourse.

On 1 December, Dominique was admitted to Queen Victoria Hospital suffering the after-effects of a bad abortion, possibly incompetent, possibly self-procured. She was released a week later, and returned to a family in turmoil. Even on the self-serving testimony of the occupants, theirs was a house in which arguments detonated like booby traps. On the last night of 1965, Lucy accused Joseph of adulteries, Joseph stormed out, Lucy enticed him back, Joseph got drunk, vomited copiously and fell asleep. Dominique remonstrated with her mother about going out, and her mother demanded she leave her bedroom door ajar on account of the men she insisted were sneaking in the window. Lucy's story of the murder was summed up to coroner Harry Pascoe by Frank Holland: 'The mother said she heard a noise in the child's room and when she went to investigate she was assaulted by two men and taken out to the garden of the house and left there'. Joseph reckoned he snored his way through it all. Police believed neither of them.

Under questioning from Jack Ford before Pascoe, however, brother Henry went back on every iota of his earlier statement, claiming he had forgotten everything he did not deny—to an extent even the experienced Pascoe could hardly credit: 'Being…your age you are not exactly mentally retarded. So you can do better than barely remember that statement, can you not?' He could not. When Joseph Kristaly finally was charged with conspiracy to procure an illegal operation and unlawful carnal knowledge, Lucy was inconsolable. 'No it's not true!' she shrieked. 'You liar! You liar!' But it now wasn't much of a case, and D Stott SM dismissed the conspiracy charge in Oakleigh Court, causing Lucy this time to run from the court, throw herself against a wooden fence and shriek repeatedly: 'Oh thank God I still have friends'. In July 1966, the Crown Law Department finally decided not to proceed with the morals charge either.

Ford was bitterly disappointed to come up with nothing from such circumstances: 'We were never able to form any conclusion on which of the two had done it. But it was always my strong opinion that one or other had done this'. It was a reminder, too, that however safe the conditions of abortions, however able the technician or sterile the surgery, the underlying events were seldom other than unfortunate, and sometimes downright brutal.

'She was only dangerous at times'

D'ye know? A chap I know, works for the sewerage board,
tells me that abortions pour into the sea at a rate of hundreds a day.
The whole thing is putrid.

The Virtuous Courtesan (1935), Jean Devanny

The debate ran all night after a twenty-hour sitting, by the end of which the sergeant-at-arms was asleep in his cutaway breeches, silk stockings and silver sword. But in July 1967, the House of Commons passed Britain's *Abortion Act*, the eighth private members' bill on the subject, this one introduced by David Steel MP, enshrining in legislation the principles of *R v Bourne.* Henceforward, abortion would be permissible where two medical practitioners certified that: (a) the continuance of the pregnancy would involve risk to the life, physical or mental health of the pregnant woman; or (b) that there was a substantial risk that if born, the child would suffer serious abnormalities.

Support for the Act crossed party lines: Steel was a Liberal with strong support from Conservative MP Chris Chataway; the Abortion Law Reform Association secretary, Vera Houghton, was married to a Labour MP. All the same, the vote of 167 to 83 didn't feel like a climactic triumph. A crucial impetus had been the harrowing sight of babies misshapen by the effects of the anti-morning sickness drug thalidomide, prescribed for their mothers during gestation. Bourne himself, appalled to be 'so closely associated with this foul operation', had joined the Society for the Protection of Unborn Children. This group freely invoked the United Nations' *Declaration of the Rights of the Child* from November 1959: 'Whereas the child, by reason of his physical and mental immaturity, needs special safeguards and care including appropriate legal protection, before as well as after birth'.

The liberal counterargument that the child's rights included the right to be wanted had barely won the day. Pope Paul VI's encyclical *Humane Vitae* a year after the *Abortion Act* reinforced the Vatican's bulwarks against 'directly willed and procured abortion, even if for therapeutic purposes'.

In Australia, nothing resembling the British Act was in prospect. Unlike Britain's Abortion Law Reform Association, local civil libertarians lacked political connections. Those providing abortion, moreover, had a vested interest in its remaining illegal: legality, and the associated regulation of fees and standards, endangered the racket which had enriched mediocre practitioners and their minions. They had an interest, even, in cultivating bottom-end providers, to cater for cases they were loath to handle themselves, and to burnish their patina of respectability.

It was this that exercised probably Melbourne's best-informed and most sophisticated analyst of abortion. Like Shannon Hicks in Kylie Tennant's *Ride On Stranger*, Beatrice Faust was 'lucky to be born'. Her mother died twelve hours after Beatrice's birth on 19 February 1939, and Beatrice's father never forgave her; she grew up anxious to please him and without hope of doing so, except, as she put it, 'by ceasing to exist'. But like Hicks, Faust grew up nursing a 'kink against authority'. Her grandfather had been educated by a fugitive Sinn Feiner in Tipperary, and was supposed to have sunk a windfall on the Melbourne Cup into the Easter Rising; her grandmother, a pacifist who had railed against conscription from the backs of lorries, believed that 'all children's questions must be answered'. 'Nobody sent me out of the room when they talked about the woman over the road who'd had an abortion', she says. 'I was brought up to think abortion was a good thing.'

To obtain sound information remained a challenge. Faust's stepmother deflected curiosity with prudery and myth: 'She gave me rough and, I later found, inaccurate descriptions of birth and menstruation—including the myth that washing during your periods sent the blood to your head and you went mad'. Faust's views on abortion were informed initially by her father's farming wisdom that 'too frequent lambing gave ewes the staggers and didn't do women any good either'. When she was old enough for it to matter, Faust gained a personal insight into the impact of practitioners performing procedures they couldn't discuss with the women concerned. She was perplexed by all three of her pregnancies, for she had had a diaphragm fitted, then a Gräfenberg ring. Unbeknownst to her, Faust's womb was heart-shaped, with an indentation at the top that rendered her contraception ineffectual. Not once did her three abortionists—Jean Field, Peter Bayliss and Max Sizeland—give her any advice. The closest she came to finding out was when Sizeland said: 'Tell your doctor it isn't his fault'. Not until she bore her son Stephen in 1965 did she grasp the reality. Rather than exclaim 'it's a boy' or 'it's a girl', the obstetrician's first reaction was to gloat to his colleague: 'I *told* you so. She's got a bicornuate uterus'.

It was her involvement that year in the founding of the Victorian Council for Civil Liberties that spurred Faust to undertake the first serious research into abortion in Australia: 'I wriggled in a sub-committee on abortion to investigate whether it could be interpreted as a civil rights/civil liberties issue... there was some hostility to its even being set up as a sub-committee'. Steeping herself in abortion's medico-legal history relative to the emergence of a feminist consciousness, she was struck by how little had changed about ex-nuptial birth. Thanks to Australia's steady postwar embourgeoisement, the social impulse to cover it up had seldom been stronger: the hasty marriage and/or the private confinement preparatory to adoption remained commonplaces. 'Nobody wants anything to do with an unmarried girl who is bearing a child', noted Lionel Bowen MLA during the New South Wales Legislative Assembly debate of the Adoption of Children Bill (1965). 'Society deplores the unmarried mother as an adulteress. Hence she is a victim of society.' Yet Faust's researches convinced her that because of the difficulty in negotiating fertility control in marriage, married women were just as likely to need terminations as the unwed. And while the well-off might have their own gynaecologists who could be trusted to handle matters discreetly, most had no guide but rumour and folklore, then were at the mercy of individuals loyal chiefly to themselves.

Faust investigated most of the providers, Rodney Bretherton allowing her to interview more than 100 patients in his surgery, and was fascinated by the phenomenon of Peggy Berman, self-made abortion entrepreneur. 'A natural conspirator', Faust thought. Her conclusions were decidedly unflattering.

> The line was drawn: doctors good, backyarders bad. In fact the doctors were corrupt. And completely unregulated. There was no upper limit on fees, for instance. And the standards were very varied. Bretherton presented himself as a clean-living, high-minded extreme left-winger, God's gift to the working class. But he let one of the Brookeses do abortions in his surgery on weekends with no medical training. Those women didn't know that he wasn't a doctor.
>
> You found that sort of thing happening everywhere. Corruption of prices and corruption of standards. Many of the men would not employ nurses who were qualified: they didn't want them talking back and didn't want them questioning the standards. This is where Peggy Berman was so dangerous around Finks and Troup. She wasn't a nurse, she wasn't going to learn nursing and she certainly wasn't going to employ anyone who was a nurse. She also tried to control the patient intake, when it should have been a doctor's decision. Is this woman well enough? Is she too advanced? To give that right to Peggy was a very dangerous thing to do.

Where the bugaboo of 'backyard abortion' was concerned, Faust saw a classic case of the phenomenon described by the philosopher Ivan Illich: '... the existence of a few charlatans or racketeers has always served the credibility of the medical guild: by denouncing their misbehaviour, the typical practitioner could legitimise the abuses inherent in his ordinary practice'.

Faust sometimes fitted the world to intellectual postulates, rather than the other way round. Almost all the women charged in relation to abortion offences *did* have professional qualifications; and Berman *did* employ nurses, even if she was disinclined to respect their expertise. But there was a deep ring of truth to her contention that this was an industry geared to the convenience of providers and concerned only at the margin with patient welfare, while her acid pen portraits were cruelly accurate. John Heath: 'Lives in immense luxury. No great skill. Genial. A large figure in many ways'. Billy Flynn: 'Bottom of the barrel. Alcoholic, senile, a lecher but friendly'. John Brookes: 'Sadist, doesn't use gloves to examine patients, nor curtains, propositions attractive girls who seek his services'.

Pricking interest in reform, however, was a challenge. The law, it seemed, was the law. One of Faust's interviewees was Justice Jack Barry, who almost thirty years earlier had envisioned the basis of a new statute; now, he told her, not unkindly, that the illegality of abortion was like the road toll: routinely deplored but a fact of life. Some, too, couldn't see the problem. The fact was that if you wanted an abortion you could basically get one. The majority of Victorian general practitioners and more than a few chemists knew where to refer you—usually in return for a kickback. It was scary, it was sleazy, but you'd be unlucky to be caught. Men didn't really want to think about it, and women who'd undergone abortion were loath to relive the experience. The left of politics, meanwhile, talked a good revolution, interested in the dividends of greater sexual freedom but not its consequences. 'The worst people were people on the left who said it wasn't time', recalls Faust. 'The revolution would come, so why bother working up a sweat? Well, a woman who's pregnant can't wait for the revolution.'

In the mid-1960s, the most active campaigners in Victoria for abortion law reform were at the other end of politics. Solicitor Charles Hider had been part of a late 1950s revival in the Young Liberals that included Alan Scanlan and Andrew Peacock; he had gone into partnership with the latter in Brighton before taking over an old firm, Rigby & Fielding. Hider wondered how opposition to abortion could be reconciled with Liberal principles of individual freedom and the right to choose. 'Personally, I didn't like abortion', he recalls. 'But what was frustrating was that the same people who opposed abortion were also against contraception; they were also against sex education; they were just not helping anyone.' Instrumental in the Liberal State Council motion for the repeal of six o'clock closing in February 1966, Hider now took soundings about a push to clarify abortion law, and found a surprising degree of support.

> The women's section of the Liberal Party were very important, very influential at the time. It was part of Menzies' cleverness. And it was the influence of middle-aged women at state council that made the difference. People like Audrey Reader [secretary of the National Council of Women] understood the pain and humiliation of abortion, and were genuinely committed to change.

Yet the motions Hider managed to have passed at consecutive State Council meetings were not binding on the government—for good reason. The political vehicle of Catholic anti-communism, the Democratic Labor Party, was a fading force nationally, its primary vote declining more than a third in the 1960s, its image among progressive voters that of a force of almost medieval reaction: 'You'd have to be a fascist, hate-mongering, racist, pope-loving, puritanical, life-hating, moralist, hung-up authoritarian prick, mentally retarded and insane to boot, to vote DLP', claimed Don in the play *Don's Party*. 'God help Australia.' In Victoria, however, the DLP remained a kingmaker. Sir Henry Bolte's premiership was gravely endangered by the hanging of Ronald Ryan on 3 February 1967. But the flow of the DLP's preferences was enough to secure the Liberal Party's re-election on 29 April: Henry Bolte's government won forty-four seats with 37.5 per cent of the total vote; Labor won sixteen seats with 37.9 per cent of the total vote. 'Politics do not transcend everything', complained the party's anti-hanging heretic Brian Dixon MLA in remonstrating with Bolte. 'That's where you're wrong, young man', Bolte retorted. 'Politics *do* transcend everything.' To Bolte, the business of government was best handled in collaboration with Arthur Rylah and undersecretary Kevin Dillon while on the train to a country race meeting, preferably with the maximum time left over to peruse the form guide. His view on abortion law reform showed all his populist instincts: 'When I was a young man in the Western Districts, we had a saying: "The girl's more scared of the calf than she is of the bull". That's the way it ought to remain. The government shouldn't help make it easier'.

~

If nothing political stood in the path of Frank Holland's ambition to clamp down on abortion, he was beginning to suspect other impediments. Detectives-Sergeant Bill Walters, Harry Morrison and Kevin Carton all came to him with complaints of an informant in Homicide.

> I said: 'Do you suspect anybody?' And they said: 'Well it's hard to pin down—but we go out on an inquiry and the doctor's just waiting for us and there's nothing doing. It's very rare we get to a place unannounced'...
>
> Now the first experience I had [myself] was with a boy who had stolen money from his employers to pay for an abortion for his girlfriend. We organised to raid a doctor's place on the basis of what

> the boy and girl told us. When our fellows arrived at the doctor's place it was quite obvious that someone had tipped him off.

Holland's comrades were right. Although Matthews was policing in western Victoria before his next promotion and Adam was shortly to retire in December 1966, Berman had both Ford in her thrall and Marty Jacobson in her pocket; she would also allege paying off Murphy, in dollar notes stuffed into a cigarette packet. Troup, too, was inclined to spontaneous generosity. Once, when a young colleague revealed that he was about to honeymoon in Hong Kong, Troup opened a satchel brimming with cash. 'So', he beamed. 'How are ya situated?' The doctor was happy enough to pay Jacobson a six-month advance so he could afford a house in Belar Avenue, Frankston; he and Berman even acted as co-guarantors of his loan.

It's unlikely, too, that Ford and Jacobson were the only information providers. Although Bretherton always denied paying graft, Cedric Ralph's articled clerk Rex Mortimore told Faust that he had acted as that doctor's bagman for many years; for his own part, Bretherton would relate that abortionists were sometimes warned of raids by switchboard girls at Russell Street CIB. Holland claimed to find the situation frustrating, citing an incident at Geelong when Homicide arrived at an empty house.

> We left a detective there and he answered the phone. One message taken from a man was about a girl who was there as a patient. We went out to interview the girl who admitted she had been at the premises and put under an anaesthetic to have an abortion. She said the next thing she knew she was in a motor car outside the premises with a nurse and a man driving the car. She said the nurse told her: 'We have just received information that the police are going to raid the premises.' The girl said they then drove around until they saw a police car pull up with my raiding party.

Yet Homicide elsewhere showed a lack of persistence at odds with their reputation. Holland's quarry for a Geelong visit on 8 June 1967 was 39-year-old Dr Mario Marchesani, whose reputation as an abortionist was as low as his community reputation among local Italians was high: he was known to rouse patients from anaesthetic and say that he would have to double their fees because the pregnancy was more advanced that his initial estimate. One Norma Wood had told

Homicide of being aborted by Marchesani and Troup, but Holland spent just ten minutes at Marchesani's Latrobe Terrace surgery, and deprecated Wood's statement as not containing 'an adequate description of the procedure followed'. Marchesani stayed in business, unencumbered by the attentions of Geelong CIB, where the officer in charge, Sergeant Eric Janetski, a veteran of the Sheep Stealing Squad, was his son-in-law.

Particularly invulnerable was John Heath—if anything, the police contributed to his sense of security. Paula Green called her boss 'a bit of a name dropper', and he could certainly boast a useful contact in former Homicide chief Bill Mooney. They had met in 1942 during Mooney's investigation of a robbery from Heath's boarding house, 'Los Angeles'. Later they both joined the Pups, the charity luncheon club founded in 1947, whose membership also featured Billy Flynn, Heath's accountant Murray Horsburgh, and Hannah Mitchell's staunch defender Percy Ridgeway. Mooney, it was known, could be called if trouble brewed. One day, Corrie Blackwell looked up to find a man standing over her, literally and figuratively: a patient of Heath's had become 'very sick', he was saying, with the implication that some money might fix the problem. The man's bravado vanished when Mooney arrived at her invitation. 'Don't touch me', he said suddenly. 'I've told a lie. *Please* don't touch me.' Mooney ran the miscreant into Russell Street to ensure he got the message.

When Mooney became deputy chief of CIB in August 1966, Heath was among his first callers. Heath was annoyed about anonymous calls and letters concerning his practice, for which he blamed 'the woman in Hoddle Street'. He complained again three weeks later. Mooney offered 'certain advice', the nature of which he did not record in his official diary, although Berman would describe a visit to 'give us the word'.

> I rang Adam, who said he had seen Mooney drive Dr Heath to the nearby grocer's shop, then walk up to our practice. The warning from Mooney was that a friend of the police was having trouble with an anonymous letter of complaint to Russell Street about illegal abortions. That was what he told Dr Troup in a loud voice.

In October, Senior Detective Francis Coates reported to Mooney and Holland a complaint by one Vivien Testro that she had visited

Heath when four-and-a-half months' pregnant, and that he had offered to abort her for $600. The expense proved too much, but Coates nursed no illusions about the good doctor: 'I have no doubt Dr Heath might have attempted this abortion if the necessary $600 could have been made available…This places grave suspicion upon him [Heath] but does not disclose he has committed any offence'. And although Coates said that Heath had not been interviewed because he was never at the surgery when police visited, something strange then happened: Heath came to see Mooney, to make his own complaint about police visiting his surgery. The perfect opportunity to address Testro's statement, one would have thought—but apparently neither Mooney nor Holland pursued it. Holland's official diary contained the notation: 'Re abortion—no action taken'.

Mooney's relations with Heath would blossom further. On 14 April 1967, Heath invited him to Burlington Chambers and asked if he would investigate troublesome telephone calls to the home of Green, who had recently defected from Hoddle Street to Collins Street, the clear inference being that Berman was the nuisance in question. Heath then ran into trouble over the exploits of a Greek nurse he had employed, despite her poor English, to handle Greek patients. It emerged that this nurse was doing a roaring out-of-hours trade in hymen repairs—a popular procedure among Greek brides-to-be. When a complaint was received by St Kilda CIB, the Greek nurse had disappeared, and Green was charged with conspiracy. Heath asked Mooney to sort it out; the charges were withdrawn.

Intermittent police visits to Heath's surgery were unavailing. Sometimes, detectives would even find Heath's solicitor Gilbert Field in situ, ready to smooth any friction, as Detective-Sergeant Noel Murphy noted in a July 1967 report, 'Activities of Abortionists Investigated by Members of the Homicide Squad': 'Over the last few years a number of complaints have been made regarding Dr John Heath of 94 Collins Street, Melbourne. These premises have been visited on a number of occasions but insufficient evidence was found to launch a prosecution against him or his associates'. With both Hoddle Street and Collins Street apparently unassailable, a decision was made to seek some easier game. Nobody could have foreseen the consequences.

~

Dr Charles Kenneth Davidson of 106 Hotham Street was Melbourne's gentleman abortionist: a handsome, cultured 52-year-old whose back-combed hair and well-cut suits lent him the look of a 1950s character actor. A man who struggled even with eye contact in conversation, his native diffidence deepened by a stammer, he scarcely seemed the type to indulge in anything illegal, or even ambiguous. He appeared, too, to have the world at his feet. His sometime girlfriend was the beautiful Janice Wakely, who had featured in the first edition of Australian *Vogue* and was a favourite of Helmut Newton and Terence Donovan. They had met on her arrival in Melbourne to model in 1956 and she became intrigued by his sophisticated tastes and walls of books. He didn't dance, disliked having his photo taken, and exhausted easily. But their relationship, sometimes sexual, always platonic, continued even when Janice was coupled with other men. 'Ken's not the marrying kind', Janice would argue. 'I could never marry Janice', Davidson would say. 'She'd run away and leave me devastated.' They were seldom parted and never for long: in 1967 she lived next door to Davidson, in an upstairs flat he also owned, with newsreader Kevin Saunders. She was often at Davidson's highly ritualised dinner and drinks, which always seemed full of beautiful women. 'I remember going to a party at his home and the whole room seemed to be full of Janice Wakelys', recalls Peggy Berman's son Peter, then a law student. 'Made me think that maybe I should study medicine.'

Davidson was no campaigner. Introduced to abortion while acting as anaesthetist to Jim Troup's father, he found it suited his way of life, enabling him to work just two days a week from his unostentatious two-storey terrace in East Melbourne. And by this shady world's topsy-turvy standards, such attitudes made him strangely appealing. 'Ken at least wasn't a hypocrite', says Faust. 'He never pretended he was God's gift to the proletariat, never said he was doing it for anything other than money. It was just a means for him to maintain a very desirable lifestyle.' But this *was* a shady world, and Davidson *had* been worrying, particularly about his near-neighbour, Peggy Berman. 'She'd invite us round for drinks and I wouldn't want to go', recalls Janice Wakely. 'She wanted to control everyone. She was unbelievably conniving.' 'We've got to be nice to her', Davidson would plead. 'Otherwise she'll cause trouble.' Crisis, Wakely sensed, wasn't far away: 'She was trying to get us to join the club, the abortionists' club. But she didn't understand

Ken. With his background, Ken would never have dreamed of bribing a policeman'.

Hotham Street residents might have imagined themselves watching a scene from *Homicide* when, at 10.30 a.m. on 1 August 1967, a formation of XP Falcons disgorged a unit of plainclothes police outside Davidson's surgery. Detective-Sergeant Fred Russell, one of Holland's Catholic core, was purportedly acting on a tip-off received the day before. Seventeen-year-old Judith Carroll, a clerk at SKF Ball Bearings in South Melbourne, was pregnant to her 19-year-old apprentice printer boyfriend, Michael Martin. Carroll wanted an abortion; Martin seems to have let something slip to a police informer. Both had been taken in for questioning and admitted to making an appointment. When police arrived, they found that Carroll had prudently stayed away, and specifics of the visit were abandoned in favour of a general look-see. In the waiting room, police found Marie Falls, a pregnant 17-year-old shopgirl from Ararat accompanied by her mother, Francis, with an envelope containing $120 cash. Davidson deflected the police's inquiries: people knew this was a standard aborter's fee and, he claimed, sometimes arrived in hope. Two-and-a-half hours' searching looked like going to waste when Russell's colleague Roy Currie lit upon the metal card file containing Davidson's patient records. 'I notice from these cards that the great majority of your patients are single women', Currie commented. 'Well, I am single too', Davidson sighed. 'That's the way things are.' Currie said he was claiming the box as evidence; Davidson would reproach himself for acquiescing. 'He shouldn't have asked and I probably shouldn't have allowed him', he recalls. 'It was unethical.'

Unethical or not, Russell and Currie thought they had struck paydirt: within three days, they were contacting the women whose names were on the cards, questioning partners and parents, laying their lives open to scrutiny, threatening conspiracy charges if they did not cooperate, dangling indemnities against prosecution if they did. On the card for 20-year-old nurse Lynette Matthews, Davidson had written: 'Long narrow face and pigtail, looks like a skeleton'. She had been ten weeks' pregnant when her boyfriend, Edward Andriessen, had driven her to Hotham Street on his motorbike to be aborted on 25 May. On the card for 19-year-old stenographer Angela Garlick, Davidson had noted her 'V mini skirt'. She had been eight weeks' pregnant to boyfriend Warwick Bennett when she had attended Davidson just a fortnight earlier. Here, detectives obtained bonus testimony from mother Wilhemina, a former maternity nurse.

> On Wednesday 26 July, I received a phone call from Angela asking if she could come and see me. She arrived about 7pm and was accompanied by Warwick Bennett...I went into my bedroom and I could see she was very worried, there was a stricken look on her face. I said: 'Darling, are you pregnant?' And she said: 'Yes.' I said 'I want you to go ahead with it'. She said: 'Mummy we are too young to marry.'

Carroll claimed that Davidson had been coy with her. 'Well, it is quite true you are pregnant', she quoted him as saying. 'You must have had some idea yourself.' He had also informed her that he didn't 'do abortions here because they are illegal', and that 'there was a terrible lot of risk involved with him doing that kind of thing'. When Martin had asked him to terminate the pregnancy, Davidson had not responded directly: 'He just told me to make arrangements for her to visit him at 10am on 1 August 1967'. Davidson had also suggested a cover story to 19-year-old Noelene Morrison, whom he had aborted on 12 July. Unfortunately, by the time police came to interview her at Bendigo Teachers' College, she couldn't remember it: 'The doctor saw me just before I was leaving and told me what to say if anyone asked me about the operation. He said to tell them something was twisted inside and mentioned a name starting with R but I do not know now what that word was'.

The card concerning Robin Ann Dunn, a computer operator at IBM, interested Russell and Currie in particular: it contained the name of her referring doctor, Bertram Vanrenen. Police accosted her on her doorstep in St Kilda near midnight and coaxed her into divulging Vanrenen's advice: 'He asked me what I was going to do. I told him I'd probably get married. He said that to be pregnant was not a good reason to get married. He said I could have the baby adopted or have an operation'. In fact, Vanrenen recalls, he more commonly referred to Max Sizeland or Rod Bretherton: 'Ken wasn't one of my usual ones. But this girl was on the other side of the river, and he sounded like a nice guy. I'd probably sent him half a dozen or so, and they'd been pleased with the attention they'd received'. On 14 August 1967,

Vanrenen had his own police visit, Russell and Currie barging into his morning surgery. Did he have a medical history card for a Miss Robin Ann Dunn? As Vanrenen accepted the card from his receptionist, Russell plucked it from his hand. '*We* will have this', he said.

~

For the last thirty months, Peggy Berman felt she had been battling: battling to protect Hoddle Street, battling to repel what she called 'the Collins Street Machine', battling to sustain her combustible relationship with Ford, battling with her health. In January 1965, she had been admitted to Hamilton Russell House with breast cancer and undergone a mastectomy. Even then, she'd never been off-duty: the police in her pay had arrived for their graft, collecting envelopes placed under her pillow by Troup. Part of her thrived on the sense of indispensability; the other part now urgently craved escape. Troup, by contrast, was confident that Hoddle Street, with all its contacts, was secure; he had even continued monthly payments to the retired Adam, just to be safe. He had recently moved in with his mistress, Maureen Philippe, in South Blackburn, and suggested Berman relax also. Norval Morris was conferencing in the United States and Europe: Troup gave Berman $1400 to join him.

On 24 August, the night before her departure, Berman met Troup and Philippe at the Menzies Hotel for a drink, then adjourned to an East Melbourne restaurant before proceeding to Berman's Oak Street home. Troup and Philippe tiffed, and when she left he bedded down on the couch; Berman and her son Peter slept upstairs. Next morning, Peter Berman was in the kitchen when he saw his mother sealing money in an envelope, which she then took to the front door. After a shower, he opened the front door to collect the milk—only to find a tall figure in grey, envelope in hand, stooped over a lifted doormat. Peter shut the door immediately and accosted his mother. 'Who's that you're giving money to and why?' he demanded. 'It's Jack Ford and I have to', his mother replied, and under further questioning became tense and angry.

It was an inauspicious prelude to her trip, and Morris's company in Chicago, Montreal, Lisbon, Rome and Athens couldn't make up for it. There were the usual irredeemable lows and indestructible highs. She overdosed on tablets in Rome, and Morris rushed her to hospital;

she also thought that the beauty of 'this ancient city' bought her 'back to life'. But when she returned to Melbourne on 2 October, she found the abortion trade in ferment. Davidson was in Sydney, trying to avoid a warrant out for his arrest. Arnold Finks had returned to work for John Heath. And, the day after Berman landed, Noel Murphy led a raid on William Fenton Bowen. After his shock a few years earlier, Fenton Bowen had resumed aborting in his own clumsy way. Max Sizeland recalls:

> On at least three occasions I knew of, Fenton Bowen attempted a procedure and failed. And some 8-10 weeks later, when the woman was sixteen weeks' pregnant and sick, I had a call asking if I could sort it out. What was outrageous was that there was never any thought of reimbursing the woman. As far as I'm concerned if you attempt something and fail, you don't charge. Fenton Bowen never gave it a thought.

Fenton Bowen had finally found an anaesthetist almost as disreputable as himself: Patrick Hickey's police record included multiple charges for drunk and disorderly, wilful damage, offensive behaviour, resisting arrest, obscene language and dangerous driving. To this, on 3 October, was added a charge of conspiring with Fenton Bowen and nurse Enid Digman to procure a miscarriage. Asked why he was carrying $1674 in cash, Hickey gave the Packeresque reply: 'I like the feel of it'.

Hoddle Street's principals still swore by Ford. Troup even trusted him to place a big bet on the Caulfield Stakes on his behalf, which paid $2500. As October ended, Berman accompanied Ford to Sydney for the Moonee Valley Cup. At the Florida Inn Motel in Potts Point, they had either a dirty weekend or a quaintly clean one: Ford would later claim that they had shared a bed but not had intercourse, as he wished to demonstrate his immunity to her feminine wiles. In between times, they met Davidson. Ford advised him to wait another week, return to Melbourne and turn himself in: he promised immediate bail. Davidson paid $500 as a 'gesture of appreciation'. So it was that Davidson attended Russell Street CIB on 3 November 1967, made an unsigned statement, was charged with twelve counts of 'procuring a miscarriage', and released on $1000 bail. Berman was confident that Ford would take care of it from there.

Yet nothing now worked as it should have. Troup went to spend his Caulfield Stakes winnings and found that ten of the $10 notes were counterfeit, forgery being rampant after the introduction of decimal currency. Diagnosed with secondary cancers, Berman received gruelling radiation treatment at the Peter MacCallum Institute. The gloomy prognosis tautened her ties with Ford, whose every step she began tracing. She would arrive at his Burwood home in a taxi and send the driver in to say: 'There is a man outside who wants to see you'. Once, in frustration at his absence, she threw a brick through the windscreen of his car; on another occasion, while he was inside, she backed her car into his to gain attention; on another, she arrived at the Police Officers' College, where Ford was teaching, and started tearing her clothes off, claiming she would tell people he had tried to rape her. Between times, there would be bizarre displays of tenderness from both. When she was ill, Berman entrusted her jewellery to Ford, saying it should go to Ford's daughter if she died; Ford gave her an eternity ring and a St Christopher's medal. Asked later why he had bought gifts for a woman he considered 'dangerous', Ford could say no more than: 'She was only dangerous at times'.

The calls were the biggest problem. Twice Ford had to change his home number because of Berman's telephone tirades; on one occasion she rang his mother pretending to be a reporter in order to get it back. And so often did Berman ring Ford at work to upbraid him for weakness and treachery that she began undermining his effectiveness as a protector. 'Jack Ford?' Holland would say.

> I never suspected him at all until Kevin Carton said to me: 'Look, she's always ringing Jack, and I hate to say it but I think she's on with him'. And then we start to look at Jack's background and we find he's always at the races and the dogs and where does he get the money?

Jacobson was already under suspicion. Holland thought him lazy, unreliable, always complaining of his financial woes; Carton simply refused to take him on raids. The relocated Matthews and retired Adam, meanwhile, were too distant to be of help. Without realising it, Berman had lost her cover. On 1 February 1968, she found out: 1087 Hoddle Street was raided.

‘Hell, we *all* do it . . .’

A lot of girls take this abortion business quite easily Bill. Of course, sometimes it ends in a dirty tragedy; but there are doctors and nurses who do the job skilfully, I know. Costs a lot—but at least you get hygienic surroundings.

Winged Seeds (1950), Katherine Susannah Prichard

The warrant was what police called a ‘bodgie’: a pretext for a search. Kevin Carton dragged a justice of the peace off Carlton Bowling Club’s green to approve inquiries concerning the ‘medical history of an unnamed foreign woman possible surname Schrey’, purportedly on the basis of an anonymous tip-off. If she ever existed, she was soon forgotten when twelve detectives hemmed Hoddle Street in.

Frank Holland took no chances. Jack Ford had been sent to run Brighton CIB two weeks earlier, and the group assembled in the muster room was brought up to strength with half a dozen Breaking Squad detectives. Nobody was told where they were going, and the party embarked initially for Footscray before doubling back to East Melbourne. Berman suspected nothing. When she had handed Martin Jacobson his monthly graft a few days earlier, there had been no talk of raids. Berman had been preoccupied with the recent resignation of Jacobson’s partner Maureen. They had fallen out over Berman’s decision to turn away pregnant girls aged sixteen and under, then Berman’s change of mind when she ‘screamed and ranted and raved’. ‘I can’t stand it any more’, Maureen said. ‘I am going and not coming back.’ But Berman had moved on quickly. She accepted Jacobson’s explanation that Maureen was ‘nervy’, and had already employed two new women: Loretta Campbell and Winifred Telgenkamp. Winifred’s husband was also a policeman, in Traffic Control. To Berman, you simply couldn’t have too many contacts in the law.

Yet all the contacts in the world were useless if they were the wrong contacts. At 10.30 a.m., Campbell answered an ominous pounding on the front door, then called to Berman in her stairwell nook: 'Sergeant Carton is here!' And as Carton flourished his warrant, his men began treading the surgery's soft grey carpets, upturning the flowers, and shouting at the dozen mainly migrant women in the waiting room, as though this would improve their comprehension: 'You have had abortion? You have had baby taken away?' As Carton began ascending the stairs, Berman blocked his path. 'You can't go in', she insisted. 'Dr Troup is operating.' Carton heard a lock turn in the operating theatre door. Electing to wait, he cursorily checked the appointment book; no 'Schrey' appeared. When Troup materialised five minutes later, police found on the gurney a groggy mother of four from Caulfield, Athanasia Sakkas, bravely trying to maintain appearances. Patients were always told to say that they had arrived already haemorrhaging, and she was repeating: 'No baby, no baby. Too much blood'.

Berman seethed quietly. 'This wouldn't happen to Dr Heath', she hissed at Carton; he looked blankly back. She sidled unobtrusively to another patient in the waiting room, Lidia Gruppillo, who had come from Springvale that morning with her husband and brother. 'Go to the toilet', said Berman sotto voce. Gruppillo looked confused. 'Say you have to go to the toilet', Berman repeated. When Gruppillo was excused, Berman made a point of leading her down the passageway. 'This way darl', she said. 'Just in there.' As the puzzled Gruppillo re-emerged, Berman thrust a schoolboy's satchel bearing the BOAC motif into her hand, whispering: 'Take this with you when you go'.

It was the best Berman could do to protect the practice's records. Otherwise, she was stupefied. She had lived in fear of such a day, but never really envisioned it: she had been so careful, so calculated, so *generous.* She rang Ray Dunn. She rang Matthews. She rang Ford. 'Who are the police?' Ford asked. She named a few with mounting fury: didn't he *know*? Both Matthews and Ford suggested she make herself scarce for a few days and hole up in a hotel while they considered their options. When Holland arrived with reinforcements to arrest Troup and anaesthetist William Crombie, Berman and nurse Maureen Young slipped inconspicuously away, accepting a lift from Telgenkamp. Much to damage them was left behind. Carton confiscated index cards describing 5000 clients. When Berman rang Jacobson at 2 p.m., she learned that detectives were also poring over the appointment books in the schoolbag that Gruppillo had uncomprehendingly turned over. It was the stuff of nightmares.

Berman checked in at Albert Park's Palm Lake Motel as 'Mrs Woods'—an alias favoured by Ford. Ford rang presently with an idea: make up six books of false records—names, addresses, medical histories—to replace those the raiders had confiscated. Ford would then arrange for their substitution with the real ones—a suggestion Matthews endorsed. Young fetched stationery from Norman Bros, and the operation was underway by the time Ken Davidson arrived in response to a plea from Berman: he contributed to a whip around to raise the bail money for Troup and Crombie, which was then conveyed to Russell Street by Troup's mistress, Maureen Philippe.

Before daybreak next morning, Berman was bound for Lalor to leave the fictitious records, wrapped in paper with $100, on the doorstep of Ford's suggested Homicide intermediary, Senior Constable Ronald Jackson. It was a desperate gambit, and it utterly failed. After doing the drop, Berman phoned Jackson from a booth. 'Mr Jackson you do not know us, but we are friends of the people you had dealings with yesterday', she said nervously. 'We are anxious to help these people and if you are prepared to exchange the books on your front veranda with the books you took there is a thousand in it for you.' Jackson froze, stammeringly refused the offer, and finally promised: 'I will be reporting this to my superiors'. Now Berman panicked. 'Thank you', she said. 'Goodbye.' She fled for Adam's rooming house, where Adam reassured her by producing a picture from his farewell of he and Carton beaming companionably. 'Don't worry', he insisted. 'Keep your chin up.' She scoffed: 'Is that a better position for the hangman's knot?'

Never was it fathomed why Ford thought Jackson eligible for enticement one day and why he proved otherwise the next. Ford explained it to Berman as circumstances: 'What you can do one day, you can't do another day'. But Jackson didn't merely turn the inducement away: he turned it in, dropping the books on Carton's Russell Street desk shortly after 8 a.m. Attempting to retrieve evidence against them, the Hoddle Streeters had provided even more—and Ford was about to ensure he went down with them. That evening, Ford drove from Brighton CIB to ask Holland for the books left on Jackson's step.

Holland wrote in his diary: 'At 5.45pm saw Inspector Ford. He made request regarding arrest of doctors Troup and Crombie—request not acceded to'. The next morning, Ford repeated the request by phone. Holland diarised again: 'Received telephone call from Inspector Ford re same as above—same result'. The evidence would help destroy him.

~

Frank Holland's crusade was now well and truly under way, with the inspector himself announcing it in a forthright interview with *The Age* on 28 February 1968. There was no liberal shilly-shallying from The Dutchman: 'The law says abortion is illegal and that is enough for me'. He dismissed *R v Bourne*: 'That decision was stated by one judge alone and it was never established that the girl's life was in danger. To say that Bourne's case has any influence in Australia is nonsense. One judge can't make a decision affecting the rest of the world'. Over the next month, more doctors and nurses passed through City Court for charging and remanding than in Victoria's history: Ken Davidson, William Fenton Bowen, Patrick Hickey, Jim Troup, William Crombie and also Billy Flynn, who was being pursued over the death of Carolyn Jamieson. With them were helpmates caught in the dragnet: June Horak, Winifred Telgenkamp, Maureen Young, plus, of course, Peggy Berman.

At last, abortion was deemed an issue worthy of media coverage. A Roy Morgan poll in *The Herald* found sizeable majorities favouring law reform, 65 per cent of men and 71 per cent of women between twenty-six and forty-five wanting a liberalisation of the laws, even if abortion for economic reasons still provoked some disquiet. Letters columns reverberated with clashing opinions. An executive of the Victorian Council for Civil Liberties, Gareth Evans, declined to blame the police: 'No reasonable criticism can be made of Inspector Holland. . . for refusing to ignore the law in the exercise of some ill-defined discretion thrust upon him because of the failure of the community and its elected representatives to face up to the question honestly'. A Melbourne University philosophy tutor, Peter Singer, chose to blame Catholics: 'It is of the essence of a free society that one group does not dictate its beliefs to the whole community. Yet that is exactly what our abortion law does'. Both appeared in a Union debate at Melbourne

University with Carlton GP Sam Benwell, where the motion 'that this house would legalise abortion' was carried 274 to 109. A lunchtime speech at the university by Carl Wood, Queen Victoria Hospital's admired professor of obstetrics and gynaecology, made the front page of *The Herald* for the claim of 25 million abortions in the world annually.

Evans, Singer, Benwell and Wood were among the sixty who met on 24 April 1968 to adopt a constitution for the formation of the Abortion Law Reform Association (ALRA), with the general purpose of pressing for law reform, and the more specific aim of securing legislation along the lines of Britain's *Abortion Act*. It was the year of the *soixante-huitards* and the armies of the night; Melbourne would host its first serious demonstrations against the Vietnam War on 4 July, police arresting twenty-six of what Chief Commissioner Rupert Arnold would describe as 'so-called intellectuals who want to change the world' for protesting outside the US consulate. But ALRA was more properly of the *bien-pensant* middle-class, like those who had taken up the cause of the death sentences on Rupert Max Stuart, Robert Peter Tait and Ronald Ryan. ALRA's president was architect Bill Dye, and its committee included 25-year-old schoolteacher and novelist-to-be Helen Garner and 31-year-old marketing manager and parliamentarian-in-the-making Ivan Trayling. Secretary Jo Richardson, a pretty Melbourne University Undergraduate from a well-to-do family, had with her boyfriend and *Farrago* colleague Lionel Pugh run an anti-hanging candidate against Henry Bolte in his seat of Hampden the year before, mischievously promoting a Young Liberal against whom Jo had played tennis at the Royal South Yarra Tennis Club.

A tiny two-paragraph item in *The Herald* also reported the charging of Bert Vanrenen, who had referred Robin Ann Dunn to Davidson—the first GP to be so charged, and an incongruously tweedy presence in the Dickensian surrounds of the City Watchhouse, with its customary cast of drunks and drifters. Waiting patiently for his wife to return from the dentist with their daughters Louise and Annabelle, he had a member of his staff ring her father, secretary of Coopers' Union at Trades Hall, to raise the bail money. Then, having been fingerprinted and questioned, he quietly returned to work, his receptionist having diplomatically rescheduled all appointments. It was almost as though it hadn't happened—but it had.

Bert and his wife Ila were establishment. Bert was a nephew of Liberal Party grand dame Jessie Sutherland OBE; Ila was the daughter of a diplomat who had founded the Canadian legation in Stockholm. The blue-blood industrialist Sir Robert Knox had spoken at their wedding, while Sir Robert Menzies had sent a telegram—they now lived two doors from Sir Robert and Dame Pattie in Malvern's Haverbrack Avenue. Now they experienced some of the paradoxes of society's views on abortion. A majority favoured liberalising the laws—but, well, wasn't it all *rather* squalid? The Vanrenen's solicitors, Blake & Riggall, didn't want to know: Ray Dunn did that sort of thing, didn't he? The Medical Defence Association, the Australian Medical Association (AMA) adjunct through which doctors insured themselves against litigation, refused financial assistance for Vanrenen's defence. The couple found themselves socially ostracised. 'I know what it's like to walk into a room full of people and have them turn their back on you', Ila recalls. One doctor's wife, for example, rang to say that her daughter would not be attending Louise's birthday party. Why? 'Because we don't *approve*', she said heavily. More seriously, Vanrenen's practice went into severe decline. 'That item [in *The Herald*] was the only time my name was mentioned in print', he recalls. 'Within a month my practice had halved.'

The Vanrenens then received some unexpected correspondence. Knowing him as one of the few GPs who did not accept kickbacks from abortionists, Peggy Berman thought Bert Vanrenen's persecution deeply unfair. Having carefully typewritten it herself, she sent a list of referring GPs, on which the Vanrenens were staggered to find almost 250 names. Surely something could be done, Vanrenen told Rod Bretherton, to have these doctors nail their colours to the mast. Could Bretherton call a meeting of the AMA?

For all his ancestor worship and private bravado, Bretherton was publicly timid. 'I've a better idea', he said. 'Why don't *you* call the meeting?' But when Vanrenen pointed out that he was no longer an AMA member, Bretherton agreed, although he delegated the business of collecting the necessary signatures to his live-in caretaker, Frederick Martorana. Martorana and Ila Vanrenen tramped round town knocking on the doors of those GPs on Peggy Berman's list. Ila was a not-so-gentle persuader. 'You know, I'm surprised you're reluctant to sign', she found herself saying. 'Because I've got this list of doctors who refer to abortionists and—isn't it funny?—your name seems to be on it.' For Ila Vanrenen, the clearing of her husband's name became an obsession. She joined the ALRA committee. She wrote to every female Victorian parliamentarian; she launched a *papierkrieg* on the offices of Bolte and Rylah; she upbraided anyone and everyone, a habit she never lost. Some years later, journalist Bruce Hanford found himself in a hotel lift on the way to a Liberal Party function, and watched Ila browbeat Malcolm Fraser at length about abortion law. Hanford was impressed by her tenacity and the prime minister's patience. Finally, Fraser said drily: 'Don't you think this is a very *slow* lift, Bruce?'

The AMA meeting on 14 June 1968 proved a timely boost to morale. A majority of the 450 doctors called for a government inquiry into 'the needs and desires of the population and the medical profession', expressing 'deep concern' at the existing laws. The Vanrenens found further support in surprising quarters. The Menzies never turned their backs. Liberal senator Dame Ivy Wedgwood became the unofficial patron of Ila's letter writing. They had sympathetic ears in Allan Hunt MLC and Roberts Dunstan MLA. One lunchtime, Sir Robert Knox accosted Ila's father at the Australia Club. 'I read about your son-in-law', he said. 'He'll be all right. What he's done is save someone from a worse fate. You should be proud of him.' And while some patients deserted, others stayed—much to Vanrenen's surprise. 'Most people thought I was part of the racket', he recalls. 'Most people didn't want to know me. But my Catholics looked after me...because Catholics have more need of abortion than any other group.'

~

For now, the fates of the abortionists lay in the hands of their lawyers, particularly Ray Dunn, who was representing Ken Davidson, Bert Vanrenen and Jim Troup. He had never been more prominent as a public figure, renowned for his wine cellar (reportedly Melbourne's best), his ballroom dancing (corpulence notwithstanding, he had dazzling footwork) and his presidency of the all-conquering Richmond Football Club (his Armadale home was scattered with tiger-skin rugs, and upholstered in yellow and black). And his role in these high-profile cases was intriguing. While Dunn had been defending abortionists since the 1940s, he had been defending police far longer: back in 1932, he had acted for Chief Commissioner Tom Blamey at a Board of Inquiry into police violence and corruption. His laceration of Brian Latch at the 'Mr X' hearings had stopped the investigation in its tracks. As Latch recalled: 'When he was cross examining me, he almost succeeded in tearing me to shreds with jibes and snide remarks that were so venomous that the board intervened…Frequently he brought me to tears as he probed, found raw nerves and played on them in the hope I would crack'. Now those formidable powers would be deployed not just on police but on police witnesses—and when *R v Davidson* opened in the City Court before RM Hudspeth SM on 22 April, he held nothing back.

The first witness was student Edward Andriessen, boyfriend of nurse Lynette Matthews. Like other witnesses, police had offered him an indemnity from prosecution under the *Crimes Act*. Andriessen was unconvinced. When Crown prosecutor Geoffrey Byrne asked him if he was a student, he replied: 'I cannot give any further evidence'.

> Hudspeth: You were asked if you were a university student, what is your answer to that?
> Andriessen: I cannot give any answer for fear it may incriminate me.
> Hudspeth: Do you think that giving your occupation would incriminate you?
> Andriessen: I still cannot give any evidence for fear it may incriminate me.

When the hearing resumed next day, the law's potential to make public spectacle of private life was also revealed. Andriessen not only reiterated his refusal to give evidence, but requested that his name be suppressed, for his identification had caused 'a great deal of trouble at home'. He gulped: 'Until last night my folks never knew anything about it and my name is spluttered all over the paper'. Dunn wasn't copping that: 'The defendant is, one, not excused from publicity and, two, is facing his trial. There seems no logical reason why the other people should be put in any different position because of that'. Hudspeth was a stickler—he would shortly gain notoriety by fining Graeme Blundell and Lindsay Smith for use of the word 'fucking' in the La Mama production of *Norm and Ahmed*. He ruled that he would not 'put any fetters on the press or the way they report proceedings', leaving Dunn to have a field day showing up the law's entailments. Beginning with Lynette Matthews, he ripped the witnesses apart.

Dunn: Now you say that he [Davidson] discussed your boyfriend with you. What was the substance of that discussion?

Matthews: What would my boyfriend say...

Dunn: Yes?

Matthews: ...and think about the situation. And oh, he suggested that would we consider getting married.

Dunn: What if anything did you say to him when he said that?

Matthews: Well I said he had—he had his studies and we didn't want to get married yet.

Dunn: Well now?

Matthews: Oh, excuse me, I feel faint...

So saying, she did.

Dunn's coup was while cross-examining Marie Falls, the Ararat girl found with her mother in the waiting room. Davidson, of course, had not aborted her...but someone had.

Dunn: Do you swear you did not go to Dr Heath's rooms in Collins Street on the Wednesday?

Falls: No.

Dunn: Just take your time. You understand that you are on oath, do you not?

Falls: Yes.

Dunn: Will you swear that you were not there?

Falls: I was there.

Dunn: Of course you were. Why did you lie about that?

Falls: [sic] To incriminate others.

Dunn pursued the police's indulgence of John Heath like a dog worrying a bone. When Fred Russell was cross-examined on 29 April, he was made to look at least rather sluggish.

Dunn: You have heard a statement here on oath by Miss Falls that the following day, when Dr Davidson said he had nothing to do with aborting her, that she was aborted in Dr Heath's rooms. Have you followed that up? Or have you *not bothered* to follow that up?

Russell: There has been a conference with Detective Inspector Holland and myself about this matter.

Dunn: No, I mean have you followed it up? I mean *Detective Inspector Holland, he has no connection with this Dr Heath, does he*?
Russell: Well, he's my superior officer.
Dunn: Well, have you been instructed to follow it up or not by him? In fact, *Dr Heath is a fairly regular visitor to the Criminal Investigation Branch, is he not*?
Russell: I wouldn't know that.

The italicised questions ooze with so much insinuation that Dunn cannot have been guessing. It seems almost certain that he was working to defeat some police with information provided by others. And while *R v Davidson* adjourned soon after, Dunn now had *R v Vanrenen* to enjoy. Despite Ila Vanrenen's entreaties to Bolte and Rylah, the case began in the City Court on 17 June 1968, with Dunn zeroing in on the unfortunate Robin Ann Dunn. The girl described being operated on by Davidson, but then, under uncannily close questioning from her namesake, tearfully admitted another termination six months later after consulting Heath. When Fred Russell appeared again, Dunn was waiting. Homicide now had evidence in two cases involving an abortionist called Heath at 94 Collins Street. Had anything happened, and if not, why not? Russell replied 'no' to the first question and 'pressure of business' to the second. Soon after, LT Griggin SM adjourned the matter, and Dunn encouraged Ila to write Bolte again asking why Heath had not been investigated. Her letter was a delicious mix of remonstrance and reprimand: Bolte would have received few such missives in his premiership.

> Monday has come and gone and I have watched the police of Victoria crucify my husband Dr Bertram Sutherland Vanrenen, that gentle man whose only concern is the health and welfare of his patients. Bother you…
>
> The present girls who have appeared in court have been pathetic nobodies. How long before they produce somebody including people that you and I know? This could become terribly nasty…
>
> Why has Dr Heath not been charged? Is it because he enjoys a particular relationship with someone which causes the police not to take action against him?

Bolte's emollient reply tactfully omitted any mention of Heath. But Dunn wasn't finished. When committal proceedings began in *R v*

Troup & Ors six weeks later, he begged no pardons. When luckless Athanasia Sakkas finished her painstaking examination through an interpreter, he ripped straight in: 'I suggest you have told lies on oath today, Mrs Sakkas, is that not so?' Again he probed the police pitilessly, especially about the relationship between Martin Jacobson the constable and his de facto, Maureen the Hoddle Street receptionist. Holland seems to have been genuinely furious about Jacobson, compelling his resignation from the force on 5 October and having Deputy Commissioner Noel Wilby designate his character 'unsatisfactory'.

Even highly regarded Detective-Sergeant Kevin Carton suffered the sharp edge of Dunn's tongue. Who was 'Mrs Schrey'? Why had she not been investigated? What about the names of referring GPs uncovered in the raid? Why was Vanrenen being prosecuted when these other doctors were not? Had there been a change of policy? Why, Sergeant Carton, why? And had a journalist been present on the afternoon of 16 September, they would have been tantalised by a scoop—from an impeccable source.

> Dunn: Well now, there is just one other matter, Mr Carton. I do not want to mention names in this thing, but with regard to the substitution of the book—you know the allegation by Mr Jackson?
>
> Carton: Yes sir.
>
> Dunn: Were you approached by a former senior member of the Homicide squad to arrange that deception? I mean nothing against you personally, but were you told of it, that this was going to be done by a former member of the Homicide Squad?
>
> Carton: No sir.
>
> Dunn: You have not been approached by a former member about this—before it actually occurred I mean?
>
> Carton: No sir...The first I knew of the substitution of the books was when Jackson rang me a little after six at home on the morning ...and then I saw them at 20 past 8 when he brought them in.

The exchange was coy, but significant: almost eighteen months before it became a scandal, a court heard hints of police corruption in abortion. The exchange soon receded to vanishing point, or at least to page 552 of *R v Troup & Ors*. But about to hove into view was a man who didn't believe in secrets.

~

Two days after the AMA meeting, Ila Vanrenen encountered in her husband's waiting room, now eerily empty, a burly, balding stranger shrouded in cigarette smoke. 'Can I help you?' she asked. The figure replied in a soft Scottish drawl: 'Oh, I have a solo practice in St Kilda, and I heard that Dr Vanrenen had a big solo practice here so I thought I'd come and have a look'. Ila scanned the room: 'Well, it's not as busy as it used to be. But we're about to have lunch. Would you join us?' Over sandwiches in the empty waiting room, the visitor introduced himself as 39-year-old Dr Bertram Wainer, a former lieutenant-colonel who had run an eighty-bed army hospital in Brisbane before opening his surgery in January 1966. Like the older man, Wainer had been confronted early in his practice by a woman wanting an abortion, and confidentially obtained a list of doctors who did them. His response to news of Vanrenen's prosecution had been 'there but for the grace of God, go I'. Now he asked: 'Bert, who's helping you?' Vanrenen admitted that nobody was. Wainer glowered: 'Nobody? Hell, we *all* do it. Why aren't the doctors helping you?' Ila laughed humourlessly: 'It's the opposite. They run a mile'. As Vanrenen explained how the Medical Defence Association had scorned his case, Wainer shook his head: it was 'cowardly conservative hypocrisy'. Nothing irked Bert Wainer more.

In common with many others in this story—Berman, Heath, Bretherton, Field, Faust, Haire—Bert Wainer's birth experiences had been complicated. When his Jewish father died while his Presbyterian mother was six months' pregnant, boy Bert grew up in penury in Glasgow's Gallowgate. His allegiances were unpredictable. He romanticised his stepfather, an illiterate alcoholic Irish-Catholic ne'er-do-well who died four years after the family emigrated to Australia in 1949, while about his new country he was perennially dismissive. 'Generally I suppose I just don't respect Australians', he admitted. 'They are into all this nonsense about ANZAC but really they have no traditions, no history. They're adolescents. You can't search for roots that aren't there.' He advanced in the new world, nonetheless, as he never would have in the old. While matriculating, he obtained work in the physiology department of Melbourne University with the legendarily salty Professor Pansy Wright, who championed his quest for a Commonwealth Scholarship in 1952. Supplementing this by working as a nightwatchman and encyclopedia salesman, he completed a medical degree. Between times, his marriage to Barbara Code, a cadet fashion buyer, yielded four children: Dirk, Rory, Felice and Sean.

Yet the handsome Wainer, who always seemed to glow with the sheen of recent exertion, chafed at confines and rigidities—they almost needed to be mandatory, as in the Army, before he could reconcile himself to them. He had a strong head for alcohol; he didn't so much puff Peter Stuyvesants as rip the smoke from them; marriage disagreed with him, and his own failed two years into his service. He developed an idiosyncratic domestic life where he spent alternate weekends with Carole Carrodus, his secretary, and Judy Small, a nurse. Wainer was a first-class, high-minded general practitioner. 'He had a magnificent bedside manner', recalls Eve Janover, who did two months' training with him in mid-1966. 'He just related to patients so well. Doctors then didn't often have a great rapport with patients. A lot of people in medicine were in it for the money. Bert wasn't.' Yet it wasn't enough: he seemed to be searching for a cause worth the candle, to absorb the unchannelled energy that he emitted, like static electricity, even in repose. He fulminated about the Vietnam War. He joined the campaign to remit Ronald Ryan's death sentence, and was one of the protestors round Pentridge on the night of the hanging, appalled at the heavy-handedness of the police in making ninety-seven arrests.

At around the same time, he was caught up in the prosecution of his brother-in-law. Small-time crook Dale Code, a traveller for S. C. Johnson Wax & Polish, was arrested as part of a ring counterfeiting the new $10 note with a Gestetner and guillotine. Code did time for the offence, but Wainer took away a recollection of Code's interrogation at Russell Street. Brought downstairs after questioning, Code declined to sign the now statutory document to say he had been well treated. 'You can go up for the same', a policeman sneered. It was the same philosophy as Jack Matthews's remark to Peggy Berman: 'It's not what you say; it's what *we say* you say'. And it angered Wainer as the earlier comment had chilled Berman.

Now Wainer wanted to help Vanrenen. Promising to pursue the matter of the Medical Defence Association, he introduced himself to Rod Bretherton, whose petition he had signed and whose AMA meeting he had attended. They clicked immediately. Wainer thought Bretherton 'a sincere and dedicated man trying to benefit humanity'; Bretherton, captivated by Wainer's energy, agreed with his plan to circularise Victorian doctors in the name of a new fund for those prosecuted as a result of abortion referrals. The $2000 subscribed for the Medical Practitioners' Protection Trust Account led to Wainer's first newspaper publicity—and it sat well with him. In September, he joined Ila Vanrenen at his first ALRA evening. In October, he called a special meeting of the Medical Defence Association, protesting Vanrenen's treatment.

> The council of the association was seated in front on a stage and the chairman announced that a decision had already been made at a previous meeting held in camera. A doctor would be defended if he had mentioned the name of a medically qualified abortionist to a patient verbally, but on no account should he write referral letters, or make the appointment with the abortionist.

It was, Wainer noted, 'absolute hypocrisy'. But the principle had been granted, and other benefits accrued: 'The about-turn of the Medical Defence Association received a lot of publicity and my name was being mentioned frequently in the press. They were beginning to label me "Dr Bertram Wainer, abortion law reformer"'. Already, some thought the label mattered to Wainer a little overmuch. Bretherton urged Beatrice Faust to meet this boisterous up-and-comer over dinner at St Kilda's Illiad, but the doctor's charm washed over the tough-minded feminist. 'How old are you?' asked Wainer. 'Twenty-nine', said Faust. 'Never tell anyone you're older than twenty-five', Wainer replied. Faust cringed: what an old roué! She was unimpressed: 'He didn't seem to know anything about anything that was significant. He didn't even know about the Bourne verdict'.

Wainer must have boned up on it soon after because he shortly interrupted ALRA's earnest convocations with the proposal that a doctor do a 'test case', à la Aleck Bourne. He went to the effort of ringing Homicide and putting the proposition to Frank Holland: 'What would you do if a Professor of Obstetrics and his staff, in a public hospital, terminated the pregnancy of a girl for reasons of her physical and mental health?' Holland replied unequivocally: 'I would have to arrest the lot of them'. Well, said Wainer, so be it. But the proposal endeared him to nobody: none of ALRA's worthies wanted to be involved in law-breaking. Secretary Jo Richardson was sent to Wainer's Carlisle Street surgery to seek his resignation, which he took in good part. 'I suppose I shall have to start my own group', he laughed. Then he asked her to dinner.

'The b-b-better man won'

Because such a solution is so obvious, so sensible and so logical, it must necessarily be impossible. We need spend no further time on it.

Justice Keith Asche

As 1968 ended, Melbourne's once impregnable abortion trade was in disarray—with one exception. At 94 Collins Street, it was business as usual. John Heath himself did little actual aborting now, preferring to wander in at 11 a.m. while other doctors like Arnold Finks and James Buchanan performed the procedures. With the closure of so many competitors, his prices had risen sharply. It was an ill wind that did not blow John Heath some good.

Heath's conspicuous sense of security, his sunny rooms always enlivened by fresh flowers, occasioned resentment and suspicion. What was so special about *his* protection? The specialness was that nobody knew how it worked. Corrie Blackwell never saw or heard of money changing hands: she simply knew that the practice had a line into Russell Street, where Inspectors Bill Mooney and Frank Holland worked in adjacent offices. And if graft was paid, it was probably not the basis of the relationship: cash in envelopes and furtive, panicky meetings were simply not Heath's style. In a sense, it was a decidedly Melbourne relationship, loose but strong, based on social overlap and mutual interest. Mooney was a member of Heath's Pups; Holland was a member of Heath's White Ensign Club; both attended the annual Pups lunch in early 1968; both attended the functions for outgoing Superintendent BH Gould and for incoming CIB Chief Inspector Colin Sharp at Heath's Delphic Club; and so forth. The deal seems to have been sealed, as it were, when Mooney reached the mandatory police retirement age of sixty on 25 June 1968, and struggled to find new employment. Heath gave him a sinecure 'managing' his rural property interests, essentially handling payroll. The difference, then, between the protection arrangements of John Heath and Peggy Berman was the difference between being an upper-class male and a lower-class female: Heath was comfortably the social equal of the police he dealt with; Berman was never even close.

Berman bore her grievances sourly, and under increasing duress. In July 1968, she was diagnosed as suffering a second carcinoma in the lumbar region. Deep X-ray treatment at the Peter MacCallum Institute left her severely debilitated, and she was excused when the presentiments were filed for the committal hearings in *R v Troup & Ors*. But her fury was unappeasable. One day at the Carlton Hotel, she threatened to turn 'Bluey' Adam in. Adam retorted that the cancer was obviously affecting her brain; if she shopped him, he would simply have her certified. Eventually she calmed down, and Adam said soothingly: 'You will be all right. You will never go for trial. They cannot send you for trial'. But when a presentiment was then filed against her, she was again inconsolable. Her only hope was that if and when Ford succeeded Holland as Homicide chief—as he was now favourite to do—the trial might be headed off.

Heath's invulnerability was summed up for Berman by an incident at 94 Collins Street on 4 December 1968, when 36-year-old Malka Buckstein, wife of a Kew physician, died after a procedure handled by Arnold Finks and anaesthetist John Levin, who insisted that it had been a routine dilatation and curettage. An autopsy revealed a pre-existing atheroma (swelling and fatty deposits) round her heart. The view of the Royal Women's Hospital registrar was that Buckstein would have been a risk to operate on for an ingrowing toenail: 'With the degree of atheroma at her age she could have died just going down the street'. Although the coroner drew no conclusion about whether an abortion had taken place, the failure of the police to investigate more fully infuriated Berman. And if she wasn't the equal of the police she dealt with, she would prove more than their match.

Early in the new year, with Norval Morris's encouragement, she agreed to meet the boisterous doctor stirring up ALRA. Although they had not previously crossed paths, Bert Wainer had referred patients to Hoddle Street, and knew of Berman as 'a cross between Mata Hari and a police *agent provocateur*'. He remembered their lunch as a mix of intrigue and flirtation.

> She was a tired, strained woman. I spent several hours talking and learned very little, but sensed that she could tell me a lot more. She was very guarded: she did not know what my act was, what my cut would be, what I was after.
>
> Despite the fatigue, the result of the tensions and stresses and ill-health of the preceding four years, her personality was vivacious, she was an excellent conversationalist with a flair for humorous remarks and, on rare occasions when she relaxed and the fatigue was dissipated, one could see her natural beauty.

Berman was instantly enamoured. Her protectors had failed, but she had found a redeemer. 'For me,' she would say, 'Dr Wainer was a gift from heaven'.

~

Other gifts were in the offing. *R v Davidson* was listed to resume in the Supreme Court before Justice Smith on 17 March 1969. But, a few days before, the Crown listed four new witnesses, added a conspiracy charge involving Judith Carroll and dropped the charge naming Robin Ann Dunn. Ken Davidson called the Vanrenens in stuttering excitement: 'I-I-Ila, m-most extraordinary news. They've dropped the charge of Robin Ann Dunn'. This was the girl, of course, whom Vanrenen had referred: chances were that if she was felt unfit for one examination, she would hardly measure up for another. The evidence of Judith Carroll, moreover, was hardly the most compelling. She had not even kept her appointment; indeed, she had born a daughter.*

Davidson was as excited as Ila Vanrenen had ever heard him: 'Apparently their c-c-case is so poor they're going through the cards trying to find more witnesses'. The Crown's late substitutions meant that Jack Lazarus, Dunn's choice as Davidson's counsel, could blamelessly delay the trial further. 'Mr Lazarus,' said Justice Smith, 'apparently about six months elapsed between arrest and

* It is an amazing aspect of *R v Davidson*, the case giving de jure legality to abortion in Victoria, that the informant in whose name the warrant was issued actually never had the abortion. A birth notice for 'Carroll' in *The Sun* for 24 February records the arrival the day before of 'a daughter (Simone Patricia) at Box Hill Hospital' to 'Judith and Terry'. During the court proceedings, Carroll referred to an uncle named Terry: he seems to have substituted in the apparent absence of the biological father, Michael Martin.

commencement of committal proceedings and now about eleven months has elapsed since committal?...Is there some explanation for this great lapse of time?' Lazarus must have smiled inwardly: 'I have none, Your Honour. I have none at all'.

Davidson, the soft-spoken dilettante who drank milk for his peptic ulcer, had always seemed a mite too genteel for the criminal justice roughhouse. His nurses, Jenny Lamble and Margaret Hamilton, had left; on his own at 106 Hotham Street, he seemed acutely vulnerable. 'We were terribly worried about Ken', recalls Janice Wakely. 'We wondered how he'd cope with the witness box. We thought he'd end up in jail, which he would never have coped with.' Yet at news that the Crown case was faltering, Davidson found unsuspected inner reserves. He was calm, stoical, organised. He enjoyed dealing with Lazarus, who would ring at unpredictable hours to discuss minute aspects of the case. Almost in spite of himself, the shy doctor began to feel excited.

At Homicide, meanwhile, confusion reigned. Holland was in his final few months of office before moving out to Malvern CIB. The department was about to take a Protestant kick, apparently from Jack Ford, although innuendo abounded. A letter was circulating among parliamentarians alleging an affair between Berman and a senior police officer: 'Mrs Berman can be found any day in her previous position booking girls for abortion in her premises at 1087 Hoddle St...Her lover or *de facto* has a good chance of becoming the next inspector in charge of Homicide'. It had reached opposition leader Clyde Holding and was said to have been read by Arthur Rylah; there was no clue to its provenance except the signature 'JH'.

Rylah himself was shrouded in rumour. The previous year, Bolte's indispensable henchman had separated from his wife of thirty-one years. Lady Ann Rylah, Victorian training leader of the Girl Guides movement, was a popular public figure who ran a veterinary clinic from the couple's five-bedroom Kew home. Then, on 12 August 1968, she had cut Sir Arthur from her will, a decision arising 'directly from his abandonment', a step preparatory to dissolution of the marriage. Seven months later, as whispers circulated of imminent divorce, two girls who worked at Lady Rylah's clinic found her comatose in the back garden suffering from a subarachnoid haemorrhage. The 'Topical Taps' column of the popular scandal sheet *Truth* on 5 April predicted: 'Inquest into death of well-known citizen will see the greatest number of barristers at Coroners' Court for many years'. But there would be no inquest: in the space on the death certificate usually reserved for a doctor's name was the notation that the coroner had ordered cremation of the body without further ado. Rylah remarried six months later.

Throughout this period, Berman and Ford were at each other night and day, exchanging complaints and threats and promises—then, bizarrely, terms of endearment. On Anzac Day 1969, Berman demanded Ford's presence at Oak Street, and when he didn't turn up had Troup ferry her to Ford's Burwood home. 'Aren't you going to let us in?' she said, pushing past him. Specifically, Berman wanted to know the meaning of the transfer of Kevin Carton, investigating officer in the death of Malka Buckstein, to the UN mission in Cyprus: a number of detectives, including Holland, had taken tours of duty there. In general, she wanted to remind him how he was compromised; how he was implicated; how he was *obliged*. Ford exploded. How dare she barge into his house—into *his life*. Furniture was scattered as he rained punches on Berman's abdomen; Troup stood by in shock. 'Let's get out of here', he said, grabbing Berman's hand. 'You shouldn't have come in the first place', Ford growled at their departing figures.

As Troup arrived home in South Blackburn a few days later at about 8 p.m., however, Ford glided up in his car. He had been talking with CIB chief Colin Sharp, Ford advised; his promotion to Homicide chief was in the bag. 'Everything will be all right when I get back in', he promised. 'Just be patient.' Troup was anxious: 'It's been a trying time. What can you do?' Ford outlined his plan to reinterview witnesses and bury the books. 'Look after Peggy', he said at last. 'She's a princess.'

Then Holland took a hand. Since December, he had been sitting on a complaint about Rodney Bretherton. Twenty-year-old Glenda Collins was a disturbed and exploited woman with three children already, two fostered to her aunt, who had become pregnant again to truck driver Benny Amato. Amato insisted on her obtaining an abortion, and his father's de facto had tried various means of procuring a miscarriage.

> [She] at that time made a hot bath for me—it was very hot—and put mustard in it and made me drink castor oil and orange. I didn't want to get into the bath because it was too hot and I was sort of made to

> get into it and told to stay there for a while. If they heard me turning on the tap they would come running in to see what I was doing...

She had finally been aborted by George Dixon, Bretherton's occasional helpmate, but on Amato scorning her requests for money had decided to turn everyone in. Collins, the Crown Law Department later agreed, was an unreliable witness: '[She is] a dull unintelligent woman with a poor social background with very poor educational standard as she can hardly read and write and presents as under the stress of real situational difficulties at all times'. But here she served the purpose of expediting a raid on John Heath's last significant competitor—timed, with a little dramatic touch, to coincide with the resumption, at last, of *R v Davidson* on 12 May 1969.

Police arrested two young women on the premises, Margaret Rowan and Lorraine Raisbeck; they spied Bretherton's bookkeeper, Noris Jaasund, secreting medical record cards among books and magazines and confiscated them too. Within days they were trailing patients of Bretherton's all over Victoria—and Ursula Raths, a divorcee with three children, wasn't going to take it. Bert Wainer had been on Helen Homewood's Channel 0 chat show *Roundabout* that week arguing for a new meeting of the AMA, and Raths arrived on his doorstep a few mornings later:

> They had asked her if she had been to see this doctor and her reason for doing so. What was wrong with her medically? They produced her medical history card with a big 'P' written on it and asked: 'What does that mean? Are you pregnant or are you on the pill? You're divorced; who's the man who got you pregnant?' Then came threats and intimidations. 'If you don't tell us what we want to know, we'll come and see you at your work. Everyone will know why we are questioning you. Give this doctor up. You'll be all right; we won't expose you if you tell us about him, but if you don't give him up we'll hound you into the ground.'

Raths would later prove untraceable, having apparently moved interstate and changed her name. But her legacy was to be the provocation for Wainer running a famous newspaper advertisement, which he and Jo Richardson somehow slipped into the conservative *Sun* late on 19 May. Headed 'Abortion Abortion Abortion', it urged women visited by police 'not be intimidated by bullying or intimidatory tactics', and promised: 'You are an Australian citizen and the law is on your side'. While Wainer was prone to grandiloquence, on this claim he would prove stunningly correct.

~

The designers of Fourth Court in Victoria's Supreme Court had nothing so plain as the mere practice of law in mind; its whole effect is to inspire a respect, even a dread, of the justice system. The ornate coffered ceiling is lofty. The balustraded cast-iron balcony of the public gallery is supported by free-standing Doric columns. The judge's presence is magnified by a tall elevated canopy in dark polished cedar; the witness stand is a lonely circular island. Nearest of all courts to the cells, and thus the most secure, it had traditionally hosted the most lurid of cases. It was here that Ronald Ryan, studying the sombre jurors about to pronounce on his murder trial on 30 March 1966, muttered to co-accused Peter John Walker: 'I think we're in deep shit'. It was now where Ken Davidson would have his day in court, being listed to appear after a manslaughter case before Justice Menhennitt. *R v Arnold*, indeed, evokes just what grim company abortion had brought the gentlemanly doctor into. Twenty-three-year-old Peter Arnold had survived a suicide pact with 19-year-old Susan Allen. The prison psychiatrist found him to be entirely alienated from mankind, aspiring only to a patch of land to grow vegetables on: 'His general view is that society is wrong and he doesn't want any truck with it. He wants nothing to do with any of us'. Disturbed by Arnold's lack of contrition, Menhennitt gave him three years.

Crime was not Cliff Menhennitt's metier. He had been an equity lawyer, best known at the bar for his expertise in Section 92 of the constitution ('Free Trade Between The States'). His most famous brief had been as Herbert Evatt's junior in the bank nationalisation case of the late 1940s; his most regular client had been Ansett Transport Industries, where his overriding instruction was to ensure that Sir Reginald Ansett never took the stand. Counsel appearing before him in criminal matters nursed a slight dread of his sentencing, which seemed arbitrary and inexact. Brian Bourke recalls representing a member of a big criminal clan, the Robinsons, on the charge of using a firearm to resist apprehension.

> Cliff gave him eleven years with a nine minimum. I mean, I just couldn't believe it. A *nine* minimum. Anyway, I go to see Robinson and I'm wracking my brains to think of something to say, and finally I tell him: 'Look, there's one consolation. This sentence is so heavy that the court of appeal is bound to reduce it.' And they did. He got four with a two minimum.

Menhennitt's reputation was for a thoroughness tending to voluminousness. One day, he drove even Justice Wilfred Fullagar, a man of famously saintly disposition, to distraction. 'But I don't *want* any more authority for that proposition', Fullagar groaned. Menhennitt was unabashed: 'Then I will content myself with giving your Honour the names of all the cases cited'. And on he continued, to Fullagar's mounting fury. When Menhennitt was mooted as a candidate for the High Court, Garfield Barwick is said to have scoffed: 'Heavens, no. We don't have time'.

Menhennitt's marriage was childless, and his manner awkward, inclining to that slightly forced effusiveness that engenders awkwardness in others. 'He was *unduly* fulsome, *enormously* helpful', recalls fellow judge Sir John Young. 'If I had an idea that he thought was a good one, he would become hugely excited by it; couldn't stop talking about what a *marvellous* job I'd done. He was immensely kind that way, almost overgenerous.' He could seem a naif, and a prude. Once, during an appearance before the Privy Council, he was alarmed to find that his opponent seemed to be expecting a female visitor...who *wasn't* his wife. He jumped up at once, spluttering anxiously: 'I have to go, I have to go'. And off he dashed into the Westminster dusk, and the celibate safety of his own lodgings.

It was the law that was his life's work. In a more leisured era for the bench, Menhennitt was a glutton for cases; toiling through adjournments, he seemed capable of almost instant judgments. His orderly mind had been honed by teaching law at Melbourne University, which barrister Phil Opas thought accounted for the expository nature of his rulings: 'It appeared to me that he wasn't just thinking of other judges but of students. His judgements were always explanatory, referring to precedents even where he was disagreeing with them and determined to overrule'. In court, he was known for immaculate manners, and a telltale mannerism. 'His lower lip would stick out', remembers Allan McDonald, then at the bar, later himself a Supreme Court judge. 'And the more it stuck out, the worse you were doing.'

R v Davidson unfolded slowly. There were twenty-one witnesses, fourteen of whom, eight women and six men, had been granted indemnities. The poor ventilation and dim light taxed attentions; the antiquated architecture taxed patience, and there was a day when Menhennitt had to discontinue proceedings because the water supply had been cut off. Ila Vanrenen lent proceedings a touch of fun, appearing every day wearing something red, then lunching at ritzy Lazar's. But Crown prosecutor Geoffrey Byrne was a ponderous advocate, whose opening address laboured the idea that Davidson was a 'practised abortionist' with a 'regular system', and whose examination could not but seem unduly intrusive: it was difficult to see who gained from knowing the interpersonal intimacies of Margaret Fletcher of Warwick Road, Greensborough.

> Byrne: Miss Fletcher, early in 1967 were you keeping company with a man by the name of Bartlett?
> Fletcher: Yes.
> Byrne: What was his Christian name?
> Fletcher: Shane or Trevor, I am not quite sure. He told me it was Shane.
> Byrne: Shane or Trevor, you are not quite sure?
> Fletcher: Yes.

For those following the story, however, there were new pieces of the puzzle. Gracie Demarco, a machinist from Lalor, testified that Davidson had decided not to abort her because she could not provide her mother's consent. He had referred her to Stanhill, where 'the doctor said he couldn't do it because he'd already been caught', and sent her on to Heath with the warning that it would be expensive: indeed, it cost $240, twice the usual charge of Davidson and Troup, and thrice Bretherton's standard discount fee. Lazarus, meanwhile, began chipping away at the police's authority by showing Fred Russell's evidently shaky grasp of gynaecology.

> Lazarus: What did you understand a curette was?
> Russell: Some interference with the uterus.

Lazarus: Did you know what sort of interference or have you any belief as to what sort of interference?
Russell: In the form of a medical operation.

Menhennitt ran what lawyers call 'a very good court'. He calmed witnesses who became distressed, referred always to 'Dr Davidson' rather than 'the accused', and stuck out his lower lip when Byrne was addressing jurors, insisting that there was 'no such evidence' when the prosecutor referred to Davidson as 'a member of a multi-million-dollar industry', and instructing him to apologise for the claim that 'if we don't get him [Davidson] this time, we'll get him next time'. He gave rapid, clear rulings, and showed prodigious recall, as when some police notes of interrogation turned out to be missing.

Menhennitt: Mr Lazarus, doubtless you are aware of *Elias v Pasmore 1934, 2 King's Bench, 164 at 173.*
Lazarus: No, I am sorry, your honour.
Menhennitt: Well, perhaps if you could take note of it. *Elias v Pasmore 1934, 2 King's Bench, 164 at 173.*

The case ran so smoothly that media coverage was minimal. On the fourth day, the courts swarmed with reporters, but none were there for *R v Davidson*: it was because Clarrie O'Shea, the Tramways Union's tempestuous general secretary, had been arrested for contempt of the Commonwealth Industrial Court. The next day, it seemed, 'the people' had thrown down the gauntlet to 'the law'. After a mass meeting at Olympic Park, 2000 unionists and students marched twenty abreast down Batman Avenue and through Swanston and Bourke Streets, culminating in a wild hour-long clash with police outside the Supreme Court. Yet even as the melee unfolded, Menhennitt carried on calmly. The Crown was about to present expert testimony from two witnesses, Dr Ian McDonald and Dr William Somerville. In order to rule on the admissibility of their evidence, the judge had to define what might constitute a legal abortion. Menhennitt painstakingly read a series of citations, ranging from Jack Barry's 'The Law of Therapeutic Abortion' in the *Proceedings of the Medico-Legal Society of Victoria* to Glanville Williams's *The Sanctity of Life and the Criminal Law*, and invited the thoughts of the respective counsels.

Gentlemen, as you will doubtless imagine, I have given some considerable thought to this matter already, but I have not reached

> any final conclusions ... I make it quite clear these are only tentative thoughts and that I have not made any final decision about the law, but I thought that counsel might be assisted if they knew the kind of thinking that I have been giving to the matter, and accordingly I hand to counsel two, one each, for your consideration and for argument, a possible view as to what is involved in the concept of lawfulness and unlawfulness.

Such civility sounded incongruous as the parties parted ways for the weekend. Victoria was in noisy industrial chaos. Cabinet was meeting in emergency session. No fewer than twenty-seven unions were planning action. Ila Vanrenen was taking Jack Lazarus to meet 'Bung' Hill, the famous obstetrician who had taught her husband, to prepare for the expert witnesses. But it almost seemed like nobody would ever make it back to court, and Menhennitt had to decree on Monday that there would be no proceedings the next day because of the absence of public transport. On 20 May, as a quarter of a million workers went on strike, the state was ravaged by power and gas cuts. The only mention of abortion in the newspapers was Bert Wainer's eye-catching advertisement, and Chief Commissioner Noel Wilby's grudging pledge to investigate. But though nobody knew it, much more significant writing was being done in Menhennitt's North Balwyn study.

That *R v Davidson* had come before Menhennitt, of course, was a fluke: judges simply took turns sitting a month in 'crime', and the case would have come before Justice Smith had the Crown not insisted on additional witnesses two months earlier. Nor was Menhennitt, perhaps, the judge whom the case would have most interested. Justice Bill Gillard puts it simplest: 'What Cliff knew of abortion would have been exactly nothing'. Yet, in other respects, he brought to an inflammatory issue a studious neutrality. For the Supreme Court bench's Catholics, serious and honourable men like Greg Gowans, Kevin Anderson and Sir Norman O'Bryan, the matter would have been challenging. As Sir John Young recalls:

> I remember sitting on appeal with Kevin in a case involving two young constables who had perjured themselves on the instructions of a superior officer ... who had then sold them out. Kevin was terribly

> troubled by the case because the constables had sworn untruth against their oath—which to a Catholic was a very serious thing. Kevin had great difficulty accepting the view the rest of us took that they had been badly done by and we ought to do what we could for them. It was too much for a Catholic. Although he finally came round to our position, his convictions made it terribly difficult: as far as he was concerned, when you swore by almighty God, you didn't go the other way.

Menhennitt might also have known a little more than anyone suspected about unwanted pregnancy. The birth certificate of his father, born Frederick Inch in Creswick to Emma Inch on 7 December 1879, is blank where normally would be inserted a father's name. When he married, as Frederick Inch Menhennett (sic) on 27 September 1911, he listed his mother as 'deceased'; in fact, she was still alive, dying a spinster on 27 August 1938. The documentation is consistent, then, with Menhennitt's father having been born illegitimate and fostered, and with his grandmother spending her life in lone disgrace: it appears they lived their lives in neighbouring suburbs, each probably unaware of the other. Did Menhennitt know? Did Menhennitt not? It is probably immaterial: he was too much the legal stickler to be guided by personal feelings. But his ruling radically improved the choices confronted by women after an untimely conception—the life-altering and potentially life-destroying choices faced by women like his grandmother.

The 'Menhennitt Ruling', given by him on 22 and 26 May, is six pages densely packed with precedent; read aloud, it would have seemed like an inky cloud of abstractions. No wonder, really, that newspapers ignored it: *The Age*'s front page on 26 May thought that the most pressing question for contemporary women was 'Are Ladies in Trousers Respectable?' On the page, however, the ruling is quite stately, even elegant, negotiating the problem that the Victorian equivalent of the *Infant Life (Preservation) Act* is differently worded with Barry's defence of 'necessity', in which Menhennitt also located the test of proportion. Abortion, he concluded, could be lawful when it was '(a) necessary to preserve the woman from a serious danger to her life or her physical or mental health which the continuance of the pregnancy would entail; and (b) in circumstances not out of proportion to the danger to be averted'. In hindsight, clarification of the law required exactly the pedantic and soporific fussiness for which Menhennitt was known. Precise in some places, vague in others, the Menhennitt Ruling offers almost nothing legally objectionable. It is not adventurous, stopping short of abortion on demand. It is not prescriptive, making no specific requirement regarding the numbers or nature of medical or psychiatric opinions. The lack of excitement it stirred is itself a kind of tribute. 'We were all rather amazed there was no appeal', says Sir John Young. 'Cases on such issues can usually be relied on to be appealed. In the end, Cliff's decision satisfied everyone. Had it been against community standards, an appeal would have been certain. But he got it exactly right.'

The ruling's influence on the jury is debateable. The skill of Lazarus was probably more material. He neutralised the prosecution experts, persuading McDonald he could not be certain what procedures Davidson had carried out, and revealing Somerville to be an active member of the Guild of St Luke, the organisation of Catholic doctors then pressuring the AMA to back away from its new position on abortion. Somerville's statement that he would not terminate a pregnancy even where a woman's life was in danger would almost certainly have sounded too severe. The case's most intriguing evidence was then provided by Davidson, who finally read an unsworn statement from the dock—choosing this method ostensibly for reasons of client confidentiality. Lazarus liked unsworn statements: they protected clients from cross-examination, and juries seldom genuinely distinguished them from sworn evidence. Davidson was thus unchallenged in his quaint assertion that the women concerned had simply imagined themselves pregnant, this being their 'inborn desire': 'This is why the women, when first interviewed by police, easily believed they were pregnant at the time of the operation and had been aborted'. The all-male jury was probably as influenced by masculine delusions about the female psyche as by the judge's fine-grained arguments. After eight hours' deliberation, they returned with acquittals on each charge on 3 June 1969.

A few days later, Davidson hosted a party at 106 Hotham Street to thank supporters, from Ray Dunn and Jack Lazarus to Janice Wakely and the Vanrenens. 'Well, the b-b-better man won', he began with uncharacteristic effusiveness, lauding Lazarus to the skies: 'I never saw him relaxed once, except after the trial was over, and then only for a few minutes'. Bertram Wainer hovered solicitously round Peggy Berman, who looked bruised and scratched. Nobody else knew, but a few nights earlier she had rung Wainer, and also Dunn, when another of her arguments with Ford had become physical; nobody else knew, but she had steadily begun spilling her decade of secrets about the corruption in Melbourne's abortion rackets.

'I don't think it has anything to do with you'

How revolting, how utterly sordid it all was!
Something to be done as secretly as if you were committing a crime.
She felt a spasm of rage. Damn them all! As though she hadn't the right
to do what she liked with her own body.

Jungfrau (1936), Dymphna Cusack

The Menhennitt Ruling is a dividing line in the history of reproductive health in Australia but it didn't emerge without warning. The big abortion cases of the mid-1960s to the early 1970s—chronologically, *R v Bayliss & Sizeland*, *R v Davidson*, *R v Fenton Bowen*, *R v Flynn*, *R v Bretherton*, *R v Field & Moran*, *R v Troup* and eventually the three cases of *R v Heath*—are a parade of attitudes, running to tens of thousands of pages of transcript and involving hundreds of statements and exhibits. They show a law falling apart at the seams, unpopular with juries, enforced with embarrassed inexpertise by the likes of Constable Alan Porter in the matter of *R v Bretherton*.

Lazarus: Mr Porter, did you at the time... equate an abortion with a curette, and believe they were one and the same thing?
Porter: Did I or do I?
Lazarus: At the time of the raid.
Porter: I didn't know what was being done.
Lazarus: I am not suggesting you knew what was being done. I am asking you did you equate the operation of a curette as being synonymous—the same thing—as an abortion—one and the same thing?
Porter: Well it is not, quite.
Lazarus: What did you believe at the time the difference was?

Porter: Well—this is when we were at the premises?
Lazarus: Yes.
Porter: I believed abortion was being performed.
Lazarus: I am asking you generally, as a matter of your own knowledge, did you believe a curette was synonymous with an abortion?
Porter: Do I believe this generally?
Lazarus: Did you at the time on the premises? We have all learned a lot since.
Porter: Well, I wasn't thinking specifically on any particular line.

Yet, because a society can be defined by what it regards as taboo, these transcripts offer an incomparable guide to their period's social beliefs and sexual mores. The idea of a single mother bearing and raising a child as an act of volition, for instance, is assumed unthinkable. As Cairns Villeneuve-Smith put it for John Heath in *R v Heath* while examining Dr Michael Guerin, a GP:

Villeneuve-Smith: Dr Guerin, as a matter of fact, if you take a single pregnant girl, she has got three choices open to her, has she not? Let me enumerate them and see if you can add any more. She can marry the boy; she can have the child adopted out; or she can terminate the pregnancy?
Guerin: Or she may perhaps have the child if there is interest in the family.
Villeneuve-Smith: She has got to have a sympathetic mum and dad…?
Guerin: Yes.
Villeneuve-Smith: Who will take it in…?
Guerin: Right.

Such exchanges reflected back to doctors a belief in the precedence of their own views. For where abortion was concerned, doctors essentially set every aspect of the procedure, including its limits. Latitudes varied. Bretherton was always most negotiable on cost, and Fenton Bowen most negotiable on term, aborting as late as twenty weeks. Heath, by contrast, seldom aborted after twelve weeks. Nineteen-year-old student teacher Bronwyn Scarff recalled a conversation with Heath's nurse, Faye Heales, at 94 Collins Street: 'She said she felt after three months it would be entirely wrong, and she thought up to that time it was only a little seed, it was nowhere near a human being, she didn't see that could be wrong'. The offer of a lot of money, of course, was an incentive to greater liberality; there were always unqualified abortionists who would take on extreme cases. But this was not a client-centred system—something with which the legal profession had something of an affinity. In a fascinating exchange with Dr John Akeroyd, a consultant at Prince Henry's Hospital, it was Heath's counsel, Peter Coldham QC, rather than the doctor who argued effectively for the primacy of a medical mandarinate.

> Coldham: In between the extremely liberal, Doctor, and the extremely conservative, there are, we have been told, shades of medical opinion. Would you agree with that?
>
> Akeroyd: I would say there were shades of public opinion, in which medical practitioners are entitled to express their own opinion also.
>
> Coldham: Is there an opinion held by medical people?
>
> Akeroyd: Yes but also by the general public.
>
> Coldham: Of course, of course. The medical men, of course, have a special advantage over us in that it is a field in which they are expert and the public is not. You follow that, don't you?
>
> Akeroyd: It is a field in which they may be expert in a technical way.
>
> Coldham: Yes that is what I meant.
>
> Akeroyd: But not necessarily in the way of having a socio-economic opinion.
>
> Coldham: Quite so. I suppose it would be fair to say... that no one doctor has found an ideal solution to the problem. Would you agree with that?
>
> Akeroyd: I would say that it is not the doctor's job to find the solution. It is the general public's.

Very seldom, in fact, do the transcripts read as though the abortionists themselves are on trial. Because the witnesses are largely younger women, and the judges, barristers, solicitors, police and jurors almost exclusively older men, they often read like moral tribunals—and while men in an adversarial system are apt to check one another, there are moments that smack of male prurience and mental cruelty, even a certain sadism. In order to cast doubt on Jean Mitchell's pregnancy in *R v Bayliss & Sizeland*, for instance, Lazarus submitted her to a bruisingly intimate interrogation.

Lazarus: Did you tell him [Mitchell's boyfriend, Allan Way] you believed you were pregnant?
Mitchell: No I didn't.
Lazarus: Why not, if you did believe it?
Mitchell: I don't know…
Lazarus: I beg your pardon.
Mitchell: I didn't want to tell him.
Lazarus: I can understand that is what you say. But why didn't you want to tell him?
Mitchell: I am afraid that is something I can't answer.
Lazarus: Why can't you answer it?
Mitchell: (distressed) Because I don't know why I didn't tell him.

Women seeking abortion were not entirely powerless, and in one respect were perhaps more powerful than today. Because men were more inclined to step back, and indeed absolve themselves of inopportune pregnancies, women wielded more unilateral discretion. This still left a two-fold dilemma: one, the choices were unappetising, being essentially between abortion or surrendering the infant for adoption; two, the women themselves were ill-placed to make decisions in isolation, and influenced by other factors. Glenda Collins, the benighted informant in *R v Bretherton* pining for her callous boyfriend, Benny Amato, found examination at least as traumatic as termination.

Lazarus: So, it is true to say that the reason you went to the police was to get your own back on Benny, isn't it? (no answer)
Foley SM: Just say yes or no.
Collins: Yes.
Policewoman: Don't let yourself be upset.
Lazarus: I think it is preferable that the policewoman does not speak to the witness in the box.
Foley SM: Do not speak to her madam…
Lazarus: Do you feel all right?
Collins: I just want to get over this.

Asked about abortifacient tablets that Amato had persuaded her to take, she confessed to being ruled by instinct.

Lazarus: I suppose you realised, did you, this could well have an effect on the child, didn't you?

Collins: I didn't think. Look, I didn't think.

Lazarus: Did you think it was possible?

Collins: No, I am sorry…

Lazarus: I beg your pardon?

Collins: I didn't. I just didn't think.

Lazarus: Just didn't think.

Collins: No.

Lazarus: You were not, I suppose, of the opinion, were you, that it was a good thing to take all this treatment during a pregnancy?

Collins: I know. I didn't want to take it really, but…

Lazarus: I understand that, but having taken it you didn't think it would be any help to a pregnancy?

Collins: I didn't know. I had never done anything like that before (witness sobbed).

Yet courts dealt more easily with a sobbing woman than a sober one. The tensest exchanges in the cases in question are not those where women break down, but where they discuss abortion as a considered alternative. Thirty-five-year-old Shirley Beasy of Swan Hill was married, with children aged fourteen and seventeen, when she was aborted by Jim Troup. The scenario perplexed Ray Dunn.

Dunn: Were you anxious not to have a further family partly because of your own health? Were you afraid for your own health?

Beasy: No, not really.

Dunn: What was the real reason?

Beasy: Well, the family was growing up and I just didn't want to have anymore.

Dunn: What type of work does your husband do?

Beasy: He is a caretaker at the Public Works Department, Swan Hill.

Dunn: Would it create some economic difficulty to further a family at this time?

Beasy: No I don't suppose so.

Dunn: Well, what was the reason?

Beasy: Well it's just that we didn't want to have anymore, that's what…

Dunn: That is the fact but what is the reason? What age are you, by the way?

Beasy: Thirty-five.

Dunn: Are you frightened it might cause you some troubles?
Beasy: No, not really.

Then there was the bewildering concept of a woman ending a sexual relationship that had resulted in a pregnancy without being driven to frenzy, like divorcee Gwenda Deacon, who let her boyfriend move to Sydney and dealt with the consequences, feeling that the relationship had run its course. Baffled by Deacon's practicality, Dunn could only speculate a ruse.

Dunn: Before he went did he tell you?
Deacon: That he was going?
Dunn: Yes.
Deacon: Yes.
Dunn: Were you still friendly?
Deacon: Yes.
Dunn: Well, did he not give you a forwarding address?
Deacon: No.
Dunn: Why not? Did you ask him?
Deacon: No.
Dunn: Why not? You see, I am suggesting to you that you are protecting the name of the man and that you are just telling this version in order to protect him?
Deacon: No I am not.
Dunn: Well now, here you are, friendly, he is the father of your aborted child. You are keeping company. Still sexual I take it? You were still having a sexual association after the operation I take it.
Deacon: No, we didn't. No.
Dunn: What, just holding hands after that, were you?
Deacon: No. Well, after that it wasn't on the same basis.
Dunn: What do you mean not on the same basis?
Deacon: Well, after it happened I felt a bit, you know, funny about it, and it didn't happen again afterwards.
Dunn: Did he contribute any money towards it?
Deacon: No.
Dunn: Why not?
Deacon: He didn't have any money.
Dunn: You asked him that, did you?
Deacon: I knew he did not have any.

Dunn: I suppose like all true lovers he promised to pay though, did he not?

Deacon: No.

In the law's eyes, ex-nuptial sex, setting at nought notions like 'honourable intentions' and 'doing the right thing', was deeply unsettling; likewise situations where women were not simply hapless victims of male lust. Twenty-five-year-old typist Helen Walsh was left pregnant by a brief fling with an officer on a Rotterdam-bound freighter, the *Wilhelmskirk*. To Dunn, that she would not then pursue marriage to the officer at all costs could only be a lie. Why didn't she write to him?

Walsh: He was going back to Holland. It's quite a way.

Dunn: I realise that and I suppose you know there are airplanes that fly?

Walsh: That's right.

Dunn: And that letters will get to him through the ship, you know that, do you not?

Walsh: Yes.

Dunn: See, what I am seeing is whether you're prepared to tell lies on oath…

Walsh: No I'm not…

Dunn: You knew you could reach him by mail did you not?

Walsh: Yes.

Dunn: And I am suggesting that you are deliberately giving us—the court—a false name to protect…?

Walsh: No I am not.

Dunn: Why did you not write to him?

Walsh: Well why should I? It is up to me. It is my decision…

Duggan SM: Your explanation is what?

Walsh: That is my explanation. Why should I?

Dunn: Just let me repeat it slowly so you will not be annoyed. Why did you not write to the man with whom you had been having sexual relations right up to the time he left?

Walsh: I tried that once before. It just didn't work. I wasn't writing another time.

Dunn: With another man you mean?

Walsh: That's right.

Dunn: But was there anything to indicate to you when he left that he would not be honourable towards you?
Walsh: Well he didn't leave his home address. That was a start.

As for a woman exercising moral judgement, that was beyond the pale. Dunn took particular dislike to Robyn Maree Rose, a Troup patient he did not think was taking her abortion seriously enough while admitting she knew immediately the reason for police inquiries.

Dunn: Why did you know what it would have been?
Rose: Well, it was the only thing I could think of.
Dunn: What, that you had done wrong?
Rose: That I had done—well, I don't think it's wrong, but I'd done it anyway.
Dunn: Well, I suppose you have done a few things…
Rose: Yes but not…
Dunn: And did you believe sexual intercourse under twenty was wrong?
Rose: No.
Dunn: Nothing wrong with that?
Rose: No.
Dunn: Nothing wrong with abortions?
Rose: No, not really.
Dunn: Well, what did you think they were after you for if there is nothing wrong with it?
Rose: Oh, because I knew they thought it was wrong.
Dunn: Oh, you knew that the law [and] your views were somewhat different?
Rose: Yes, that's right.

Dunn erupted. 'Is this trying to divert my attention?' he demanded. 'This beautiful stroking of the hair like Cleopatra? Could you just…?' The magistrate chided him: 'That is only a comment, Mr Dunn'.

After the Menhennitt Ruling, scope for disagreement actually grew rather than contracted. It was no longer necessary to deny an abortion's occurrence; it was imperative instead to demonstrate that continued pregnancy would have incited the patient to mental breakdown or self-harm. It now was not merely socially unwelcome for a woman to be rational; it was legally inconvenient. It happened anyway. Twenty-one-year-old Andrea Jacobsen calmly organised an abortion with James

Buchanan, not telling her boyfriend, a Catholic, or her father, a member of the Exclusive Brethren, while confiding in her mother Wanda. Heath swore that 'her mental condition was such that termination was required'. Yet her condition seemed distinctly sane. Of her boyfriend, from whom she parted, she told the court: 'I didn't tell him anything that went on. I just told him that everything was all right…I do not really believe that when a girl is pregnant she should get married. That is not necessarily the basis of a good marriage'. Of her father, she said: 'I wouldn't say he's a strict man; he's got some funny ideas, you know'. Wanda Jacobsen exhibited quiet pride in her daughter, whom she thought 'the best balanced person I know', for behaving so responsibly: 'Well, she was upset naturally at the fact that this thing had happened and the fact she had broken off with the boy…But psychologically she was still mentally well-balanced. She had gone ahead and arranged everything herself'.

When Barbara Harland-White, a divorced costing clerk who lived with two of her four children, consulted Heath in August 1970, she recalled his preparatory spiel: 'We have to put down some particulars about why you are having this done. Shall we say that you have been under a nervous strain?' In fact, she proved to have a remarkably retentive memory, noticing the crowded appointment book, and also that the bed into which she climbed was warm from another body. She showed, too, an independent streak, deciding that Heath need not know the name of the father, a married man; she gave instead, rather mischievously, the name of a detective from Box Hill CIB whom she had recently met, Edgar Snell. Such impertinence hardly endeared her to Heath's counsel, Peter Coldham.

Coldham: Now I just ask you again, since your memory is so accurate …You maintain that you told a lie in answer to the question that was asked you at 94 Collins Street in August as to who was responsible for the pregnancy?

Harland-White: That's correct. I do not think it has anything to do with Dr Heath who the father of the child is.

Coldham: You think it is irrelevant?

Harland-White: That's correct.

Coldham: But it is very relevant when you get there, isn't it, to take a peep in a book you are not supposed to see?

Harland-White: Well, they are not supposed to be left on the table.

Coldham: Well, have you never heard of the word 'trust'?
Harland-White: There is no such thing.
Coldham: Do you know what it means? (no answer) Why did you put his name down, poor old Edgar Snell?
Harland-White: Because he was the first man that came to my mind.
Coldham: I see. And I suppose he was the first man that came into your mind because you thought he was responsible for your pregnancy.
Harland-White: No, he was not.
Coldham: Who was responsible for your pregnancy?
Harland-White: I do not think it has anything to do with you.
Coldham: You don't think it is relevant.
Harland-White: No.
Coldham: Well if it wasn't Edgar Snell, who was it?
Harland-White: I don't think it has anything to do with you.

When Coldham submitted to Harland-White that her children would have been ashamed of their mother's pregnancy to a man who was not their father, he could take no more of such temerity. A sensible woman making an informed choice was no help to his client; at another level, it threatened his male authority.

Coldham: What do you think those children would have thought of their mother if they had found out she was pregnant?
Harland-White: I think they would have quite accepted the situation.
Coldham: Did you have any anxiety as to the reaction of your children when they found out you were pregnant by a man who was not their father and to whom you were not married?
Harland-White: No.
Coldham: None at all?
Harland-White: No.
Coldham: I say this to you bluntly: I suggest to you that that is a lie, isn't it?
Harland-White: It is not a lie.

In hindsight, it is hard to see why details like names of fathers were ever relevant, even under the law of the late 1960s and early 1970s. But, especially for the unmarried, the pressure for full confession can be considered part of the shaming process. The woman had done wrong. The first step to restitution was a full account of her misdeed with no detail excluded. As she had surrendered her honour to a man, so she could surrender her privacy to the court. The embeddedness of this belief is such that Harland-White seems to have been the only witness who stood her ground on the issue.

In hindsight, too, it is as well that the Menhennitt Ruling, with the pressure it placed on counsel to demonstrate that their doctor clients were simply taking pity on women momentarily unhinged, would be so seldom applied in court. Its benefit proved to be symbolic: simple but explicit acknowledgement that pregnancy was not always an unmixed blessing. *R v Troup* and *R v Heath* are both post-Menhennitt cases, and it is noticeable how much more confident witnesses had become, no longer feeling the pressure to lie or merely economise on the truth. The confidence led to some exploitation, with psychiatrists cultivating a lucrative racket in $50 opinions about women's 'mental health', and there would be excesses of guileless optimism. One abortionist complained bitterly to Beatrice Faust:

> The patient thinks she [is] all right as long as she's got a letter. Letter! Jesus, Mary and Joseph! The last letter I had said: 'This patient is sixteen weeks' pregnant and in excellent health.' Some of the others are nearly as bad. They think 'Menhennitt' is a magic word.

But in the immediate aftermath, concern was with the robustness of the ruling, how it would be tested, and by whom—although, in retrospect, there was never much doubt about the answer to the last.

‘Look here Doctor, I might have to arrest you’

He would deliver babies. He would deliver mothers too.
The Cider House Rules (1985), John Irving

‘Abortion Abortion Abortion’: what had that fellow Wainer been thinking? A word taboo for most of Australian settlement had been splashed all over a newspaper—and by *a doctor*. For many peers, it was unconscionable behaviour; for the Australian Medical Association, it smacked of advertisement, the profession’s own taboo, and the association’s ethics committee formally reprimanded Wainer on the evening of 6 June 1969. He left the meeting perhaps as impenitent as it is possible to be: he had in mind publicity beyond the imaginings of hidebound colleagues.

Wainer had developed parallel objectives. Still he aspired to a ‘test case’ to ascertain the extent of Victoria’s laws, something of which he had boasted in *Truth* on 25 January. ‘DOCTOR DARES’ screamed the headline, describing the daring doctor simply as ‘a bluff man prepared to say his piece and hang the consequences’—albeit not so bluff that he hazarded identifying himself.

> A Melbourne doctor is seeking a suitable woman on whom to perform an abortion as TEST CASE of Victoria’s anti-abortion laws.
>
> The doctor says that when he has performed the operation he will INFORM THE POLICE and invite them to take action against him.

To this plan, an impediment existed. Wainer was not trained to perform abortions, and was too scrupulous a clinician to try. And although he by now knew Rod Bretherton and Peter Bayliss, neither shared his self-immolating propensities. Until Frank Holland’s campaign, in fact, they had hardly been interested in abortion as a cause at all. That original *Truth* headline, however, had introduced Wainer to its features editor, Evan Whitton, who would prove integral to Wainer's second objective: revealing the police corruption which abortion's illegality had nurtured.

Since their November 1968 introduction, Wainer and Peggy Berman had courted one another warily. She would tease him with enigmatic remarks. 'I do not have cancer at all', she insisted one night. 'I have Smith of the liver, the spine and the heart!' Wainer asked who Smith was. 'He's a policeman', she answered breezily. 'But don't ask any more questions about it.' After six months of euphemisms and evasions, she had finally introduced Wainer to Troup, who talked of Hoddle Street's dealings with police dating back ten years. These stories resonated with hints that Bretherton had given him of graft, and Wainer shared them, without divulging any names, with Superintendent Keith McLeod when that officer visited him to discuss the *Sun* advertisement. McLeod suggested that complainants come forward. 'It would be like asking an escapee from Belsen to return and discuss his complaints with the camp commandant', said Wainer, rather hyperbolically. 'We're scarcely as bad as that, are we?' McLeod replied. Wainer warmed to McLeod, but took his inferences no further.

Finally, Berman admitted that 'Smith' was Jack Ford, newly installed as head of Homicide—and, as if in confirmation, rang soon after in hysterics. 'He's here, he's here', she shrieked. 'Ford's here and he's beating me.' A male voice commandeered the line and told Wainer to mind his own business. But a few days later, at Davidson's acquittal party, Berman's injuries were plain to see. What had started as parallel objectives were shortly to become violently zigzagging ones in which it would be difficult to tell who was using whom and for what. Nobody sent those lines in crazier directions than irrepressible, indefensible Stanley Charles Wyatt.

~

Charlie Wyatt would try anything once: he even joined the police in February 1948, staying a year. But in the main, he simply liked money, and would consider any end to acquire it. He first made a good living as a contract slaughterman at the South Melbourne abattoir to provide for his five children with wife Alice May. Yet, from his deportment, you would hardly have guessed his occupation. He got around town in a tan Chevrolet. He liked smart suits, with a preference for baby blue; he was seldom seen without a raffish pork-pie hat, which kept in place a regrettable ginger hairpiece; he was never sniffed without the overpowering odour of the male scent Aramis. His great pleasure was the punt, and he was twice convicted of being 'found in a common gaming house'. Then, in February 1961, he was found jointly liable in a cattle duffing case brought by the Victorian Producers Cooperative, and a sizeable judgment against him cost his family their Noble Park house and Rye holiday home. Ever resourceful, he ran an SP book in Carlton's Red Lion Hotel, whose licensee, sometime abortionist Belle Moran nee Lewis, became his mistress. Her boys, Lewis and Desmond Jnr, specialised in collecting SP debts. Their standard technique was to identify the defaulter, break his collarbone with a baseball bat, *then* demand the money—the success rate was high.

Wyatt didn't bother keeping his relations with Moran a secret. Indeed, he continued spending one or two nights a week with his wife regardless—for very good reason. In December 1962, Wyatt was arrested for his SP activities by Senior Constable Ronald Jackson of the Gaming Squad. Luckily, he had well-connected lawyers. Roy McMennemin had been practising as a solicitor since April 1960 and had built a big casebook of work for ex-policemen through father Harry, a forty-year veteran of the force. The McMennemins got Wyatt off his charge on a technicality, then bore with him through creditors' efforts to send him bankrupt. When Wyatt started a television rental and repair business in Geelong in his wife's name, he used conjugal visits to Alice May as an opportunity to have her sign cheques which the McMennemins then cashed for him. Wyatt knew enough about televisions to turn them on and off, but the upfront payments provided him with a useful cash pool. He kept a line into the police by acting as an informer for, among others, Ron Jackson, the officer who had arrested him. On the top floor of Geelong Television Services, meanwhile, Harry McMennemin plied his entrepreneurial trade, which was mainly off-course gambling, and also maintained links with the unsavoury local abortionist Mario Marchesani.

Belle Moran was less lucky. After Wyatt's arrest, licensing authorities forced her to sell the Red Lion. She was confused by Wyatt's comings and goings, especially when he bought his wife a house in Footscray and began plaguing Jean Field to resume her abortion business. 'She asked me if I wanted any staff as she was going to put her head in a gas oven', recalled Field. 'She was desperately placed, apparently.' Field was reluctant, but her invalid husband needed looking after, and she finally agreed to some procedures in March 1966 at Moran's home in Langs Road, Ascot Vale. She began at once to regret it. She loathed Wyatt. One day he engaged her in a long conversation about his friend, trainer Roy Shaw—Field simply *had* to meet him. So long did he go on that it seemed he was trying to delay her leaving, and when she returned home she found it had been robbed. In October 1967, he also tipped Ron Jackson off about the abortory run by Field's sister, Bessie Watts, with her husband Ken in Bundoora. 'There is more where this came from too', he promised.

By now, Wyatt had sold Geelong Television and started King Size Television in Footscray, still staying a step ahead of creditors by using the McMennemins to cash his wife's cheques. There were lots of these, because Wyatt lived large. He bought a racehorse using his daughter's name: Ammate won $20 000 in ten races. He bought an $8500 Jaguar in his wife's name, with money bilked from the finance company that provided his hire purchase funds. He staved off the law by selling televisions and radiograms to police at knockdown prices, and by providing part-time employment to members of the local CIB. But whenever he appeared before the trustee in bankruptcy, he mysteriously had no money to pay creditors, and would lead the trustee's barrister, Peter Brusey, a merry dance.

Wyatt: I do various jobs for people, working commission etc.
Brusey: Where from? Where is the money from?
Wyatt: There is always odd money coming along.
Brusey: Where from?
Wyatt: It comes from various places.
Brusey: Tell me one?
Wyatt: There are chaps...
Brusey: Listen to my question first of all. Has it come from any kind of employment at all?
Wyatt: No.
Brusey: Very well. Has it come from gifts?
Wyatt: Well, call it gifts.
Brusey: Yes or no, has it come from gifts?
Wyatt: I call it gifts.

In fact, Wyatt had one very particular job. On Moran's urging, although against Field's judgement, he had become the 'male voice' for their abortory: the man in a mask who made reassuring doctor-like noises before the anaesthesia. Moran explained: 'It speaks and says "good morning" and "what is the little girls' name?" and so on'. Field and Moran were now making reasonable money accepting referrals from Fenton Bowen, and Wyatt eyed their income jealously. He spent time with Marchesani, learning the tricks of anaesthesia himself, then unceremoniously ratted on Field and Moran to another of the police he informed for, Detective-Sergeant Eric Suttie.

On 3 April 1968, Homicide detectives hid in pine trees overlooking Lot 2, Highbury Road, Tally Ho. Others trailed Belle Moran in her blue Cortina as she picked up two pregnant women outside a Nunawading bank. Finally, bursting the flywire, they found Moran, Field, Field's sister Annie Shaw and her husband Donald with $800, two foetuses and three patients: a suburban librarian, a country housewife and a country schoolteacher. Suttie was taken aback. Moran was Wyatt's lady, wasn't she? She received rather different treatment from her co-conspirators, being allowed to drive into Russell Street in her own car, then released without questioning. Suttie would introduce Wyatt to Frank Holland at Swanston Street's Oxford Hotel as 'the fellow who gave us the information about the arrest', a meeting where Wyatt asked: 'See if you can do anything for her'. Apart from that, he seemed prepared for his mistress's incarceration as the price of removing Field: Moran was eventually charged like all the rest.

Suttie couldn't understand Wyatt: 'I knew him to be a man who seemed to have studied the book *How To Win Friends and Influence People* and had studied it a bit hard'. But even he, a decorated policeman, allowed himself to be influenced, placing bets for Wyatt and also collecting money: at one stage, he had $3900 of Wyatt's cash at his house. Asked why, he replied: 'Because he asked me'. Wyatt's police connections, when fully revealed, proved amazingly extensive, reaching as high as the CIB chief, Inspector Colin Sharp, to whom he gave a Pye Black Box radiogram. He networked ceaselessly, turning customers into acquaintances, punting police into pals. The trick, perhaps, was that no one person knew the full extent of his criminality. Wyatt's measure is only really gained from thorough perusal of the 1500-page transcript of his bankruptcy file, containing such exchanges as:

Brusey: Was the business [King Size Television] honest?
Wyatt: Honest?
Brusey: Yes.
Wyatt: I don't know what you mean by 'honest'. The business 'honest'?
Brusey: I will let the answer stand.

King Size Television was decidedly dishonest, dealing regularly in stolen goods and collecting pre-paid income for maintenance contracts on which it never intended delivering. And, in December 1968, Seaboard Finance found that Wyatt had been scamming them, reporting hire purchase arrangements in fictitious names, then pocketing the money. They received a call from Belle Moran asking why she had received a solicitation notice. Seaboard manager John Gleeson reported: 'She denied any knowledge...and implicated Charlie Wyatt and said it was one of his shady deals. She indicated to me that this had happened before...I could not get any further information from her as she sounded rather drunk'. Gleeson visited King Size and found frauds aplenty. Wyatt's friend Bruce Johnston bailed him out, with money from Moran. And around this time, perhaps because he was caught short, Wyatt decided to tackle abortion seriously, contacting Fenton Bowen, who agreed to refer patients to him in return for a $50 kickback on the standard $220 fee; they would meet every week at Fenton Bowen's Masonic lodge to reconcile their accounts.

With so many doctors out of action, Wyatt had a money-spinner on his hands. He and Moran used Langs Road as their base, plus houses in Yarraville, North Sunshine and Box Hill, scheduling as many as forty operations a week: Melbourne had not had an unqualified operator as active since John Brookes. Wyatt shared Brookes's cavalier attitudes, too. After a while, he didn't bother with anaesthetic. He was lazy and brutal, sending a fair proportion of his patients to hospital with perforations and infections; some turned out to still be pregnant. Nor was he a man to share his pelf. As the principal of King Size Television, May Wyatt was stunned to receive bills from suppliers worth $17 000. All she had ever done was sign cheques; latterly, Wyatt would admit, he'd been forging her signature, because he 'didn't want to trouble her'. She fled to a relative's place in Bairnsdale. Wyatt followed and, during an altercation on 1 February 1969, fired a shot at her, for which he was charged.

Much later, Wyatt would be painted as a loveable rogue. In fact, he was a dangerous, incorrigible and self-serving criminal. Peggy Berman had his number. She was horrified when she heard he had entered the abortion trade. When word of her horror reached Wyatt, he said cheerfully that he would have her killed. Berman complained to Matthews, who had just returned to Melbourne to head the Traffic Control Squad, and Matthews sent word via mutual friend Harry McMennemin that Wyatt should come to his office in Dawson Street, Brunswick for a chat. Berman was sick and mad, Matthews explained, always embarrassing his family with interminable late-night phone calls. Matthews was under no illusions about Wyatt's activities, and made him an offer: for between $200 and $300 a week, depending on patient numbers, he would ensure that Wyatt was never raided. Wyatt jumped at the offer. With his firearm charge returnable on 1 May, he could do with another friend in high places.

Wyatt had another reason to avoid his wife: she had been declared bankrupt, and a trustee had been appointed to investigate King Size Television's affairs. Wyatt remained pathologically defiant. To keep them beyond the trustee's reach, he organised for the furniture to be stolen from the house in Footscray, and for the records to be stolen from King Size. The local CIB showed no zeal about investigating either incident—not surprisingly, given that some members had been part-time King Size employees. Perhaps Wyatt's greatest act of hubris was to open another business, Mr Big TV, less than a mile away two weeks later, this time with Belle Moran as nominal owner, plus many of the same workers. A visit from solicitors of the bankruptcy registrar soon revealed that parts of television sets missing from King Size were on Mr Big's premises.

Wyatt was developing a reputation. Peggy Berman was terrified. Bert Wainer was appalled and enthralled. *Truth*'s Evan Whitton was following his trail. Matthews, meanwhile, was willingly doing Wyatt's bidding, and had presented a plan. In the event of his hearing of a raid, Matthews would forward him a message via Robert Lord, a Footscray chemist: '*Don't go to the races, Charlie*'. The firearm charge had been upheld, but Wyatt was appealing, and it didn't stop him hosting two gossipy lunches with McMennemin, Matthews and Colin Sharp at South Melbourne's Walnut Tree Restaurant.

Thanks to his new prominence, Wainer was now receiving information, reliable and otherwise, from many quarters. On about Monday 2 June, he was visited by 19-year-old Frances Davidson from Carnegie, aborted a few weeks earlier by Wyatt, and her father. She had been spirited by Moran from outside Armstrong's Body Works in Flemington Road, crudely aborted without anaesthetic, and left sterile by a perforated uterus. The father gave Wainer the name of Fenton Bowen as referring doctor and the telephone number the girl had rung. 'I could use it any way I liked,' Wainer recalled, 'so long as they were not involved'.

On 4 June, Wainer stormed into Russell Street and for the first time accosted Jack Ford, the new Homicide chief. In such circumstances, however, Wainer could be awkward. He began by bemoaning Homicide's failure to investigate the evidence of Gracie Demarco and Marie Falls, the two Heath clients in *R v Davidson*—not an unreasonable request, although Ford had been in his new job just two days. Wainer then told Ford about Frances Davidson, but without mentioning a name or address, asking that he be given until the following Monday, 9 June, to persuade the girl to talk to police. This, of course, was an action he had a fortnight earlier urged women in a newspaper advertisement not to undertake, and he did not deliver on his promise. Ford waited a few days and rang Wainer: this time the doctor gave him the name, partly reneging on his promise to the girl's father, but no address. With the name Davidson and a check at Fenton Bowen's surgery, Detective-Sergeant Noel Murphy found his way to the family home, where he learned it was too late: the girl had gone to Queensland and refused to be interviewed. Questioning other women on a referral list from Fenton Bowen, however, he began assembling the elements of a case against Wyatt.

For all his energy and fearlessness, Wainer could be a frustrating informant. He could later point with justification to his suspicions about the police he was dealing with, but part of him also craved a role in the chase, as a Sherlock Holmes to these flat-footed Lestrades. Wainer made an oath: 'I determined to track down these vultures who, by their greed, ignorance and stupidity, left a trail of death or mental and physical mutilation behind them'. The irony is that it would be the police who finally tracked the vulture Wyatt down, and Wainer who would befriend him.

~

The first abortion to test the lie of the post-Menhennitt land in Victoria was shrouded in mystery for legal reasons that later became mythological. Wainer left multiple accounts of the story, each subtly different, and each omitting a crucial detail. The first and fullest account is in Wainer's book *It Isn't Nice*.

> In theory a doctor could now lawfully terminate a pregnancy if he believed the danger of continuing the pregnancy was greater than the danger of terminating it. This meant that if a woman came to a doctor threatening to suicide or resort to a backyard abortionist, the doctor could legally abort her. Or could he?... I rang a number of senior gynaecologists and asked them to do a test case abortion quickly so that other doctors could follow with safety. If the doctor was arrested after publicly announcing that he had performed the abortions then his trial would test Menhennitt's judgement. If he were not arrested then other doctors could operate with impunity. However, no one was prepared to take the chance of fifteen years' gaol. One doctor stated that he had no desire to be the 'Doctor Bourne' of Australia.

Wainer first found his ideal patient: Wilma, a dressmaker's apprentice from country Victoria.

> As she walked in she looked wilted, bruised and injured, as if she expected to be abused and punished. No patient ought to come to a doctor looking like that. She had desolation, despair and defeat written all over her. She was slender, with honey blonde hair and large eyes—these eyes were kept downcast as she commenced haltingly and between sobs to tell me her story. She was twenty-one. At fifteen she had given birth to a child. Her father had condemned her bitterly and never let her forget her 'disgrace'... She told me of the trauma of the adoption of her baby, how she stared at every child of that age, wondering if it were hers.

Left pregnant by another man after 'drinks and promises', she turned desperately to Wainer, projecting him into his favoured redeemer's role. By 1985, when Wainer was interviewed by journalist Gloria Frydman, the story had become even more dramatic.

> She told me her story and then she said to me: 'I want you to do the abortion'. I told her I could give her $120 and send her to an abortionist. But then she sort of put it on me with: 'Well why are you talking about abortion? I've read about you and you said you would do an abortion.' At that stage I'd done lots of d & cs [dilatation and curettages] but I hadn't made a practice of doing abortions and I had certainly never thought of becoming an abortionist myself. I told this woman that I could refer her on but when she said 'but what about you?' I knew it was there lying between us. I knew that something was going on in that room that day and it's very difficult to explain it to anyone else. So I told her I would do her abortion for her, providing she would let me tell the police afterwards.
>
> So Wilma had her abortion. By some stroke of common sense I also called the media and told them I had done an abortion. I then drove to the Homicide Squad and told them what had happened… I turned up at the police station with my solicitor and every television and radio station was there. I walked into the Homicide Squad and told them what I'd done…The next thing that happened was the media made headlines about it and that's a matter of history now. After that every woman in Australia who was pregnant wanted to come and see me.

The abortion certainly took place, on Wednesday 11 June 1969, at Evancourt Private Hospital, 1017 Dandenong Road, East Malvern, where Wainer knew the general manager. The crucial detail omitted is that the abortion was done by Rod Bretherton. Wainer did not have the skills and never seriously cultivated them. There was good reason for Wainer to take the credit at the time—Bretherton was facing charges following the raid on his premises a few weeks earlier. Why Wainer continued to take credit long after it was necessary, and appears to have rather embellished the story, stemmed almost certainly from the men's later falling out.

Another element to the events is added by Beatrice Faust. She was at Bretherton's Brighton home on Saturday 14 June, where a protest was being organised for his imminent appearance at the City Court in Russell Street, when Dr Maurice Nissen, a friendly gynaecologist, suggested that Wilma, a patient aborted the previous week, would make a suitable test case. Wainer's response, she remembers, was initially dismissive. But on Tuesday at 10.45 a.m., journalists turning up to see Bretherton being remanded were instead treated to the sight of burly Bert Wainer bounding up the steps of police headquarters across the road to offer himself for arrest.

Wainer bore a letter addressed to Ford outlining the abortion, stating that he had three psychiatrists' opinions that 'a grave risk to her life and mental state would exist' if the pregnancy continued, and referring further inquiries to solicitor David Murray of Collins Street's William Murray & Son. Ford read it carefully. 'You're infringing on the trade a bit aren't you?' he said finally. 'Do you think it's a job for a GP?' After a few more questions, the policeman advised: 'Look here Doctor, I might have to arrest you'. Wainer smiled: 'OK. I'll be waiting'. He sauntered back into the street, and onto the front page of almost every newspaper in the country. And if Wainer was not perhaps 'the Bourne of Australia', this was an inspired act of opportunism, proof of Gough Whitlam's wisdom that 'quite small and ineffectual demonstrations can be made to look like the beginnings of a revolution if the cameraman is in the right place at the right time'. Alongside the page one splash in *The Age,* a sidebar headed 'This Was Supreme Court Ruling' gave Justice Menhennitt's deliberations their first media outing. 'If Bert hadn't stacked on his act, the Menhennitt Ruling would have been a sleeper', Faust observes. 'The fact he wasn't immediately charged publicised that Menhennitt existed. I don't think that any of those guys at the time fully appreciated the use of Menhennitt. Ken [Davidson] certainly didn't. He was just glad not to go to jail.'

Whatever the coverage of the mainstream dailies, the story was still owned by *Truth*. Whitton grabbed the scoop of the only interview with the girl herself: 'I took a train to Melbourne by myself. I told Dr Wainer everything...I knew the danger. I was prepared to take the risk'. And afterwards? 'I was very happy. Really, I couldn't believe it was over and done with...I was terribly relieved.' Wilma also revealed how two Homicide detectives had swooped on her home, questioning her at length.

> They said they'd like to speak to me at the police station. They said this was what Dr Wainer wanted... When I got down to the police station and they asked me a few questions I didn't like to answer, I said, 'do I have to answer these?' and they said 'yes.'
>
> I was at the police station from about 3.30pm. They let me go at 10.30pm. I signed each page of a six-page statement. At the end of it was a sentence saying I made the statement of my own free will. I realise now that I didn't have to say anything at all to the police and I'm sorry I made the statement... I think they're trying to knock Dr Wainer down, pin something on him. I think they will pounce as soon as they find some little fault.

They couldn't. The following week, Attorney-General George Reid confirmed that Wainer had acted 'within common law as established by Menhennitt's ruling'. Indeed, he told Channel Seven that Wainer was well aware of 'the fact that he had not committed a crime'—which from Wainer brought the obvious rejoinder: why, then, had Wilma been questioned so exhaustively? Wainer was confident enough now to be asking other, more serious questions. On the day of his visit to Russell Street, he had told Superintendent Keith McLeod that four people, granted indemnities, would testify to having paid graft to police: these were Berman, Troup, Bayliss and Bretherton, who had alluded to it. On 21 June, Whitton threw down Wainer's public gauntlet in *Truth*. Under the headline 'ABORTION DOCTOR ACCUSES POLICE OF BRIBES', Wainer claimed to having 'the names of three persons who, if given indemnities, will testify they have paid bribes to certain police officers in the belief that the money would protect them from being raided'. The slippage from four to three seems an early sign of Bretherton's equivocation, and publicity had the effect of making everyone a little more cautious. When Fenton Bowen went on holiday, so did Wyatt and Moran, spending a few days at Stewart's Hamilton Hotel in Brisbane, then joining friends in Kirra, near Coolangatta. Enjoying the sun, the races and beers at the Burleigh Heads Hotel, Wyatt could forget about being under a three-month jail term for that pot shot at his wife. In fact, Wainer's parallel objectives still had many zigzaggings ahead.

~

There was a story here, a big story—Evan Whitton could feel it. He was fast becoming Melbourne's most respected, and reviled, reporter. A self-described 'failed Catholic', he had taught English at Toowoomba's Downlands for fourteen years before chancing his arm at journalism in the *Toowoomba Chronicle*. He then responded to an advertisement placed in the union newspaper by *Truth*'s new editor, tabloid guru Sol Chandler: 'Wanted. Australia's best journalists. Highest pay. Apply: *Truth*'. Whitton's first story involved going to Pentridge to watch Ronald Ryan's return from Sydney; he later attended Ryan's execution.

Melbourne's newspapers at the time—the morning *Age* and *Sun*, the afternoon *Herald*—were as prudish as they were profitable. Thanks to Managing Director Jack Williams, *The Herald* was also solidly Catholic. 'We used to say the *Herald* had more sacred cows than the whole of India', recalls reporter Kevin Childs. 'I remember Jack [Williams] pulling a feature they'd already blurbed [promoted on the front of the newspaper] on the slang used by used car salesmen. He said: "This has some overtones that the gentleman concerned might not be honest. We have a lot of car salesman who advertise in *The Herald*"'.

Truth, however, was a zesty paper, a haven of half-humorous hyperbole in which 'the train of death' (the *Southern Aurora* after its crash at Violet Town in February 1969) and 'the dogs of death' (dogs at the Lost Dogs' Home) met 'the Van of Danger' (a Fairlea Prison van involved in an accident). Whitton revered the hard-bitten, brandy-swilling Chandler, an alumnus of London's *Daily Express*, and never tired of quoting his mots. 'The art of journalism is the art of getting it in without committing libel or adultery', Chandler opined. 'There is *always* a form of words... Sometimes they come to me straight away; sometimes it takes as long as ten minutes.' Even Chandler's sacking was magnificent. When John Gorton was first mooted as Harold Holt's successor as prime minister, Chandler was leaked information by Billy McMahon supporters about Gorton having swindled his father's mistress of a share in the family fortune. Chandler decided not to run it until Gorton's ascension had been approved, explaining: 'It's much more interesting to run this about a prime minister rather than a would-be prime minister'. Shortly, a telegram arrived from proprietor Rupert Murdoch: 'Resignation accepted'.

Fear that Chandler's loyal staff would walk meant promotions all round, and Whitton was able to recruit a smart young offsider. Bruce Hanford had arrived in Australia in September 1966 as a 20-year-old draft dodger from an Oregon logging town. The radio licence he had obtained as a DJ got him a job as a small-boat sounder for Brisbane Harbours and Marine, before the flies forced him south. 'Melbourne was then very small', he recalls. 'There were only 200 people out after 10pm and I met all of them in my first two weeks.' He found that he excelled in journalism of a very detailed nature: his 8000-word 'The Great White Housing Leviathan' in *The Age*'s short-lived 'alternative' magazine *Broadside* so incensed Victoria's all-powerful Housing Commission that they demanded right of reply. To put some distance between himself and the FBI, he then decided to go sailing, but got no further than Gabo Island, where he was wrecked and rescued. Now Whitton threw him a lifeline.

By 1969, *Truth*'s front page was a carnival of carnality. There was: 'A young bride of only five days has heard how her husband tried to seduce another girl after she showed him roses tattooed on her breasts'. There was: 'A 59-year-old man claims that by "mere touch"...he can improve the bust of any girl with a power given to him from the spirit world'. But inside, the newspaper covered crime and the courts more comprehensively than any competitor, running stories to impressive detail, and undertaking series of sometimes inordinate length. Whitton's 'The Naked People', an investigation of nudism, ran to six instalments, in one of which the journalist placed third in a heat of the naked men's swimming championship. Abortion, at the shared border of sex and crime, suited *Truth* as no other newspaper.

A week after his coat-trailing accusations of corruption, Wainer saw to Bretherton's carrying out a termination on a 40-year-old Italian woman, Maria. Wainer found it curious that her Catholicism was apparently not a consideration. She explained that she had nine children between seven and twenty-three and didn't think raising a tenth in poverty helped anyone. 'The Pope?' she said. 'He no play the game, he no make the rules.' This time Wainer added to the provocation by stating that he would not be questioned; he was available only to be arrested. He appeared instead on the ABC's popular *This Day Tonight,* likening himself to conscientious objectors to the Vietnam War: 'If a young man can go to prison on his conscience,

I guess a middle aged man can too'. If this comparison was not a stretch, his comment that 'the police will look foolish indeed if they don't arrest me' almost certainly was. Police were puzzled about how to treat Wainer, but arrest was no longer a serious option.

Wainer also had a particular of the corruption incorrect. In his next interview with Whitton, Wainer claimed to know eight police involved in corrupt practice. He described Wyatt without naming him, then suggested that Homicide was his protector:

> There's a guy who's running a backyard operation behind the front of a business. This guy used to be in the gaming squad and he's still got plenty of pals in Russell Street. And there's a doctor who refers girls to him. Can you imagine a doctor referring girls to a backyarder? Why would he do it? For $50 a time that's why. I have done everything possible to sink this backyard man. I'm so angry he's still going. I've turned him in to the police. I've given his name and address and the patient he operated on. That's four weeks ago and there's been no action.

Wainer was wrong. Homicide *had* been investigating Wyatt, and Murphy *had* now found twenty of the women from Fenton Bowen's referrals, which would eventually form a long charge list against him. What had retarded the investigation was Wainer's own advertisement, because potential informants, wakened to their legal rights, were refusing to answer Murphy's questions. But Ford appears to have been worried about *not* doing his job. When Berman complained to him that he wasn't doing enough to help her, he countercomplained that everyone was watching him because of the rumours about their affair.

Wainer's wrong guess, nonetheless, was also right. Wyatt *did* have a protector, Jack Matthews, although not until Wyatt found common cause with Wainer did the reporters realise the misplacement of their initial suspicion. 'When Wyatt started complaining about "Jack", we initially thought it was Jack Ford', Hanford recalls. 'Evan confronted Ford about it and he was very indignant. In fact, "Jack" was Matthews, and Ford kind of fell beneath our wheels.' At this stage, Wainer, Whitton and Hanford knew perhaps less than they were letting on. Hanford remembers Whitton counselling him on one story: 'Try and make this sting a bit. I don't know what the guy's guilty of, but he's guilty of something'.

'Didn't you know they were so close to you?'

Isn't it enough to have the whole neighbourhood talking without killing yourself in my house and getting me into trouble? Out you go!
The Joyful Condemned (1953), Kylie Tennant

The price of dealing with one social grievance, Wainer had found, was becoming heir to many. Some days, his Carlisle Street surgery resembled not so much a waiting room as a hoping room.

> On any one day in my surgery you might find a criminal, fresh from gaol, with information about a friend of his who had been unjustly convicted; an old age pensioner with complaints about the local council and removal of her garbage; a drug addict complaining about his treatment by the Drug Squad; an elderly man, veteran of the First World War, who wished me to help him further his claim for a pension dating back to 1917; an academic who claimed he had been unjustly certified insane. And, of course, there were women with their unwanted pregnancies who were coming from as far away as Perth and Darwin under the mistaken idea that I was an abortionist!

Wainer would actually oversee just one more abortion, arranging the termination of a 16-year-old rape victim, this time in his surgery because Evancourt's administration was wary of further police visits. Wainer believed that this termination would push the limits of the Menhennitt Ruling: 'There was no danger that she would commit suicide, there was no danger to her physical and mental health'. He may have been worrying unnecessarily—the abortion was strikingly similar to *R v Bourne*—but his concern was understandable. Becoming notorious suited him personally, but was becoming a problem professionally. One day he returned to his surgery to find that his partner, Dick Salts, had upped and left. Catholic Salts had always been uneasy about Wainer's activities; he had also become irked by the distribution of work. Wainer got lucky: the young Jewish doctor who had trained with him in May 1966, Eve Janover, offered to fill the breach. Other pressures were harder to relieve. Wainer was easy to find, and knew it by the volume of threatening phone calls, angry letters and hostile stares. He came to believe that his phone was tapped. He installed an alarm in his Daimler, and asked visitors to flat 6D, Edgewater Towers in St Kilda to give three long and three short identifying raps. He began surrounding himself with like-minded souls, who formed themselves into a sort of Baker Street Irregulars. Among 'The Untouchables' were a St Kilda chemist, Bryan Bennett, and two journalists, Michael Stewart of the *Sunday Observer* and Lionel Pugh of *The Australian*. In the early stages, Peter Bayliss and Rod Bretherton formed part of the inner circle; likewise Wainer's sister, Beryl, and his sometime girlfriends Judy Small and Carole Carrodus. Others whirled through, attracted by Wainer's charisma, and the whiff of danger.

> Michael Stewart was with me one night when we were pursued at the speed of 80mph in a Keystone Cops episode around St Kilda. Michael was driving and there were four Latin-looking thugs in a car chasing us around the side streets. Then for one absurd moment, we were chasing them until we suddenly realised what was happening; a screaming U-turn by both cars and the chase was on again. Ultimately we lost them thanks to Michael's superb driving.

Whitton was unenamoured of the group, whom he thought a danger to themselves. 'What are you doing with these jokers, Bert?' he would ask. 'You have to work with what you've got', Wainer would reply. Bruce Hanford was equally dubious: 'People started talking about arming themselves. I said: "Are you really prepared to shoot a policeman on suspicion? Because if you *do* arm yourself you run a strong risk of being shot by your own gun"'. In the Wainer papers at the State Library of Victoria are the beginnings of a Chandleresque typescript concerning The Untouchables, with Bert the world-weary narrator.

> I got out of bed and stretched. I viewed my body with displeasure and thought, that is undoubtedly a pot belly my lad. I covered the

> offending protuberance with a dressing gown, eased on slippers. I walked out of the bedroom through the hall and into the kitchen, made some tea and had breakfast, three cups of tea and four cigarettes. As I puffed on the last cigarette I wondered would they arrest me this time and if they did how I would respond to no cigarettes and confinement.

It peters out after three chapters but conveys the sense of role-playing in Wainer's dramas, the idea of watching himself *be* Bert Wainer. 'Bert had a great need for attention, this enormous need to make something of himself', recalls Hanford. 'And being "Bert Wainer, abortion law crusader", suited him to a tee. He also very sincerely believed that his own life was under threat. We were in the middle of the kind of media frenzy that makes people crazy.' Few escapades were so crazy as the Sydney sortie that Hanford and Whitton made with Wainer on 10 July 1969.

~

The Sydney abortion scene was far rougher and more corrupt than Melbourne's. After the death of the vile Dr Reginald Stuart-Jones in June 1961, police ran it for their own benefit, CIB chief Donald Fergusson and confederates Ray Kelly and Fred Krahe essentially taking a cut of every procedure. From time to time, Sydney threw up cases of shattering horror. In August 1962, 19-year-old Jennifer Kirkwood of Lane Cove fell pregnant to her deckhand boyfriend, Gerald O'Halloran. They chose to wed. But her parents insisted that the disgrace of forced marriage was too much, and compelled her to see Fergus George, a dentist with a sideline in abortions—who killed her. Locals were spellbound in November 1964 by the discovery of the body of 21-year-old Dianne Horler, French mistress at prestigious Ascham, in the Woollahra flat of well-known abortionist Dr George Smart. Newspapers covered the appearance of Smart before Murray Farquhar SM in lavish and voyeuristic detail, likewise Farquhar's conclusion that while 'a great deal of suspicion' attached to the matter, it 'did not add up to a *prima facie* case'. In time, of course, Farquhar would be as infamous in the law as Smart was in medicine.

This bore little on Melbourne until Frank Holland's crusade, which forced many women to seek help in Sydney, from which they returned with morbid tales. 'Belinda' told South Australian researcher Barbara Baird of visiting a Potts Point 'surgery' to which she was directed by a frightened Melbourne abortionist.

> It was disgusting, like a cattle call. There were these wooden cubicles with a bit of flimsy material over each one and you were told to get undressed and to put on a Modess belt. I was standing there with a Modess pad hanging down like a rabbit's tail, which I felt was undignified to say the least... It felt like a production line, like being in a factory, an abortion factory. You went into these cubicles and you were called out one by one and you went through a door and there was a very simple operating theatre set up with a plastic bucket at the end of the table.

Even a place that tried holding itself aloof of corruption, like the Heatherbrae Clinic, was affected by the general climate of haste and fear, recalled Jane Holland.

> Anyway I got a taxi to the Heatherbrae Clinic and when I knocked at the door the woman who opened it peered out behind me into the street and said: 'Come on in quickly'. And then sort of glared at me and said: 'Have you got the money?' I gave her the money and she stood there and then she showed me into the waiting room which was to the right and said: 'Take your clothes off'...
>
> They strapped me into the dentist's chair and put my feet in stirrups, I think, and gave me an injection and I passed out. When I came to I was in a room on the left of the passage and... I think she was slapping me and I wasn't terribly groggy. I recovered, got dressed and they said: 'You can get a taxi at the end of the street.'

Wainer had been invited to join a 2GB radio debate on abortion law, and resolved that while there he should present material concerning corruption and brutality in Sydney's abortion scene to Chief Commissioner Norman Allan. To this idea there was always a surreal aspect: police knew abortion in Sydney to be corrupt and brutal because they kept it that way. The planned trip soon developed a paranoid edge. When Bennett received a call saying that Wainer would be a dead man if he went to Sydney, Wainer started worrying. 'All they needed to kill Kennedy was a high-powered rifle', he fretted. 'If they could do that to him, they could do it to little old Bert Wainer from St Kilda.' Wainer insisted on arming himself, and invited a well-known gun dealer to his flat. George Joseph, straight from the mean streets in his broad-brimmed hat, arrived with two disassembled shotguns in a suitcase. 'Oh no, that is no good to me', said Wainer. 'I want something smaller. I am in fear of my life.' Whitton's partner, Noela McMahon, looked on with suppressed laughter: it was so... *Guys and Dolls*! Joseph found Wainer's behaviour odd, his speech 'a little incoherent', and thought he 'had been drinking'.

Wainer, Whitton and Hanford chartered a twin-engine Piper Aztec; a 'decoy' booking had been made on TAA. En route, Wainer decided he didn't want to meet Allan after all, and wished to avoid the Police Administration Centre in Surry Hills; Allan, if he wished, could come to 2GB. While Wainer was there, a deputation from Allan actually arrived: Donald Fergusson himself with two younger colleagues, Noel Morey and Roger Rogerson. They adjourned to the boardroom, but an impasse developed when the eagle-eyed Rogerson noticed that Whitton was taping the conversation: no confidences would be divulged in front of reporters. As Wainer was wont to, he developed an exorbitant opinion of Fergusson, who 'emanated an aura of power and ruthless strength' and was 'undoubtedly the smartest and toughest policeman I have ever met'. But apart from providing Whitton and Hanford with a readable story—'Wainer's Flight of Fear'—the trip accomplished little. Its chief impact, believes Rogerson's biographer, Duncan McNab, was 'confirmation of Rogerson's role as the anointed one'. Seven months later, Fergusson would be found shot through the right temple in the washroom of his Surry Hills office. 'Fergusson was one of those cops who believed the clean quid was OK', says Whitton. 'Casinos, working girls, abortionists. But he drew the line at drugs, wouldn't do heroin.' Others would.

~

If Wainer knew little about the Sydney scene, he still only knew some of the Melbourne scene. He decided for the first time to assemble those of the city's leading abortionists he knew: in a reference to 'Don Vito' Genovese's fabled Mafia gathering, Jack Ford would christen it 'the Appalachian meeting'. Bretherton hosted Bayliss, Berman, Davidson, Fenton Bowen, Finks and Troup at a buffet lunch in the wood-panelled lounge of his mock-Tudor Brighton home. Wainer wanted to unite them, but they weren't easily led: 'Here were these men, certainly not friendly with one another, grouped together in one room, discussing their various hobbies such as farming, sailing, real estate and skiing. Anything but abortion'. He explained his test cases and the principles they established. 'If you seven will help each other, you need never fear arrest', he continued. 'Furthermore, those of you who are paying police graft can cease doing so and the price of an abortion can fall.' He noticed that at the mention of graft, there was not so much as a twitch.

'An attractive, beautifully-tailored group', thought Berman: she sensed that most would be perfectly happy if someone simply told them who to pay off. And what Wainer called the 'port-after-dinner atmosphere' was deceptive. For all the vexations of graft, these doctors had flourished amid illegality. One, Finks, had other plans altogether: he was leaving for London in a few weeks, reckoning that there must be more scope for his talents under Britain's *Abortion Act.* Another, Fenton Bowen, was eagerly awaiting Charlie Wyatt's return.

For, although out of sight, Wyatt was never out of mind. On 26 July, Whitton and Hanford published the fruits of their research into his past as a policeman and his present as a bankrupt, referring to him as 'Harry the Backyard Abortionist'. As part of their investigation, Noela McMahon had dialled the telephone number given to Frances Davidson for her abortion: it connected to Mr Big TV. Times had tightened for Wyatt in his absence. His medical certificates for angina hadn't been accepted by the bankruptcy registrar or the County Court, and, despite the efforts of McMennemin and Matthews, there was a warrant out for his arrest on the firearm conviction. Wyatt drove with Moran to Sydney, where from room 610 of the Masonic Club he made a series of telephone calls to Melbourne. Fenton Bowen buoyantly told him there were 'loads of girls' in need of abortions. Matthews also believed the coast was clear, providing that protection money was delivered to his home rather than work. Finally, Wyatt's friend Gert Rose confirmed the availability of his house in Dunedin Street, Maidstone as a surgery.

Yet, a lot had changed in a few months. At 9 a.m. on the day that Whitton and Hanford published their expose, four Brighton CIB detectives began a stake-out from 83 Collins Street, diagonally across the road from number 94. After ninety minutes, during which sixteen people entered, four Homicide detectives muscled in too. Corinne Blackwell was having her hair done on the third floor when she noticed the mass of police cars outside, and was halfway down the passage to Heath's surgery when a policeman blocked her path. 'You can't come any further', he said. 'There's been a raid.' She scoffed: '*Who's* raiding *what?*' Her incredulity was understandable. Heath had operated with profitable impunity since World War II. Now there were police all over the place, executing a warrant to search for the medical records of two women aborted at the practice. The police found rather more, including two women in the recovery room, a third in surgery undergoing a procedure at the hands of James Buchanan and anaesthetist Robert Manser, and a black attaché case bulging with cash. The waiting room was also full, and the raid would change the life of one patient: 19-year-old Julene Banks from Box Hill South, two months' pregnant but expecting to wed her sign-writer boyfriend, Peter Cumming. The raid must have seemed like providence: they changed their minds, married a week later, and became parents to a daughter on 30 January 1970.

Heath had sensed he was under surveillance and had logged a complaint at Russell Street some days earlier. But it wasn't like the good old days of Holland and Mooney. There hadn't even been time to secrete the red appointment book, receptionist Beth Stuchberry shoving it hastily onto a high shelf in the pantry. Heath maintained equanimity. 'Come on Beth', he said. 'They have a warrant. We will get them the book.' Others were nonplussed. Heath's arrest was an event Wainer had not anticipated. The police had taken a course of action he had urged, and he was perplexed. Berman was not about to help him understand. The likelihood is that Ford initiated the raid on her urging, but admitting as much would have damaged her status as a wronged woman and helpless victim. Her autobiography decries 'the Collins Street Machine' as the centre of all evil, but omits to mention its overthrow. Wainer's attention shifted quickly anyway: he would trust a clean-up only on his own terms.

This had consequences. Word reached Wainer that Wyatt's return was imminent when a blonde in her mid-twenties came to his surgery with the news that she had been referred to Wyatt by Fenton Bowen, and was due to be collected at 8.30 a.m. on 15 August near North Melbourne railway station. Wainer hatched a plan to substitute one of his 'female assistants' for the girl in question, then follow the contact car to its destination with police in tow. Yet his methods were confused. Late the night before, he rang the Barwon Heads number of Superintendent McLeod, another policeman of whom he held quaintly golden opinions: a 'soft-spoken, freckled man who would have fitted well into the Highlands of my native Scotland, whom I instinctively trusted'. But Wainer did not trust him sufficiently to explain why he needed his help. McLeod would recall that he 'could not get much sense out of him [Wainer] but he impressed on me that it was urgent'. The police arrived on one corner at 7.45 a.m. the next morning; Wainer arrived a quarter of an hour later at another corner, stationing Lionel Pugh nearby as an observer disguised as a council gardener. Realising that the rendezvous had been botched, Wainer had to call the exercise off. He complained bitterly to McLeod, and felt he had 'reason to disbelieve' in a misunderstanding. But his desire to lead the hunt, and his imparting the minimum information to police, had contributed to the plan's failure.

Wainer was further unsettled by an incident late at night as he drove to Edgewater Towers and believed he was being followed by a car, culminating in a bruising encounter.

> There was a small man looking at the back door of Edgewater Towers and the car which had been following me was now in a position facing the back door. In other words I would have been theoretically between the car and the man in the foyer. The man heard me open the front door. I was running and he obviously recognised me and started to pull something out of his pocket which looked metallic and looked like a pistol. This took place in split seconds. I kept running and hit him...with my shoulder, and hit him on the way down.

Wainer believed he had been the victim of an attempted assassination, and would recall a conversation with Ford in which the policeman ventured that the McMennemins were the likeliest perpetrators—a conversation Ford would deny. Whatever the case, Wainer decided to beard the McMennemins in their own den, and took Pugh to their Dudley Street offices. Wainer challenged them: 'I've come to see you because it has been said you want to kill me and I would like your side of the story'. Harry McMennemin denied it, brandishing his savings passbook at Wainer as proof of probity. 'Look for yourself', he said. 'I have only $150 in it.' Not bad for one who had cashed tens of thousands of dollars of Charlie Wyatt's cheques over the last few years. Though the death threats to Wainer were probably more wardings off than anything else—as Evan Whitton observed: 'If someone is going to kill you, they don't usually tell you about it'—the doctor had come a crucial step closer to his backyard abortionist quarry.

Wainer was also right about Wyatt: he *was* back in town. On 14 August, Wyatt had visited Matthews's home at 287 Gillies Street, Fairfield and paid him $300 as an advance on his protection. He overheard Matthews have a heated telephone conversation with Berman and a quieter one with Ford, and took Moran to work the next day feeling secure—oblivious to Wainer's panting pursuit. But Wyatt's sense of security was about to be tested. Planning a day at the Sydney races, he headed for Essendon airport on 16 August. At 11 a.m., however, Moran answered a telephone call at Maidstone from Matthews: Homicide was acting on a complaint about the premises, so they had 'better get out'. After reuniting with Moran that evening at the Marco Polo Motel in Flemington, Wyatt took another $200, six longnecks and a bottle of whisky to Gillies Street, where he and his protector talked business over Grace Matthews's roast lamb. He and Moran then moved on to Footscray's Palm Motel.

During the final chase after Charlie Wyatt, it was by no means clear who was working for whom. On 19 August, Jack Ford briefed Senior Detective Kevin Evenden about information from Berman that girls named Wallace and Bonner were to be conveyed to a Wyatt abortory the next morning from a Surry Hills tram stop. Shortly after 7 a.m. the next day, Evenden visited Wallace in Domain Road and persuaded her to permit a policewoman being sent in her place. An hour later, Wyatt had just begun work in Allendale Road, Blackburn when he received a call advising him of the entrapment, and had to 'bustle down' to the tram stop to intercept Moran.

Wyatt, Moran and Gert Rose's wife, Marion, set up the next day in a house in Drew Street, Yarraville that was occupied by Gloria Lawrence, who worked for Wyatt's Footscray chemist contact. The steriliser was on, the dilators were boiling up and two patients were waiting when Matthews rang: next door had smelt the Dettol and complained. By his own account, Wyatt shouted: 'Everybody out! The police will be here in half an hour'. The two girls 'just got dressed in a hurry and ran'. Ford asked Footscray CIB to wait until Evenden got there, but Wyatt, Moran and Rose had made good their escape by the time he arrived. Wyatt claimed to have cheekily changed into a tracksuit and jogged around the park opposite, watching the raid.

It was never ascertained exactly how Wyatt beat these stings—whether Matthews was his sole protector or acted with Ford. The temptation is to believe that Ford, already proven corruptible and always in need of money to subsidise his gambling, was cooperating, and Wyatt would do his best to implicate Ford later, claiming that Matthews had asked him to obtain $2000 for the Homicide Squad chief from Fenton Bowen. Yet Matthews could also have been acting unilaterally. Monitoring traffic on the police's D24 network was easy. He was by now special assistant to the chief commissioner, in charge of complaints—not an onerous role, at least as he saw it. 'They come in here, dear, and I give them a good sympathetic hearing', he explained to Berman. 'When they go I just screw up the paper and throw it in the wastepaper basket.' Wyatt's cry that the police 'will be here in half an hour', meanwhile, smacks of a confected detail because he actually left in such haste as to abandon his gear. Police found the steriliser, an operating table, suitcases full of surgical instruments and a red telephone book inscribed with patient names: it does not sound like an orderly withdrawal with a comfortable half-hour to spare. Ford also had good reason to delay the raid slightly for Evenden's arrival: Wyatt had lots of friends at Footscray CIB and had employed some of its members. The possibility exists, then, that, perhaps as a means of further placating Berman, perhaps out of the same zeal that motivated his raid on Heath, Ford actually *was* trying to catch Wyatt. Certainly *some* police were—one would shortly do some inspired sleuthing.

After a day's aborting in Blackburn on 24 August 1969, Wyatt made a beeline for Gillies Street to hand over another $100. He was by now so familiar there that Grace Matthews carved him roast beef sandwiches. Late in the evening, he rang for a Silver Top Taxi to run him back to the Palm. Early the following morning, Senior Constable Ronald Vienna from Footscray CIB happened to be investigating some break-ins at that motel when the proprietress confided her suspicions regarding a guest called Lee who claimed to have come from Queensland, and offered Vienna the key to his room, number 53. It was the Aramis that betrayed its wearer: Vienna had caught a whiff of Wyatt at the local police station and never forgotten it. Scanning the room, he spotted some of Wyatt's trademark hats, and shirts with the laundry mark 'Lewis': Belle Moran's maiden name and sometime alias. In the sleeve of a pink shirt was found $2480. In the hotel car park was a Holden with a boot full of surgical instruments—the car was registered in the name Frank James, but it turned out that every payment on it had been made by Wyatt.

Vienna called Evenden. By mid-afternoon, Wyatt was in the City Watchhouse—and he was *not* happy. He happened to meet CIB chief Colin Sharp in the men's urinal. 'Didn't you know they were so close to you?' asked Sharp out the corner of his mouth. Wyatt seethed: no, he bloody well hadn't.

~

Both Heath and Wyatt had been arrested. Troup and Berman were back at work. The government and police seemed inclined to respect the Menhennitt Ruling. But Wainer was unappeased. The doctors, he had decided, were weak and self-interested. First Bayliss, then Bretherton, were resiling from earlier admissions of paying graft. As Bretherton's daughter Di says, it was typical of him to mouth sentiments he shrank from acting on:

> My father was good at self-deceptions. For instance, he wasn't a Communist Party member but he liked sometimes to think he was; he certainly had communist friends, but he was just a member of the local Labor party. On abortion, he was very outspoken round the dinner table. When it came time to do something publicly, he preferred to hide behind Bert, then grumble that his contribution hadn't been recognised.

Wainer still hankered to provide unignorable proof of the venality of the abortion trade, perhaps partly to justify how the issue had consumed him. He worried about the debate disappearing, for bigger stories suddenly abounded. Great Train Robber Ronald Biggs was somewhere in Melbourne. The cast of *The Boys in the Band* and distributors of *Portnoy's Complaint* faced obscenity charges; likewise British comic Jimmy Edwards for using 'fuck' in a joke at the Chevron. *Truth*, meanwhile, was preparing to run such lengthy extracts from Christine Keeler's autobiography that the paper had room for little more than Jack Dyer, Ron Barassi and the saucy 'Heart Balm' advice column. Wainer complained to Whitton that there remained work to do. 'Sometimes,' says Whitton, 'I had to remind Bert that I was working for Rupert Murdoch, not for him'. On Friday 12 September, Wainer sent a fascinating twelve-paragraph letter to the editor of *The Age*, part philosophical musing, part manifesto. He deplored the cowardice of doctors, likening them to Nazis:

> I submit that the position of these people is no more defensible than that of war criminals, who at Nuremberg defended themselves by saying it was the law or that they were only obeying orders. The Nuremberg tribunals and history have passed judgement on this matter, and left forever a stain on the conscience of the human race to show what can happen when a man or a group of men elect to evade the responsibilities of personal involvement.

Having tested it successfully, Wainer now thought the Menhennitt Ruling insufficient, and wanted it 'clarified by being written into Statute law'. He called for 'all others who so believe' to 'barrage the newspapers, radio stations and politicians with letters, phone calls and other positive action'. Wainer would be taking unspecified steps:

> I have consequently decided upon a course of action which within the next few weeks will bring me into headlong conflict with the law as it now stands. I do not take this step as a crusader, reformer, or, as some people have suggested, out of a desire for publicity. I do this because there is no other course open to me. I do this because I believe deeply that women have this right.

This unspecified plan was implemented the day after the letter's publication when Wainer met Jack Ford outside Albert Park's basketball stadium. According to Wainer, he put to Ford a proposition: a ring of Melbourne abortionists would pay Ford a cut of each case, as much as 10 per cent; Ford, he claimed, agreed to Wainer taking 2 per cent himself. Wainer also made solicitous comments to Ford about Berman, saying that she had a 'love-hate complex' where the policeman was concerned: 'If you cannot love her then she wants you to hate her'. It ended up being Wainer's word against Ford's, for the Homicide Squad chief would deny any such agreement.

Forty years later, it is hard to surmise who said what in a conversation so full of mutual distrust. It seems unlikely that Ford would have agreed to any arrangement on the spot, least of all with someone so close to the press; Berman called Ford an 'each ways man' for his sliding one way then the other when propositions were before him. By the same token, Ford was perennially short of money, and the Spring Racing Carnival was in the offing. The prospect of a reliable cash supply can hardly have left him entirely uninterested. Wainer left the conversation feeling that Ford was 'purchaseable', but also that he had really 'achieved nothing', and the next day he was hospitalised with pneumonia, run down and worn out. So much for his 'course of action'.

Waiting two weeks, he divulged his version of the conversation to Michael Stewart of the *Sunday Observer*, without naming Ford. The article claimed he would seek an appointment with Arthur Rylah and 'produce signed affidavits' about graft from four doctors: himself, Troup, Bretherton and Fenton Bowen. The threat was empty. He had none of them. Troup could perhaps be relied on, but the invocation of Bretherton's name finally estranged them for good, and Fenton Bowen had just days before been found guilty in his long-delayed abortion trial. Because he had suffered a stroke two years earlier, a sympathetic judge imposed a three-year bond, but Fenton Bowen was not a man around whose evidence any crusade could safely be constructed. Publicly, Bert Wainer boasted an arsenal. Privately, he was shooting blanks.

~

It had been a gruelling period for Fenton Bowen, a mediocre doctor fond of his comforts. The trial had been prolonged by the discharge of the first jury, and Fenton Bowen's attempts to talk the star witness out of her testimony had been embarrassingly revealed. For the three days between conviction and sentencing, he had been confined to bed in Pentridge—nor was his ordeal over. On 1 October, the 64-year-old was charged again, this time with twenty-four counts of abortion: twelve on his own account, the rest with Charles Wyatt and Belle Moran.

For Wyatt, the trip south had also become a disaster. It wasn't just being behind bars: it was that everyone knew where he was. When police wanted to charge him with abortion, they could. When the registrar in bankruptcy wanted him, he had to attend. Under such circumstances, Wyatt knew only one course: lie. And the lies he told before the registrar on 9 October were not just minor misstatements; they were flagrant falsehoods. With the benefit of affidavits filed in support of the new case against Wyatt, his old nemesis, Peter Brusey, started fishing for information about his abortion activities, beginning with his knowledge of Jean Field—whom Wyatt simply denied knowing.

Brusey: Do you know anybody who is in any way connected with the medical profession under the name of Field?
Wyatt: No.
Brusey: Or a nurse?
Wyatt: No.
Brusey: Or in any way connected with the medical profession even in the most lowly capacity?
Wyatt: No.

Nor did Wyatt know anything about the Holden full of abortion instruments outside the Palm Motel.

Brusey: You have got nothing to do with abortion in any shape or form?
Wyatt: No.
Brusey: And Mrs Lewis, the same applies to her?
Wyatt: I don't know about Mrs Lewis. Not to my knowledge...
Brusey: Well, Mr Wyatt I have got some news for you...

Brusey must almost have chortled as he explained that the payments on the car were all in Wyatt's name. He had documents. Just *look* at these documents. Even Wyatt began faltering.

Brusey: Do you mean to deny that any such payments to GMAC have been made by you?
Wyatt: That's right.
Brusey: If it is established, can you explain it?
Wyatt: Yes.
Brusey: You can explain?
Wyatt: Yes. (pause)
Brusey: Do not keep us in suspense. You were paying for a car which was found outside the motel when you were arrested? (pause)

Deputy Registrar: You said you could explain.
Wyatt: If there is anything to explain, I said I would explain.
Brusey: Explain it.
Wyatt: I can't explain it.

Brusey was not interested in abortion per se; all he wanted was the cash of Wyatt's rightfully due to his long-suffering creditors. So could this man Frank James have anything to do with the instruments in the car?

Brusey: Is he in the abortion business?
Wyatt: I do not know. Possibly he could be.
Brusey: Do you think he might be trying to incriminate you?
Wyatt: I do not know.
Brusey: Do you think he might be leaving his car outside your hotel with abortion instruments in it to get you into trouble?
Wyatt: Who said he was in the abortion business?
Brusey: Some people are in the abortion business. The question is who. I am not interested in any abortion business you are in except to find out about money.
Wyatt: I think it is most unfair that there are these allegations.

Life must have felt awfully unfair to Charlie Wyatt. Everyone was complaining. His wife Alice May wrote pleading to be left alone.

> You should know by now that I do not want any part of the assets you have. You are entitled to the horse and the house and all that goes with it as it was all your money that went into it. But please do me one thing and that is clear my name... All I ask is leave us all in peace and let live.

His de facto Belle Moran was then caught by a process server as she left the Watchhouse after visiting: she started running, but the skilful server slipped the summons between her arm and body. All these people's problems. What about him? He was *in jail*. All those palms he had crossed to stay on the right side of the law; all that information he'd provided; all those televisions he'd damn near given away; all those lunches and beers down the years. That bludger Jack Matthews had *somersaulted him*. 'Nobody somersaults Charlie Wyatt and gets away with it', he told whomever would listen.

Wyatt wasn't to know, of course, but he hadn't been somersaulted at all. Had Senior Constable Vienna not visited the Palm Motel that 25 August, had the proprietress not asked him to look in on the obnoxious visitor from Queensland, had Wyatt not been so obsessively fond of Aramis, he might have continued under his old mate's aegis. As it was, another fate lay in store. On the basis of a complete misapprehension, Charlie Wyatt, backyard abortionist, bankrupt conman and serial liar, was about to join forces with abortion's white knight, Bert Wainer.

'I don't know whether to shoot myself'

Corruption happens in every country. The disquieting thing about it in Australia, as in the United States, is that people do not feel very much about it when it is happening—and forget all about it soon after.
The Wild Men of Sydney (1958), Cyril Pearl

Charlie Wyatt was released on 12 November 1969, Belle Moran having persuaded a friend to post bail. This was an act of some generosity on her part. In a month's time she would be going to jail, with Jean Field and Donald and Annie Shaw, for the abortions at Tally Ho—charges that had only come about because Wyatt had shopped her. Life with Charlie was like that.

Perhaps the last word of commendation for Charlie Wyatt had been on his Victorian police service record, which described his character as 'good' when he left in March 1949. In the twenty years since, he had done nothing to justify that faith. He had been a spiv, a snitch, a bankrupt, a bully. He had owned houses, cars, businesses and a racehorse, and paid not a cent to creditors. He had served jail time for firing a gun at a wife whose life he had ruined. He had cynically manipulated and exploited his de facto when it suited him. Answering the bankruptcy registrar's questions, Belle Moran described Wyatt as an enigma even to her.

> I have always thought he knew what he was doing and I have just gone along. That is all. Perhaps I have been very silly...You are always referring to me and saying I live good. I haven't got anything. All I have ever done was work, everybody knows that...Mr Wyatt told me very little and very little about his family or anything...He is a very quiet man Mr Wyatt and never told me very much. Anything I found out I would have to find out some other way.

Yet redemption was at hand. Wyatt contacted Bert Wainer via Wainer's ex-wife, Barbara, who worked at a gym Wyatt patronised. They agreed to meet at the Southern Cross Hotel on 20 November 1969. Wainer was immediately smitten.

> A man approached with extended hand. He said, 'I'm Charles Wyatt.' His whole appearance was a shock. I had a picture in my mind of a sinister, furtive and shady looking man. Here was someone who emanated confidence and good health. He was blond, tanned, had an open, frank face and the look of a man with a clear conscience. He was immaculately groomed, well-manicured and wearing a small pork-pie hat and his suit looked as though it had just been delivered from the best tailor in town.
>
> I had anticipated a duel of wits, with Wyatt trying to find out how much I knew whilst I fenced with him and attempted to extract information. Nothing could have been further from what happened. Charles proceeded to unburden himself of the details of his own particular police graft network. Names and sums of money flowed over his gin and tonic without reserve. It was all too easy.

Indeed it was. Wainer heard the 'underlying tone of bitterness'; he heard more of it when he accompanied Wyatt to Fenton Bowen's Lonsdale Street surgery.

> When Dr Fenton Bowen saw us both together, his face registered a number of emotions; fear, amazement, confusion. To his mind, the entry of his erstwhile colleague and myself, apparently on good terms, must have been shocking. He knew that I was intent on seeing legal abortions introduced and that Wyatt should have considered me a deadly enemy.

The opposite, of course, was also true. Wainer had proclaimed an 'intense hatred' of backyard abortionists: those 'vultures', with their 'greed, ignorance and stupidity'. Now he had met the epitome of that class, a man whose prosecution he had demanded and sought to engineer for the last six months—and he had invested him with the appearance of 'a man with a clear conscience'. Wainer heard Wyatt and Fenton Bowen complaining about their charges, how the police had 'double-crossed' them both, and saw in his former quarry a catalyst for his dormant crusade. 'All too easy'—but such good fortune wasn't to be scorned. The pair took a taxi to the Caroline Street flat of Peggy Berman, who, despite her loud disapproval of backyard abortionists, was similarly charmed.

> I opened it [the door] and there unexpectedly stood a pleasantly open-faced, smiling man with Dr Wainer. 'I'm Charles Wyatt,' said the stranger. I was non-plussed. 'I believe we have good friends in common,' he said. He smelt highly of after-shave lotion, wore a flamboyant baby-blue suit and his jewellery was all glitter and gold… Here was Wyatt the self-confessed backyarder chuckling over our efforts to catch him, and telling us in minute detail about payments, amounts, times, dates and personal characteristics of Ford and Matthews. This left me shocked, and for once even Dr Wainer was speechless.

Seldom can open physiognomy and snappy tailoring have worked such magic: in a few hours, sworn enemies had become inseparable allies, amid a nimbus of cigarette smoke and a clatter of empty bottles. Finally, Wainer made a suggestion. Wyatt should prove his bona fides by ringing Matthews then and there. Easy, said Wyatt.

> Wyatt: Hello Jack, Charles here, Charles Wyatt.
> Matthews: Hello Charles. How are you?
> Wyatt: Not too good. Just got out of you-know-where. I've lost a lot of weight. The food wasn't good. It's not the food Grace cooks.
> Matthews: I know. I know.

Then Wyatt let fly. Why had Matthews told him it was safe to return from Queensland? Why had he been turned in? Why was he on charges? Matthews temporised. Wainer 'had made things too hot'. Wyatt shouldn't worry. It would be two years before he came to trial—plenty of time to sort things out. But it was too late. Wyatt turned the phone over to Berman, and then to Wainer. 'But doctor, these people you are talking to are criminals', Matthews spluttered. 'You must not listen to their stories.' Wainer retorted: 'If they are criminals, from what I have heard they are small time compared with you'. After Wyatt's departure, Wainer made a suggestion to Berman. Why not tape the conversations on the telephone line at Caroline Street? They wouldn't spend money more wisely than on the NEC MyCorder, a reel-to-reel machine with a phone attachment, acquired the next day from Melbourne Tape Recorders in Elizabeth Street.

Over the next few days, Wainer spent more time with Wyatt, whose allegations grew graver, and more grandiose, by the day. He complained of betrayal by the McMennemins. Roy McMennemin had buried him before the bankruptcy registrar, claiming dubious ignorance of Wyatt's financial affairs: 'I have to plead stupidity...It not only appears he has put it over me but a great deal of other people in Melbourne'. Now Wyatt told Wainer that the McMennemins were at the centre of 'Crime Incorporated', a syndicate through which they ran crime of all descriptions. Homicide? They had Rylah in their pocket because they'd stayed out of his wife's death. Breaking Squad? Vice Squad? Crooks to a man. But Charlie Wyatt? Honest as the day is long. And the fact is that Wainer *wanted* to rely on him. This exotic figure was the passe-partout to a criminal netherworld that Wainer had been scrabbling to enter.

Wainer's plan, again, was to get himself arrested and thereby be free to divulge what he now knew. It is not obvious why this was the only means to this end. Wainer would say it was 'because the Parliamentary forum was closed', although the media forum was open, and would prove cavernously so. More likely it evinces Wainer's theatricality. Since his test case abortions, he had fallen in love with the idea of being arrested, perhaps like the conscientious objectors to the Vietnam War he had invoked. He had failed to interest Ford in arresting him in Albert Park two months earlier; now he set out to provoke Matthews. Matthews's deadpan diary entry for 24 November cites a call at 11.35 p.m. suggestive of two men each far from sure what the other was up to.

> This man's voice was most peculiar and it appeared that he was either under the influence of alcohol or had taken some drug. He informed me that he again wished to interview me about the allegations against members of the force. I again informed him that if he had any allegations to make he should make them to the chief commissioner of police. The caller informed me that he would not do this. Because of the peculiar behaviour of the caller I asked if he was feeling well. He replied that he was tired after having dealt with seventy cases in his surgery. I then terminated the conversation.

They hadn't heard the last of one another.

~

Berman had always viewed Wainer as a valuable means of keeping the police on their mettle, and perhaps also of prejudicing her eventual trial. But essentially she wanted to keep working, legally or illegally, and still saw Ford as her simplest means of doing so. The pressure of charges on Heath looked like an opportunity. But, to her frustration, 94 Collins Street remained open for business. Indeed, Heath became interested in the premises that Arnold Finks had left behind at 123 Collins Street, which Berman and Troup wanted for their own activities.*

Continued corrupt relations between Berman and Ford are consistent, too, with the freedom of their conversations after 24 November—conversations Berman was now taping on her new recorder. It is unclear whether Berman was paying Ford for protective services at the time; it is clear he was providing them, and to an increasingly restive customer. Berman seethed with complaints. What was happening about her trial? Why was Heath still operating? Little did Ford realise that his interlocutor was fishing for incriminating remarks—which he proceeded to offer. On 25 November, for instance, Ford dragged himself to work despite illness only to learn that Hoddle Street was having a day off. He complained bitterly:

> There was no need for me to be . . . here today if you're not working. When I took a day off one day you screamed like a banshee. What will happen if you want me every day? I never take a day off. I'm here every day looking after you.

Strung up to a pitch of exasperation, he decided to go home to bed: 'So goodbye for now at any rate. I'm going home, I'm sick and I'm going home. I shouldn't have come in here today. I only come in here to look after your interests'.

---

* Ford actually seems to have acted for Berman in this transaction. Finks, it appears, had given her tacit approval to take over the lease on 123 Collins Street; Heath and James Buchanan had then made a counteroffer. This, at least, is the inference of a telegram that Ford sent to Finks's Hyde Park flat on 28 October 1969: 'Suggest keep to original offer Collins definately [sic] no deal Jayare [presumably "JR" Heath]'. The wire was signed 'Arnold Friend'. Finks took the advice, for Berman and Troup began to make use of the premises in December.

The next day he sounded depressed, like a man who couldn't remember how he had started something, yet could not work out how to finish it.

Ford: I wanted to go home yesterday because I was sick.

Berman: Well, you told me that you were only staying there for us.

Ford: That's right too.

Berman: Well, who was looking after us while you were away?

Ford: Nobody... all right, well shut down then. I don't care what you do but I'll do everything I can for you. I'm protecting you here all the time.

Not that Ford knew, but it was getting close to finishing itself. That day, Wainer also called Whitton: 'Wyatt tonight, at my place—eight o'clock'. Berman too? 'Peggy Berman, too.' The journalist was not without misgivings. This time-consuming saga had lately been short on immediate rewards. He told his partner Noela he was 'sick of it'. She changed his mind: 'You've got to stay in there because this might turn into a worthwhile story'. That story, 'The Night of the Hearse', published in *Man* magazine and anthologised in Whitton's *Amazing Scenes*, is a genre classic, Wainer presiding over a chaotic, alcoholic evening at Edgewater Towers like a medieval lord of misrule, to the peals of Wyatt's manic laughter: 'Aaaark! Aaaark!'

Provoke Matthews? Just watch them! With a series of prank calls over the course of the evening, Wainer sent to Gillies Road a squad car, an ambulance, a fire engine and finally a hearse. 'Jesus, Bert', said Whitton at one point. 'You're playing cops and robbers.' Wainer replied weightily: 'I must'. Matthews's poker-faced diary entry records his return home at 1 a.m. to find his household in uproar and a familiar voice asking if there had 'been any callers'.

> The reception was particularly bad and was not assisted by this person being close to the phone and shouting. The person who had previously telephoned me announcing himself as Dr Wainer came on the phone and insisted that I should see him some time in future. I again informed him that the chief commissioner was the person whom he should interview. There was a great deal of background noise and I could hear the sound of at least one woman talking. Dr Wainer's rambling conversation went on for some time and I at last terminated the conversation.

The evening failed in its stated objective, for Wainer remained unmolested by the police. Chances are that word of it also caused a few policemen to begin covering their tracks. But, somehow, it bonded the participants as no previous event or gathering had. Egged on by Wainer, Berman and Wyatt started using their new-found tape-recording capabilities—for the sound of the woman talking that Matthews heard was one of Berman's tape-recorded telephone conversations, through which Wyatt was shouting: 'D'ya wanna hear any more, ya bludger?!' There would be plenty more to hear by the time they had finished.

Berman rang Ford constantly—but then, she always had, so the policeman suspected nothing. She bombarded him with pleas, complaints and threats about the case against Hoddle Street. Ford had always expressed confidence about obtaining her a Crown Law Department nolle prosequi—an agreement not to proceed. But the publicity surrounding Wainer had made it difficult, and Ford always had at the back of his mind the rumours associating him with Berman.

> Look you're not going to get to Court…that's first of all. I've been working on fellows for months. You're bloody stupid at times…I've done everything exactly right. If they were watching me twenty-four hours a day, they would get nothing from me from the day I got here. I've not put a foot wrong and there's one thing in mind—to get you out of bother…There's only one person who can damage me in any way—is you.

This dawning awareness of his vulnerability to Berman's caprices did not prevent him venting his volcanic temper: 'Look, you had the chance of getting a nolle…All you had to do was keep quiet and let your friends try and help you and all you did was just create a stink and brought yourself under notice and destroyed any chance'. At times he let slip hints of higher corruption:

> Ford: You lived in luxury for years because people helped you and as soon as things go wrong you turn on them. You are the only people who have turned on anyone…
>
> Berman: You are kidding…
>
> Ford: I don't hear Heath singing out about Mooney and Holland…I don't hear anybody…

At other times, he also let slip Berman's influence over him—which Berman, for the tape, was always anxious to play down.

> Ford: I knocked up Heath and don't forget...
> Berman: I don't care whether you lock Heath up or not...
> Ford: Liar. You begged me to.
> Berman: No I didn't bloody beg you to.
> Ford: You liar. You did and there are plenty of records of it, don't worry about that.
> Berman: Plenty of records I begged you to lock up Heath?
> Ford: Yes, put him out of business so that you could get the business.
> Berman: Oh, is that the story?
> Ford: That's one of the stories. There are a lot of them.

Once in a while, Ford forgot himself, and brooded on how he'd let his guard down.

> Ford: You know, two things I can always remember about you, I always remember two things—the first time I ever met you alone you said 'you've got to trust somebody'.
> Berman: That's true.
> Ford: The second thing is, you said 'you'll never come to harm through me'. Two things I remembered I believed. I never trusted anybody till then. And it didn't do me much good.

The vengeance Wyatt and Berman wrought on their police protectors, Matthews and Ford, would be devastating. The irony is that it was based on false assumptions. Matthews had *not* betrayed Wyatt. And Ford *had* been seeking a nolle prosequi for Berman, and was very close to it. The Crown Law Department file for *R v Troup* contains Ray Dunn's urgent application for a nolle on 24 October, supported by a medical opinion from top oncologist Cyril Minty outlining the extent of Berman's cancer and its secondaries. The opinion of Crown prosecutor Alan Dixon was that 'while the independence of the doctor should be checked', he thought 'at first sight the case against Berman should be nolle'd'. On 21 November, Dunn wrote with the additional advice that Berman's condition was deteriorating and that attendance at court would be deleterious to her health: 'The strain of a lengthy trial will be far too much for her to stand, and it could quite possibly have a fatal effect on her'. Chances are that, as Ford indicated, Berman would not have gone to trial, except that on 4 December she accompanied

Wainer and Wyatt to the opening day of *R v Field & Moran*, where the trio's high spirits were obvious—the nolle, Ford told her, was off. 'I go and tell them how sick you are and you waltz in with Wainer and Wyatt on your arm', he lamented. 'You're being plain stupid... You can commit suicide as far as I'm concerned.'

With that, perhaps, he signed his own suicide note. Berman had always shied from incriminating Ford; so, strangely, had Wainer, believing that the Homicide Squad chief might turn out to be a useful informant in the future. Now both Berman and Wainer were out for him, as well as the rest. On the morning of 5 December, Wainer rang Victoria's solicitor-general, Tony Murray, asking if he would receive evidence of police corruption: Murray offered him an appointment at 3 p.m. He solicited *Truth*'s interest in publishing the story: Whitton hastily agreed, with the stipulation, on the advice of *Truth* subeditor Bill Murray, that the material come in the form of statutory declarations.

So it was that Wainer corralled Wyatt, Berman, Jim Troup and Maureen Young on the verandah of Fenton's Bowen's Lonsdale Street surgery, and advised that the time had come to document what they knew. At Temple Court, 422 Collins Street, Whitton waited with Wainer's solicitor, David Murray, to oversee the swearing of their affidavits; Wyatt cajoled a reluctant Fenton Bowen into joining them.

It soon became obvious that Wainer had underestimated the duration of such an exercise: by 3.45 p.m., only three affidavits were sworn. Fenton Bowen was particularly coy, and at first 'didn't want to sign anything'. Wainer rang Murray again and asked for another couple of hours. Murray gave him until 6 p.m. At about ten minutes to six, Wainer burst into the street, affidavits in hand, concluded there was no time to find a taxi, and commenced running towards Spring Street. He arrived at his destination, dishevelled and sweat-soaked, on the stroke of six. He returned via *Truth*'s office, where Whitton was already pondering how best to display his hard-won scoop in the midweek edition the following Tuesday.

Berman felt spent: 'With this part of the battle over, I was exhausted'. But Wyatt was exuberant, intoxicated, cachinnating crazily. 'This stuff you're printing: it's just muckraking', he told Hanford. 'Wait till I make my bail. Then I'll really give you something.' He accompanied Berman and Troup to Caroline Street, regaling them with bigger and wilder tales, and felt an overpowering need to gloat to someone. He settled on Senior Constable Ronald Jackson, who had arrested him all those years ago at the Red Lion Hotel for SP bookmaking, and to whom he had subsequently sold a cheap television and plied with many beers—the dirty little bastard. At 11.06 p.m., Wyatt dialled his number and switched on the MyCorder. Ford and Matthews, he told Jackson, would be getting what they deserved.

Jackson: It goes back to the old times, does it?

Wyatt: Old times and new times. It will do them good. It won't hurt them, but all the young blokes are all right, thank Christ because... they are going to feel the punch you know... the impact is on them.

Jackson: Yes, it would... Where is this coming from—from the Berman sheila?

Wyatt: Oh, Berman is mixed up in it, yes. Not only is she mixed up but—do you know when all those blokes there were... copping the brunt of everything, Ford was right in the big payola business, you know...

Jackson: Yes, I understand that...

Wyatt: You knew that...?

Jackson: Well, I was led to believe—pretty strong feeling...

Jackson remained perplexed that it had been his doorstep on which Berman had dropped the fake Hoddle Street records. Why hadn't she used Jacobson, whom everyone knew was crooked?

Jackson: I don't know why they never used that man up there—why they never used him. I'm buggered if I know...

Wyatt: Which one was that?

Jackson: Jacobson...

Wyatt: Jacobson yes... but how silly were they for Ford and Matthews to engineer that and not bring you into it?

Jackson: That's right...

Wyatt: Yes... it shows how desperate they were.

Wyatt assured Jackson 'from the bottom of my heart and as a personal friend' that the young policeman would not be mentioned. Having hung up, he handed Berman the tape implicating him. The best revenge, eh? Served cold.

~

'Read it regularly', Henry Bolte would say of *Truth*. 'And I like it.' The edition of Tuesday 9 December 1969 would have been an exception. Whitton's opening paragraph paid homage to his old boss Sol Chandler's love of eye-popping capitalisation: 'SIX people, including three Melbourne doctors, have lodged sworn affidavits with the solicitor-general NAMING senior police officers alleged to have been running an ABORTION "PROTECTION" RACKET'. When Jack Ford arrived at Russell Street, he was greeted by silence and stupefied looks. He rang Berman and she cringed from his ire as he read out the headline: 'On the front page…"WE PAID OFF COPS" by Evan Whitton…fucking mongrel bastard'. Berman denied everything: 'I knew you'd always put it back on me. You've put everything back on me, and you always have done, but never the good things'. Ford wasn't listening.

> Ford: I'll be moved from here. I have doubt whether I'll last the rest of the day out here as a matter of fact.
>
> Berman: Darling…
>
> Ford: I'm finished. I don't care. I don't know whether to shoot myself or not. I don't think I will. I think I'll fight it out and let people get in the witness box.

With Wainer, then, Ford was in agreement: there would have to be an inquiry. Just the other side of the Yarra, the doctor was holding court at Caroline Street to an audience of reporters, explaining that he believed there were as many as thirty police involved and a dozen doctors, and claiming that one senior officer had taken $156 000 in graft—Jack Matthews, although 'Senior' was not named. 'I think this may well shock the people of Victoria', he said. 'And the revulsion they experience…may lead to enlightened law reform.' Not if Arthur Rylah could help it.

Rylah knew the pressure would be on him to do something eventually. His solution was to do as little as possible immediately. His appointment to inquire into these allegations would be…the chief commissioner of police. 'I believe the government and general public are entitled to a quick explanation', said Chief Commissioner Noel Wilby. Quick, however, did not appear either thorough or independent, and Wilby and Assistant Commissioner Angus Carmichael spent two weeks being chauffeured around Melbourne in a grey Humber trying to obtain information for an investigation that nobody had any faith in.

Wainer was evasive, giving some answers but not others: 'You can go on putting questions to me all day. I do not know which questions I am prepared to answer and which I will refuse to answer'. Ford, Matthews and Timmins gave interviews a week before Christmas, but Berman, Wyatt, Fenton Bowen, Troup and Young all refused to co-operate. When Wilby called on her, Berman even rang her former lover for advice.

Ford: That might be the chief himself coming to see you. It's a bit awkward being the chief's car.
Berman: They wouldn't have a warrant would they?
Ford: They've got nothing to have a warrant for.
Berman: Well, I won't open the door and that's that. He's got a few problems of his own hasn't he?
Ford: I know, love. How are you apart from that?
Berman: All right.
Ford: Let [me] know, sweetie, how it goes.

Bolte was defiant. At his press conference on 15 December, in his spacious, wood-panelled, air-conditioned office furnished with a portrait of the Queen and a bust of Winston Churchill, he was a study in insouciance. 'Sir Henry, what's happened to the Aboriginal affairs department?' asked one journalist. 'I rang them this morning and I was told they'd moved down to Queen Street.' Bolte laughed: 'Yes, they've gone walkabout. I don't know why'. On the matter of abortion, he sipped his tea inscrutably.

Question: Is the government going to have an inquiry into abortion now that Dr Wainer has presented his affidavits alleging police have been taking bribes, Sir Henry?
Bolte: Both Arthur [Rylah] and Tony Murray are examining the affidavits now. They'll decide whether there'll be an inquiry or not.
Question: Would you say there's the possibility of an inquiry?
Bolte: I'm not saying anything.
Question: Would you say there's no possibility of an inquiry?
Bolte: I'm not saying anything.

The premier received a second cup of tea on a silver salver. Lighting a Turf, he dismissed Wainer contemptuously.

Question: Dr Wainer was interviewed last night? Did you see it?
Bolte: Naw! He's pathetic. He's probably certifiable... I'm told he was involved in that $10 note forgery case recently. Who was it? Anyway, they used his house. Now that's rather interesting. I think we could make some use of that.

But his gauleiter, Rylah, normally such a supple strategist, was losing his touch. The government was taking a drubbing. *Truth* was still running rings around *The Herald*, *The Sun* and *The Age*, printing more allegations, more investigations, compelling others to follow. But on their own, Murdoch's mischievous sprites could have been seen off. In fact, Whitton believes he was lucky to get as far as he did. Murdoch hated the abortion story, writing from London to executive editor Neal Travis that he wanted no more of it. Travis told Whitton years later that he had stuck the memo in a drawer. Whitton was momentarily piqued. 'The freedom of the press wasn't fought for to make proprietors rich', he declaimed. 'You're wrong about that, you know', replied Travis drolly.

So for all their inky lumbering, the big papers were now mattering more and more, and these were now united in their criticisms of the appointment of a policeman to investigate the police. They advocated law reform; they called for a public inquiry; they ridiculed Rylah's efforts to keep a lid on the matter, by, for instance, having Wilby present his confidential report on Christmas Eve. They had done the government a lot of damage over Ronald Ryan—and Bolte and Rylah now feared a repeat. Catholic Jack Williams at the Herald & Weekly Times was unlikely in the long-term to tolerate sympathetic coverage of abortionists, but David Syme & Co managing director Ranald McDonald and *The Age* editor Graham Perkin were obvious pinkos. The Victorian government went to Christmas riding a media tiger with a growing appetite.

~

Throughout December, Wainer was trying to keep that tiger fed. The media could be fickle; Wainer strove to keep it interested. *Truth* ran stories concerning police officers promising to roll over and other doctors who might step forward. It also greeted Christmas with the front page screamer 'EX-NUN IN STRIP SCENE': after leaving a convent, a former nun was appearing in a play in King's Cross with nude scenes. How to compete?

One way was to bruit Wainer's political ambitions. He foreshadowed these early in December by placing an advertisement in *The Age* seeking like-minded souls interested in forming a political party, with the expectation of fielding candidates in the state election due the following April. Wainer's ideas did not begin and end with abortion: he wanted to run on a general 'clean up Victoria' platform. The response was prompt and promising, from university students to disaffected socialists, nature lovers to Bolte baiters: they would, early the following year, come together as Wainer's Progressive Reform Party.

One Wainer stunt, however, almost went badly wrong. On 23 December, a 'Mr Brett' called Wainer's surgery saying his girlfriend was pregnant. Mr Brett insisted that he would use an address he had for a backyard abortionist if he could not obtain a referral to a proper doctor. Wainer swapped a referral for the address: 377 Malvern Road, South Yarra was a flat-roofed, single-storey premises consisting of a small workshop and a front office rented by a 60-year-old Scottish insurance broker, Charles Gardiner. When Wainer called on him at 5.30 p.m. that afternoon, he was satisfied that Gardiner was suspicious, and cajoled Berman into keeping watch.

Things then went a little weird. According to Wainer, Berman accosted a Greek couple who had pulled up outside in their white Valiant station wagon, and who confirmed they were there for an abortion. Berman told them there had been a delay and that they should orbit the block for half an hour. When they returned at about 7.15 p.m., Wainer told Berman to ring the police, then five minutes later watched as 'three men emerged carrying bundles and ran up the street to waiting cars'. This and the delayed police response to his call he construed as proof of further protection for backyard abortionists. He detained the couple when they returned while he waited for the police, then let them go, although his taxi driver had already taken their and other licence plate numbers.

When testimony was heard on 'the Malvern Road Incident' a couple of months later, the evidence was less cut and dried. Gardiner testified that Wainer had peered round the door at 5.30 p.m. asking for a loan, but was apparently under the influence of alcohol. 'If he was sober I would have done business if I could', said Gardiner. 'He was incoherent, he was swaying and hanging on to the door.'

After buying some Christmas gifts across the road, Gardiner had left at 6 p.m. In response to the complaint, he was visited the next day by Detective-Sergeant John Baker, as was Wainer. Wainer initially declined to help. He said he had the licence plate of the Greek couple but would not divulge it, for fear they would be harassed by police. Then he apparently changed his mind, for Ford gave Baker a bunch of licence plate numbers on 29 December. The cars, however, checked out: everyone concerned had reason to be in the vicinity, or could not have been there, having probably been taken down incorrectly. And Angelo Yancos of Reservoir, the male of 'the Greek couple', denied that he had spoken to anyone, stating that he had come by Gardiner's premises to arrange some insurance cover for the stock of his electrical goods store over Christmas: he brought the four cover notes he had bought the next day. He also told the story of being raided on 19 January…by Michael Stewart and another member of The Untouchables. After ignoring some late-night phone calls, Yancos and his wife were woken by banging on their front door.

> I said, 'Look I can't let you in. It's twelve o'clock at night.' They said, 'Let us in. We want to talk to you…You can help us regarding the Malvern Road incident'…They said that Dr Wainer spoke to me and they wanted to know what he said and all that sort of thing. I said, 'Dr Wainer? What are you talking about? I do not know anything about this.' He said, 'You had a woman to get aborted'. I said, 'What woman? That was my wife.' He said, 'Was it your wife?' They were surprised. After a chat at the door they wanted to use the telephone so I let them and they were talking to someone by the name of Charles or something, I do not know. Then they handed the receiver to me and said, 'Talk to Dr Wainer'. I said: 'Get out of my house.'

The police were slow to react to Wainer's call, although Wainer had also been slow to make it, and as an investigation it was a shambles, laying Wainer open to the same charge of harassment that he had levelled at police. Berman would give only equivocal testimony about the incident, failing to corroborate Wainer's claim of sudden activity behind the premises, and would omit it from her autobiography altogether. The taxi driver was forgetful and disorganised. Another witness, who had arrived with Wainer, left too early to see anything of significance. There were actually a variety of other explanations for the evening's events—including that Wainer had been set up by the mysterious Mr Brett.

Nonetheless, Wainer added 'the Malvern Road Incident' to a new series of allegations he made when further unsworn statements were taken from Berman, Troup, Fenton Bowen and Young at Caroline Street on Friday 2 January 1970. The bulk of the material, he thought, would be sufficient to force the government's hand. Indeed, he had amassed so much that when he solicited the interest of *The Age*, reporter Kevin Childs promptly requested support from his office. 'You'll have to send someone down to help', he told his chief-of-staff. 'Otherwise it'll take weeks.' The bulk did the trick. When cabinet discussed his latest salvo on the Monday morning, they concluded they could stall no longer. A meeting of the Executive Council—Rylah, Governor Sir Rohan Delacombe, Attorney-General George Reid and public works minister Murray Porter—took just eight minutes to constitute a 'Board for the purpose of inquiring and reporting ... by all lawful means whatsoever' into police corruption 'connected with illegal abortion practices in Victoria'.

'See you in hell, sweetie'

'Get a pencil,' he ordered. He was going to give her a telephone number. He was going to give her the telephone number of the only man in Los Angeles County who did clean work.
'Then we'll see... I'm not promising anything,' he said.
Play It as It Lays (1970), Joan Didion

Although telephone conversations between Jack Ford and Peggy Berman in the last weeks of 1969 provided little of evidential significance, Berman mechanically recorded them anyway—a seemingly endless loop of anger and recrimination. When Berman wished him a happy Christmas, Ford recoiled in horror.

Ford: You have my full assurance that I'll have a beautiful Christmas. I have the full assurance that I'll be out of here in a couple of days and I have the full assurance that I'm finished. The full assurance that my family are ruined... my old father and everybody. Not because I did anything wrong but because I tried to help you. That's all I've got, a full assurance that my life is finished, thank you very much.

Berman: Darling, are you blaming me?

Ford: Well yes, you bred Wainer. You have told him these things.

Berman: I did not breed Wainer... Everyone breeds Wainer. The system breeds Wainer.

When Ford wished Berman a happy new year, she retaliated.

Berman: You just want me to go to jail in February and in your own sadistic fashion wish me a happy new year.

Ford: I don't want you to go to jail at all.

Berman: Well, why did you take the money for two and a half years and then not do anything?

Ford: I did not take the money for two and a half years and I did try and help you.

When Berman offered her love, Ford became incandescent with rage.

> Ford: With somebody like you to love me I don't need anyone to hate me. Goodbye.
>
> Berman: I didn't do anything like...
>
> Ford: You have crucified me and you have done it in the most vicious way...and he [Wainer] is a fucking liar. I'll give him something for his corner in the witness box.

Ford was particularly incensed at the allegation he had agreed to the deal mooted at Albert Park in September, insisting he had rejected Wainer's proposition. When Berman quoted Wainer credulously, he sneered: 'See you in hell, sweetie'. But first, they had a date in the Twelfth Court of Melbourne's new County Court on William Street, where representatives were foregathering of the *Board of Inquiry into Allegations of Police Corruption in Connection with Illegal Abortion Practices in the State of Victoria.*

Nowadays, inquiries have been routinised; in Henry Bolte's Victoria, they were uncommon, and the commission of William Kaye QC was generally unwelcome. Kaye was vice-chairman of Victoria's Bar Council—twenty-four years at the bar, eight as a silk, and a safe pair of hands: shrewd, severe, sometimes censorious, with little patience for unorthodoxies and irreverence. One day he was hearing a case in a courtroom occasionally visited by a rat that scuttled along the top of the judge's canopy. Kaye had been rubbing Bill Nettlefold QC the wrong way all day when the rat made a well-timed appearance. Nettlefold pointed weightily to the bench: 'Ladies and gentlemen of the jury, there is a *rat* up there'. Kaye was on the point of declaring the silk in contempt when he was informed that the remark was, strictly speaking, true: many barristers envied Nettlefold his opportunity.

Kaye's counsel assisting was the unmistakable Jack Winneke, still as gangling and rangy as when he had played fifty games for the Hawthorn Football Club, before retiring in favour of the law. Winneke's instructing solicitor was Garry Trollope of Blake & Riggall; the inquiry secretary was Howard Race from the Crown Law Department; and that, a few stenographers aside, was that. Winneke recalls:

> Bolte hated inquiries, said you never knew where they were going to lead. He agreed very reluctantly, and he was pretty keen to get it over

with. So we just dragged ourselves along by our own bootstraps. He may have felt Bill was the sort of bloke who could keep a lid on things. In fact, I think they probably made a mistake, because Bill was very thorough, wanted to chase every rabbit down every burrow.

The novelty of inquiries had another effect. The affair was covered in voluminous detail in *The Age*, *Sun* and *Herald*. The Kaye Inquiry led *The Herald* virtually every afternoon, identified by the medically explicit motif 'Abortion Probe'. In fact, this was somewhat misleading, because the proceedings examined abortion almost by the way: this was an investigation of police graft. And here was an opportunity squandered. Not a single patient was heard from. The reasons abortions were sought went unaddressed. The place of abortion in the *Crimes Act* went undebated. A mainly female predicament was argued over in an exclusively male forum. There was not a single woman at the overpopulated bar table, and the women who constituted just twenty-one of the inquiry's 140 witnesses were left isolated and exposed. Maureen Twisse broke down during her examination and cried for more than a minute amid embarrassed silence.

Nonetheless, among the women was the show-stopper: Peggy Berman, Victoria's most infamous woman, withstood thirty-four hours of questions, nearly a tenth of the total. She was vigilantly protected by her counsel, Bob Vernon. But for a witness whose lawyers had claimed could be killed by the strain of a protracted trial, she was incomparably resilient, cheerfully confirming her affair with Ford.

Winneke: During the period of time following your initial contact with him what sort of relationship have you had with him?

Berman: The relationship did develop into a personal relationship.

Winneke: What sort of personal relationship specifically? Did it develop into a sexual affair?

Berman: Yes.

Winneke: Does that mean that on occasions you had intercourse with him?

Berman: Yes it does indeed.

This was racy stuff in a state where Arthur Rylah railed against the 'flood of filthy literature' and demanded 'an alternative to sex in the lives of our children and in the lives of the community'. There was never a dull moment as Berman described the fear she felt of her law-crossed lover.

Winneke: What were you afraid that he would do? What was your fear of him?

Berman: He was a very strange personality.

Winneke: A lot of men are strange personalities and a lot of women are strange personalities too. What was it about his personality that made you afraid of Ford?

Berman: He is known in the underworld.

Winneke: I want to know what *you* thought.

Berman: He said to me once that—I did not know how to handle this—that you want to be like a snake. The snake licks its victim all over and then swallows it.

When Ford and Berman were pitted against one another, it was like eavesdropping on a private conversation.

Ford: You were quite friendly towards me in 1962–3, weren't you?

Berman: I don't follow the question.

Ford: You were in love with me at this time, weren't you?

Berman: It doesn't always mean the same thing.

Ford: Never mind that, you were in love with me.

Berman: Yes.

Ford: In 1964 I went to America. Do you remember that?

Berman: Yes.

Ford: Do you remember writing to me in America?

Berman: Yes.

Ford: Were you frightened of me then?

Berman: Yes.

Ford, like colleagues Martin Jacobson, Ron Jackson, Charles Petty, Gordon Timmins and eventually Jack Matthews, elected to represent himself at the inquiry, arriving daily hefting a Gladstone bag of documents. It was a mistake. Not simply was it a case of the legal maxim that the man representing himself has a fool for a client, but Ford was angry, and it showed. Accustomed to police interrogations where he made the rules, he clashed constantly with Kaye. The only thing that cheered him was that his nemesis Wainer was having the same trouble.

~

Wainer had to remind himself every now and again that he was still a doctor, for he hardly ever seemed to do any doctoring anymore. When not in the grip of the law, he was obsessed with politics. The Progressive Reform Party first met on 5 February 1970, where proposals were heard for seven different branches, the first sallies were made at a constitution, and a donation of $1000 towards expenses was received from Dr William Fenton Bowen. Wainer was at his charismatic best, delegating roles, philosophising extempore. Away from the limelight, he was more troubled, confiding in new party colleagues George Hardy and Ted Dugdale about his straitened financial circumstances. They proposed a means of keeping their new leader afloat: the 'B. B. Wainer Trust Account', registered at the ES & A Bank in Swanston Street, would solicit donations to 'support a brave man', with the aim of raising $1 each from 50 000 people.

At the inquiry, Wainer was also receiving rather less respect than he thought his due. He had originally seen himself as a kind of co-prosecutor, rather elaborately presenting Winneke with his credentials.

> At my first meeting with Winneke I offered him certain articles: an article, published in the *Australian Army Journal*, written by me; a research article on malaria; a photograph of myself taken at the passing-out parade of the Queensland Police Cadets; a letter from the Queensland Police Public Relations Department which stated that during the years I had spent in Queensland I had been a close friend of the police and always welcome in the Police Club; a photograph of myself conducting the then Minister for the Army, Dr Forbes, around an Army Hospital and a letter from Major-General Colin Gurner in which he stated that until 1966 I had commanded two large units in the Australian Army and had been responsible for stores of a value in excess of one million dollars.

It was a well-meant but clumsy gesture. Winneke, wary of Wainer's political ambitions, perused the offerings and returned them tersely: 'These won't be required'. In the witness box, Wainer came across as quick to allege but slow to prove, which did not endear him to the acerbic Kaye. The inquiry pored fruitlessly over 'the Malvern Road

Incident' and complaints of police inaction in the case of Frances Davidson. But what chiefly antagonised Kaye was Wainer's demeanour, on which he lavished an uncharacteristically colourful passage of his final report.

> Certain characteristics displayed by Dr Wainer while he occupied the witness box did not commend him as one upon whose testimony unqualified reliance could be placed. His behaviour, particularly on Monday morning 23 February, was extraordinary. He appeared to be struggling with sleepiness and heavy with malaise. His eyes were discoloured, his speech was weak and slightly slurred, and at times, while seated, he supported himself by both arms stretched along the top of the witness box. Yet there were moments when he rose to his feet expressing answers with clarity and undue vehemence.

The inference of drunkenness caused Kaye to dwell on an incident in Wainer's past. On the night of 28 January 1966, Wainer had been breathalysed in Beaumaris and charged with drunk driving, shop breaking and stealing—for somewhere on his path, he had made off with an iron from a shop he'd broken into. Wainer had blamed the happening on medication, been fined and given a bond, and there was an element of spite in Kaye raising the embarrassment four years later. Wainer, though, allowed himself to be riled, thundering that the whole thing was 'trivial'. Kaye began: 'Is that your considered opinion, Dr Wainer, of the moral propriety of what you were alleged to have done—broken a shop window and…' Momentarily shaking off his lassitude, Wainer jumped to his feet. 'I think it is absurd to hear things like this pertaining to a $4 iron when I was obviously ill', he stormed. 'I have never heard anything so farcical in my life.' Kaye glowered: 'Is that the best you can do doctor?'

The other doctors in the inquiry cut figures less impressive still. The inquiry's penalties for non-appearance of witnesses were paltry fines under the *Evidence Act*, and even those who turned up could not be compelled to testify. Kaye allowed them to answer questions in camera, but Ken Davidson, Max Sizeland, Peter Bayliss, Lister Catchlove, Rod Bretherton, Billy Flynn and John Levin all avoided summonses until the very last moment, and John Heath refused to answer questions at all. Fenton Bowen, whom Winneke privately thought 'ga-ga', disowned his own affidavit: 'It was very amateurish.

Words were thrown at me . . . Dr Wainer was telling me what to say and Mr Wyatt'. Bretherton even had the nerve to sue Winneke for defamation. Winneke recalls:

> One thing I was really concerned about was making allegations in a public forum that I didn't know were right or wrong. I told Bill: 'Look, I'm very worried about this. We have no protection.' He said: 'We've just got to get in and do it.'
>
> The day after I opened the inquiry I got a writ from Bretherton for saying he'd bribed the police, when really I hadn't a clue. I was simply going on what Peggy Berman had told us. Basically I was alleging he had committed a number of criminal offences, and couldn't claim the defence of truth because I was simply repeating somebody else's allegations.
>
> I remember the process server arriving and saying: 'Can you tell me where Mr Winneke is?' I say: 'That's me.' And he hands me the writ. Then he says: 'Can you tell me where I can find Bill Kaye? I laugh and I say: 'Oh I most certainly can.' So I knock on Bill's door and tell him: 'Hey Bill, I've got a friend here.'

As allegations grew wilder and woollier, Kaye and Winneke grew tenser. Charlie Wyatt represented himself when his celebrity counsel, Frank Galbally, went to appear for celebrity client Wilfred Burchett in Noumea—and none too well. 'He was a real bloody no-hoper who you wouldn't trust in a fit', recalls Winneke. 'A cop gone bad and a real sleazy bloke, too.' In Wyatt's favour was that he admitted being an abortionist, basically because he had to in order to exact revenge on Matthews. The trouble was that this proved him a liar, for he had just denied it to the bankruptcy registrar. In other words, to believe Wyatt now, you had to assume he had mended a lifetime's ways overnight. Wyatt's credibility was particularly shaken by Jean Field, who had initially described paying protection money for many years to Superintendent Charles Petty, but who then said that Wyatt had put her up to the allegation. When Wyatt retaliated by claiming she was angry because he had denied her sexual favours, she seethed: 'How wicked can you get? You are an animal'. Kaye snapped: 'Unless you [Wyatt] have something to substantiate, I don't want to hear any more'.

Ultimately, the witness who had done more than anybody to bring the inquiry about was regarded with acute scepticism, while it was a witness for whom nobody had much time who made the difference. Jim Troup had always appeared a slightly ridiculous figure, with his cash fetish and sartorial affectations: he attended the inquiry with a rudimentary pager on his belt that never seemed to ring. Yet in the stand he proved poised and persuasive, waiving the offer of in-camera privileges, while not obviously striving to show himself in a favourable light. 'Troup was unusual', says Winneke. 'Didn't have an obvious axe to grind. Seemed to be doing his best to tell the truth. I admired him because he didn't make a fuss.' Troup's quiet but firm support lent Berman's testimony a credibility it might not otherwise have enjoyed, for in these times a little calm went a long way. Bruce Hanford recalls:

> As journalists, we had hot shit coming through the telephone every day. Everyone wanted to talk. Charlie Wyatt was telling us these incredible stories. I kept having to remind myself: 'The uncorroborated testimony of an accomplice is not evidence.' Because in this environment it was very easy to freak out. Like Lionel did.

~

Twenty-three-year-old Lionel Pugh was a young man in a hurry, albeit without a destination. He was freckle-faced, fast-talking and flippant, and hankered to make his mark; he just wasn't sure how. Unseated as editor of Melbourne University's *Farrago* by the charismatic Pete Steedman, he tried out his social concerns on *The Australian*, sending them a long account of his work with the Student Anti-Hanging Committee. 'REPRIEVE RYAN', read their reply. 'HANG PUGH.' *The Australian* later took him on, and he showed the nerve and vitality of a good reporter in the making. But his persona, like his cravat, was self-conscious.

In particular, Pugh became profoundly upset when his sometime girlfriend, ALRA secretary Jo Richardson, first declined his proposal of marriage, then began withdrawing from their relationship. To revive Pugh's spirits, Jo introduced the raw reporter to the activist doctor. The meeting of minds seemed momentous. Pugh became a member of Wainer's ersatz Praetorian Guard, The Untouchables, undertaking such tasks as driving the doctor's Daimler round of an evening to confuse anyone following him. Nobody was more stalwart; perhaps nobody was acting out of such confused impulses. In the second half of 1969, Pugh moved into the Walsh Street house that Jo shared with her sister, Susan. But when Jo reiterated that she had no wish to reunite, and in fact would shortly move to Sydney with the ABC, he became inconsolable. He made a will, appointing Susan his executrix. He failed Economics A for the third time, jeopardising his university enrolment. He lost his licence for dangerous driving, and for refusing to give his name and address to police. He resigned from *The Australian*, was taken back, resigned again to accept an offer from the *Sunday Observer*, then saw that offer withdrawn. Susan found him 'very bitter, disillusioned and cynical about prospects for the future'. She also found him falling out of love with his mentor and, for unknown reasons, reacting 'strongly against Wainer to the extent of being hostile towards him'.

Finally, Pugh obtained a part-time position in the ABC newsroom. However, when he attended the Kaye Inquiry on 20 February, he was shocked to hear Wainer describe him as an associate, and anguished about the ethical implications. He quixotically wrote a resignation letter, although he does not seem to have sent it, requesting rather that he be reassigned. Nor did he send Jo two deeply loving letters also betraying his disillusionment: 'I am inclined to think that idealism, recognised as so desirable in our circle is little more than the hope of attaining self-gratification'.

At a Progressive Reform Party meeting on 1 March, Wainer foreshadowed his plan to run against Arthur Rylah himself in the blue-ribbon Liberal seat of Kew, pitting his party's best asset against the government's worst liability. There was concern about another decision to make the party eponymous: 'Dr Wainer's Progressive Reform Party'. It didn't sound like the participatory democracy the party had originally espoused. But when one member stated the obvious—'This party *is* Dr Wainer'—it was hard to demur. Some had been wary of Wainer's association with The Untouchables; this consent may have been a means of securing his commitment.

Pugh wasn't at the announcement. A couple of nights later he rang Geoff Hjorth, Sue Richardson's boyfriend and a party member, asking for the return of a borrowed shotgun. When Hjorth arrived, Pugh suggested they go to the nearby Harp Hotel, from where he rang Jo on a payphone at 9 p.m., saying that he still loved her and didn't want to live without her; the conversation ended inconclusively. With Hjorth, though, Pugh seemed his usual self, and he piled into a taxi when they parted about 2.30 a.m. Four hours later, in secluded parkland on Parkville's Gatehouse Street, Pugh was found dead, sprawled on his back with a gunshot wound in the chest, shotgun barrel nestled in his lap, cravat still tight around his neck.

Wainer suspected foul play, arguing that Pugh's arms were too short to have reached the trigger and discharged the fatal shot. But he did not come forward at the inquest, where measurements and photographs by the investigating officer suggested otherwise, and where the coroner found that Pugh died from 'the effects of a gunshot wound to the body inflicted by a gun under his control and management'; nor, although it is dedicated to Pugh, did Wainer elaborate on these suspicions in his autobiography. If assassins *did* wish to stop Pugh and authorities *did* wish to conceal this, furthermore, they chose their target uncommonly well, for his lovelorn letters and maudlin moods in the preceding few months scarcely made suicide an impossibility. 'Lionel wanted to be good', says Whitton. 'He just wasn't very good at it.' In that sense, in this story he is far from alone.

~

If not a pyrrhic victory for Wainer, the Kaye Inquiry took its toll. In particular, he suffered a second mild coronary occlusion on 13 March and was hospitalised for three weeks. While he was out of action, the inquiry, heading towards a total of three million words, seemed simply to be growing longer rather than deeper. And the same was true of the constitution of the Progressive Reform Party, which was fast becoming a mishmash of vaguenesses. Its education policy was to 'offer children the opportunity to develop in their own way in their own time', and its development policy was to shun 'flat erection, suburban sprawl, high-rise hideousness'. It demanded additional tests for every driver who intended exceeding 35 m.p.h. (56 km/h), and agreement on a 60 m.p.h. (96 km/h) maximum speed for all cars. Wainer then refused to allocate preferences, decrying such deals as 'political expediency'. Several hundred people attended Wainer's address at Melbourne University on 24 May; his decision would deprive their votes of a good deal of their impact.

The inquiry hearings ended two days before the state election, with Winneke savaging Wainer at length in his final address as a 'grandstander' who sent police on 'fishing expeditions': *The Herald*'s headline was 'WAINER IS DISCREDITED'. Not, however, where it mattered: he attracted not quite 10 per cent of the vote in Kew, and Rylah's vote shrank almost a third. The party's other candidates fared less well, but Wainer had the authority to deflect complaints about the party's indifference to preferences: to exchange preferences, he insisted, would be to 'damn ourselves in the eyes of the community' and 'lose the vote of the young, enlightened virile voters'.

At the party's election post-mortem, Wainer also divulged more about his personal circumstances. 'I have been advised that I should go bankrupt', said Wainer. 'This will scotch certain ideas that I have made a lot of money out of abortions and will enlist public sympathy.' Whether or not he invited it, his affairs nosedived soon after. A week later, he was served with an eviction notice on his surgery, where he was six months behind in the rent. His Daimler was repossessed. Banks foreclosed on his small but dearly loved block of land at Lakes Entrance. He was by now living mainly on the trust account that the party had established for him, which never met projections but provided $850 between April 1970 and June 1971.

Wainer was increasingly obsessed with writing 'the book', by which he would vindicate himself. He insisted on the party remaining independent, but also wanted that right for himself. Deputy leader George Hardy was alarmed.

> Hardy: Whatever you do is connected with the party—whatever you do *is* the party.
>
> Wainer: We must work towards the point where this is not necessary.
>
> Hardy: We need more members—members who are prepared to think and work.
>
> Wainer: We must not sacrifice our identity for the sake of becoming a popular party.

Wainer seems to have decided unilaterally that the dream was dead, that what he wanted was not so much an alternative political force as The Untouchables redux. He saw poor attendance at the annual meeting at Melbourne University as confirmation.

> I am feeling rather a flop. In February, 500 people turned up to the meeting at this university. Tonight there are only about 40...At the request of the party I disbanded the Untouchables. I think this was a

> grave mistake. I feel we are now too ineffectual to play any part in the political scene in Victoria... I would prefer to act as an individual rather than as a member of [the] Progressive Reform Party which is just putting forth a lot of hot air. I had the idea of rallying people round me who had the same ideas. I don't want to be a member of a conventional political party. Are you with me or not?

Little wonder that members decided to adjourn and heckle a DLP meeting nearby. Hardy was not replaced when he resigned in frustration soon after. And, although it survived a while in name, the party was effectively over.

~

There was always action aplenty around Wainer at this time. For Wainer was now not just famous but a poster child of the protest movement, bracketed with the likes of *Oz* editor Richard Neville and Monash Maoist Albert Langer, even if he perhaps more closely resembled *un homme sérieux* like Jim Cairns—indeed, he would shortly march alongside Cairns in Melbourne's Vietnam Moratorium rally. Like Cairns, too, who was attacked and badly beaten by gate-crashers at an ALP fundraiser at the end of August 1969, he would have to live with threats to his safety. Wainer had the momentary satisfaction on 15 September 1970 of sitting in the Parliament House public gallery as Rylah enumerated Bill Kaye's recommendations, including charges against Matthews, Ford, Adam and Jacobson. But the next night, a petrol bomb was lobbed into his sister's house, causing serious damage. Jo Richardson had returned from Sydney, and he moved into her share house in Walsh Street, South Yarra.

While the Taxation Department bankrupted him by day, Wainer wrote by night. He also commenced a relationship with Jo that would last the rest of his life, one that began with a fugitive feel. One night, for example, Wainer emerged from Walsh Street to find two men with their heads beneath the hood of Jo's car. They met the onrushing doctor with a cosh that fractured his cheekbone and left him bearing a vivid scar. Anxious about his safety, Wainer admitted to his circle a bodyguard cum detective, Tom Eriksen. Eriksen purported to specialise in protection, never travelled unarmed and always affected quasi-uniformed authority; he would later be prosecuted for impersonating a policeman. In April 1971, when there were rumours of a threat to Wainer, Eriksen had Walsh Street ringed by twelve armed men with rifles and batons. Jo found Eriksen as scary as any threat he might have stared down.

> I've met very few evil people in my life but he was one. A horrible man with this tiny wife that he bullied, and had five children with... He offered Bert his protective services and Bert took them, but it was almost like they were spying on each other.

To extract himself from this contracting world, Wainer travelled to East Pakistan to take stock of its border war with India. He wrote a long, detailed and frankly unpublishable account of his time there, but felt better for the freedom, and elected on his return to quit Melbourne. After a few months as a locum in Portland, he learned that Caloundra in Queensland was seeking a doctor to run its fourteen-bed hospital, built as an election promise five years earlier and never used. Wainer's application caused a fuss, with the state's health and police ministers vying for the opportunity to reject it: he fooled both by electing to work as a GP instead. Towing a trailer behind her Volkswagen, Jo began the long drive north with Wainer, sons Rory and Dirk, and Flash, the family dog.

The drive itself was therapeutic. At about 8 p.m., on the freeway near Newcastle, they heard an insistent tooting behind them. They accelerated fearfully, but it proved to be a wharfie trying to flag them down. 'You know you've been losing things all the way down the freeway?' he said. 'I've been picking them up.' Judging them in need of rest, the man took them into his own family home for the night, and helped them repack the trailer before sending them on their way with a hearty breakfast. 'We'd forgotten humans were capable of such great kindness', recalls Jo. Soon after arriving, Wainer fell ill with painful and incapacitating pancreatitis. But Eve Janover, who was working in a Brisbane hospital, again filled the breach, first as a locum, then as a partner. Wainer married Jo in November at Nambour.

The practice encountered little call for abortions in Caloundra at first; indeed, there seemed a somewhat different attitude to unwed expectancy. One day Wainer did a pregnancy test on a teenage girl and dolefully confirmed it was positive. Her eyes lit up. 'That's *fantastic*', she exulted. 'I've got him now.' Then, in January 1972, Wainer finished writing the manuscript he now called *It Isn't Nice*. Its release coincided with that of Peggy Berman's *Why Isn't She Dead!*, published by Gold Star, an imprint whose specialty was pornography. But where Berman's book was mostly backward looking, Wainer's mix of memoir and manifesto was clearly casting forward. He brought into his practice a South African, Dr Josh van Offdenbach, who did abortions on the quiet, and became involved with the Brisbane-based Children by Choice, which had opened a family planning clinic behind an old Red Hill shopfront amid familiar menaces. He was susceptible, therefore, to a phone call from Peter Bayliss.

Bayliss had become an increasingly rebarbative personality, estranged from his family by constant philandering. 'You spend all day looking up snatch', his lawyer Andrew Fraser once joked. 'Why do you spend all night chasing it?' Bayliss leered: 'Butchers are the biggest meat eaters'. Since his 1966 acquittal, he had nursed an outsized sense of invulnerability. He called his nominee company Nichevo (Russian for 'fuck off'), and boasted the motto *Nemo me impune lacessit* (Latin for 'No-one touches me with impunity'). Former comrade Sizeland had decided it was all too much: 'Peter was pestering me, saying things like "people who've suffered together should stay together". I finally said: "Look, why don't you join Wainer? There's all these people looking for abortions and they'll go to Wainer because it's the name they recognise"'. Bayliss justified the exercise to Wainer as 'unfinished business', while promising Wainer that he would only have to deal with 'front of house'. Although their relations had been strained by the Kaye Inquiry, Wainer agreed to come south for a few months to get him started.

Bayliss's brittle extraversion, however, was not up to the task. Gripped by nerves at the sight of his clinic on *This Day Tonight* and the front page of *The Age*, he abruptly sought to back out. Fortunately, Wainer thrived on the attention, and the scent of battle revived his inner warhorse. Arraigned before the Medical Board for acting 'so as to promote your professional advantage', he held his ground and escaped censure. Defamed by 3AW's Norman Banks, he sued and won. 'After that, Bert thought he was bulletproof', says Fraser. Above all, loath to return to Caloundra as a perceived failure, he pursued Bayliss's idea himself. Premises for the 'Fertility Control Clinic' in East Melbourne's Wellington Parade were spartan. In a building shared with unlikely tenants—the Liberal Party, Parents Without Partners, Alcoholics Anonymous and publisher Max Newton's porn empire—patients who could not find a bit of borrowed furniture sat in the hall. Bayliss did the work; Wainer took the brickbats and, as time passed, the bouquets too. Jo finally acknowledged that Wainer would not be returning to Caloundra and retraced her steps to Melbourne, where the clinic carried out 5400 procedures in its first two years. It was a new world—parts of it, anyway.

~

John Heath had not returned. After he was raided a second time in August 1970, the Crown applied to revoke his bail, and he was persuaded by his solicitor, John X Smith, to undertake not to practice until the trial ended. Then the jury deadlocked and a retrial was ordered; *that* jury had to be discharged because of prejudicial articles in *Truth* and an editorial in *The Age*. Seventy by the time his prosecution petered out, Heath felt unable to start again, and retired somewhat ingloriously. Sizeland finally felt sorry for his old mentor. 'I was upset when John was charged', he says. 'I'd say: "It's wrong. He's an old man. He's helped a lot of people". I remember someone saying to me: "It's not what he does; it's what he is". John always had a reputation for avarice.' The Hoddle Street defendants, meanwhile, were finally winnowed to three—Troup, Berman and Young—on one charge. The prosecution, sick of the matter, offered the trio a choice of judge in return for a guilty plea, and liberal-minded Justice Leo Dethbridge handed out bonds and fines. Troup spent only a year off the medical register before moving to Mildura in December 1971 to run a clinic.

Otherwise, it was a bit like The Who's new single: 'Meet the new boss/Same as the old boss'. Many of the same practitioners kept on keeping on, now with the reassurance of the Menhennitt Ruling, and without the distraction of police graft. Like Troup, Fenton Bowen regained his medical registration. Bretherton, Sizeland and Catchlove flourished. Davidson married the sister of the junior counsel in *R v Davidson* and they had two sons. Some practitioners did not outgrow old habits: Bayliss and Buchanan continued to be the subject of complaints for carelessness and overcharging, and Wainer eventually formed an alliance with Dr John Levin; and not for forty years would the law catch up with Mario Marchesani, when he was convicted of exchanging shots of pethidine and morphine for sexual favours from drug-addicted prostitutes. Yet, while the practitioners were mainly the same, the power dynamic *had* begun changing. An anonymous letter to *The Digger* in January 1973 had the nerve to condemn Wainer's works on the basis of Bayliss's obnoxiousness.

> I don't think his [Wainer's] set-up is a 'service' at all since in my personal experience he withholds information on available abortionists and refers everyone wanting an abortion to only one guy, who is apparently a masterful surgeon but, as I found and Wainer later admitted, an arrogant and inhuman cunt! On top of this you suffer the rude and superior attitude of this guy's nurse and in my case wait for nearly three hours after the appointed time…
>
> I found Wainer's surgeon such an unfeeling and arrogant bastard that I left his place five minutes after being with him, upset and crying. I returned to Wainer's place where his objectionable receptionist had delight in telling me that I'd blown it by walking out of the surgeon's place and there was no-one else in the whole of Melbourne who was performing abortions. Wainer repeated the same information and only after my insistence that this couldn't be so and a further flood of tears would he divulge alternatives to his pig surgeon.

The letter embarrassed Wainer and was partly responsible for his estrangement from ALRA. But it and similar complaints were also grounds for optimism. There are no means of recourse in an illegal system, no protections for the unwary. The doctor was still powerful, but no longer all-powerful, and by now the dynamic was changing all over Australia.

Epilogue
'The choice for me'

It's over. Feel better?
Surfacing (1972), Margaret Atwood

When abortion law yielded to the siege laid on it, the citadel was found strangely deserted. As *R v Davidson* commenced in May 1969, abortion was illegal everywhere. Within two years, three-quarters of Australia's population could contemplate abortion knowing that they need not become criminals in the process. In South Australia, the *Criminal Law Consolidation Amendment Act*, passed by both houses in December 1969 on the initiative of Steele Hall's Liberal/National coalition, actually insinuated the Menhennitt Ruling's principles into the statutes. Abortion was permissible if more risk to the pregnant woman's physical or mental health would be posed by continuing rather than terminating the pregnancy, or in the event of substantial risk that the child would be seriously handicapped. The legislation, brainchild of Attorney-General Robin Millhouse, with the assistance of the local branch of the Australian Medical Association, stopped short of so-called 'abortion on demand'—to counteract the fear that South Australia would become to abortion as Nevada to divorce, it included a two-month residential requirement, the abortion had to be performed in a prescribed hospital, and required the approval of two doctors. But, in a skilful piece of undersalesmanship, advocates stressed its evolutionary rather than revolutionary nature. 'The Act codifies what we have been doing for years', said local AMA president JR Margarey. 'It really doesn't do a great deal more than that.' It was bolder law-making than anyone desired to admit.

The ramparts of New South Wales looked taller and steeper. Doctors and police were earning too much money; politicians saw too few benefits from reform. In February 1970, Premier Robert Askin stressed: 'Several years ago I gave church leaders an assurance that I would not tinker with the laws on abortion and homosexuality [and]... there will be no change by any government I have the honour to lead'. He boasted of a full-time squad of twenty-seven officers policing abortion—how great was their personal rake-off is anybody's guess. As Jeannie Dempsey recounted, abortion was widespread and its secrets open.

> The address was...in a block of flats in Maroubra. I hopped in a taxi and said the address and the taxi driver turned around and gave this sneer, and I thought: 'He knows. If taxi drivers know, police know. Wainer busts were nothing...Here I go, front page of the paper again'.

The front page was nearer than imagined. In March 1970, the ABC's *Four Corners* screened a detailed investigation of Sydney's abortion trade, as part of which they invited Chief Commissioner Norman Allan to appear. When he responded blankly to the question of whether abortionists operated in Sydney, film was screened of a surgery operating just a block from the Police Administration Centre. A crackdown commenced, reputedly starting with those services that refused to pay graft, among them the Heatherbrae Clinic in Curlewis Street, Bondi, which was raided at 9 a.m. on 11 May 1970. A 37-year-old single woman from Newcastle awoke on the operating table to find 'a lot of noise and men taking photos'. Multiple charges were laid.

Yet juries in New South Wales were as reluctant to convict as those in Victoria. In Newcastle Quarter Sessions on 27 October 1970, for example, Dr John Stephen and nurse Rose Wallace were acquitted of aborting a 17-year-old girl. They actually admitted to the procedure, but claimed in defence that the girl's immaturity and hypertension rendered continuation of the pregnancy a mental and physical risk. Stephen, a government medical officer from a family of distinguished doctors, made an impressive defendant. 'I believe any pregnancy could have killed this girl', he stated. When the Heatherbrae defendants appeared in the District Court the following year, they were fortunate to come before liberal-minded Justice Aaron Levine, best known for sparing the mischief-makers of *Oz* magazine a jail term on obscenity charges; he had also been the judge in the case of the tragic abortion death of Jennifer Kirkwood. Now he assimilated the Menhennitt Ruling by allowing for legal abortion in the instance of 'serious danger to the pregnant woman's life or to her physical or mental health', extending it to allow for those dangers to be 'any economic, social or medical ground or reason' arising at any time during the pregnancy, albeit with the restriction that the abortion had to be performed by a medical practitioner.

In retrospect, this was remarkably orderly. The late 1960s and early 1970s are remembered as an era of protest. But there were no abortion suffragettes, no conscientious abortion objectors. The marchers who menaced the Supreme Court during *R v Davidson* were protesting the persecution of Clarrie O'Shea, not demanding respect for *R v Bourne*. Even Bert Wainer, though he urgently courted it, was never arrested. The crowd that watched Wainer ascend the steps of Russell Street police headquarters to confess his first test case abortion was there to support Rodney Bretherton, and was hardly in uproar: the protestor who appeared on the front page of next day's *Age* was not a flower child or a wild-eyed firebrand but a spherical Prahran clergyman whose placard read 'Reform in England—Why Not Here?' Other displays of civil disobedience were also muted. Thirty women staged a 'quiet and orderly' demonstration at the committal of the Heatherbrae defendants on 1 June 1970; the twenty women wearing tunics reading 'Abortion on Request' who attended the appearance of Dr Isidor Ackerman on abortion charges on 15 December 1970 left when asked.

Why was this? Abortion sat ill with the masculine accent and often ludic intent of the 'protest movement'. 'Anything can be made into an issue', promised *Oz* editor Richard Neville in his protest manual *Playpower*. 'An irritating state occasion, the awkward presence of a police car, the untimely sacking of a university lecturer. All can provide pretext for a youthful show of force.' But what was playful about abortion? If anything, it invited the aspersion on the permissive society that it begat more unplanned pregnancies and diminished sense of male responsibility. This was a generation keen on lampooning all hypocrisies—except its own.

At least in its initial stages, too, most of the pro-choice campaign's chief protagonists were men—it was perhaps the last exercise in female emancipation in Australia where this was so. At its inception, for instance, ALRA's Victorian patrons included only one woman (Lady

Janet Clunies-Ross) among five men (Bishop Felix Arnott, Rev. John Westerman, Rabbi Dr Saenger, and Professors Norval Morris and Roderick Andrew), while its expert committee was all-male (Professors Carl Wood and Peter Brett, Doctors Stan Gold and Sam Benwell). The women were in the main well educated, socially privileged and/or, in the case of Faust, highly intelligent; they were not the type to storm a court or egg a premier.

Not until Kate Millett's *Sexual Politics* reached Australia in 1971, arguing that heterosexual relations were political and governed by a 'theory of patriarchy', was the promotion of 'women's issues' perceived as the prerogative of women, and did collectives like the Women's Action Committee in Melbourne and Women's Liberation in Sydney lend a militant edge to pro-choice polemics. Abortion then became almost a feminist rite of passage—Germaine Greer famously skipping down the street after hers—while reform-minded doctors began to seem anachronistic. 'Over time, the attitudes of my father and his peers caught up with them', notes Rod Bretherton's daughter, Di. 'By the time abortion became legal and there were opportunities to bring women into the practice, they didn't take them.' Even Wainer's relations with the new feminist establishment grew strained as his clinic faced harassment by the self-styled 'pro-life' movement. Where was his 'army of women'? he complained in 1985: 'When I was physically fighting the Right to Life Association outside this clinic, there were no feminists helping... Essentially I think this is because it's much easier to give lip service support only'.

The army of women were probably occupied elsewhere. For out of early experiences in the push to liberalise abortion came deeper understandings of the advancement of 'women's issues'. After encouraging Monash University medical students to solicit MPs' attitudes on abortion using the name 'Parliamentary Abortion Lobby', Faust conceived of a vehicle for organised feminist influence on the political process called the Women's Electoral Lobby (WEL), the inaugural meeting of which was held at her home in February 1972. After similar meetings round Australia, WEL members surveyed all 600 federal candidates for that year's election on a host of 'women's issues', with the results published in a lift-out in *The Age*. The least cooperative was a DLP candidate in Bennelong who threatened to throw his interlocutors out if they used the word 'sex' again; Gough

Whitlam vindicated his high score by removing luxury tax from the contraceptive pill, introducing paid maternity leave for public servants, and promoting benefits that enabled single mothers to keep their children. In April 1974, too, items covering abortion were included in the Medicare schedule.

Success in liberalising abortion also mobilised an oppositional movement. The forerunner to Right to Life, the Human Life Research Foundation, was petitioning Victorian parliamentarians within six months of the Menhennitt Ruling. Campaigners met early success in Western Australia when three private members' bills for the decriminalisation of abortion introduced by James Hislop, a flamboyant physician turned Liberal MLC, were defeated. But law was harder to undo than prevent. A bill which would have restricted abortion to cases of rape and serious foetal deformity in South Australia, introduced by a Labor Catholic, Terence McRae, was also defeated. The pro-life movement in Australia has been neither so ambitious nor so aggressive as that galvanised by the US Supreme Court decision of *Roe v Wade* in January 1973, which decided that the constitutional right to privacy was 'broad enough to encompass a woman's decision whether or not to terminate her pregnancy'. But it demonstrated political power five months later when Labor backbenchers David McKenzie (Diamond Valley) and Tony Lamb (Latrobe) tabled a Medical Practice Clarification Bill to legalise first-trimester abortions in the Australian Capital Territory. There being no female members in the House of Representatives, WEL erected a tent embassy outside in emulation of the Aboriginal outpost erected the year before. Right to Life, however, overshadowed the embassy with their own marquee, while three archbishops led prayers for the bill's defeat at Manuka's St Christopher's Cathedral, and a motion that the bill be read a second time was defeated ninety-eight to twenty-three. A year later, Right to Life presented its maiden manifesto to a 'Pro-Life Rally' in Treasury Gardens: 'Abortion . . . is not a question of private morality, but a civil rights question. The notion that a woman could have a private right to an abortion cannot be sustained without a complete denial of the child's inherent right to life'.

Yet, if a defeat on the day, 'McKenzie–Lamb' was a whetstone on which talents were sharpened. One key opinion former, having her first experience of serious lobbying, was a 28-year-old journalist. 'I felt I had been born to it', Anne Summers recalled. 'I was exhilarated by the intrigue, the organizing and the keeping tabs on the numbers.' She would be, inter alia, First Assistant Secretary of the Office of the Status of Women in the Hawke government. Giving her first public speech in the tent embassy was a 31-year-old WEL member. Susan Ryan, later the first woman to hold a cabinet post in a federal Labor administration, would recall the occasion as 'the official end, I suppose, of my Catholic status'. It was also soon an ironclad rule of abortion availability in Australia that publicity invited hostility. The public seemed content for abortion to continue quietly; they did not relish being reminded of unpleasant realities or less fortunate lives.

So it proved in Queensland, where Peter Bayliss put up his shingle at a clinic in Greenslopes in November 1979. An ABC report invited the wrath of Right to Life, then a retaliatory campaign by the new Women's Campaign for Abortion. Rumours of restrictive legislation were confirmed in April 1980 by the Liberal member for Salisbury, Rosemary Kyburz, who courageously divulged the contents of the mooted Unborn Child Protection Bill to the ABC's *AM*: abortion would be permissible only where a woman's death was imminent, with compulsory notification to the department of health; doctors, nurses, social welfare workers or even friends who helped a woman to obtain an abortion would face long jail sentences with hard labour. For this, she was vilified by loyalists of Premier Joh Bjelke-Petersen, like Des Frawley, MLA for Caboolture: 'Her outbursts have been those of a bitter, angry, frustrated woman who has shown herself to be emotionally unstable'. Yet polls suggested that Kyburz's concerns had majority support, and a modified bill was defeated at the second reading stage the following month.

Right to Life renewed their offensive on Greenslopes five years later, using a patient complaint about complications in her hysterectomy. Operation Lost Cause involved fifty-four policemen seizing records for 47 000 patients, and combing the premises with video cameras while plumbers searched the drains for foetal matter. Television cameras and news photographers, mysteriously tipped off, thronged the building, capturing images of the scatter of terrified women. Bayliss and anaesthetist Dawn Cullen were charged, and the District Court case was led by Director of Public Prosecutions Des Sturgess.

As with *R v Davidson*, however, prosecution had an equal and opposite effect. Ruling on the relevant section 282 of Queensland's *Criminal Code*, Justice Fred McGuire arrived at Menhennitt's position: for abortion to be legal, the doctor must believe on reasonable grounds that the operation was necessary to preserve the physical or mental health of the mother, and was not out of proportion to the danger to be averted. The jury acquitted after three hours. Bayliss relished the subsequent Fitzgerald Royal Commission, trailing a sign behind his private plane: 'Face It. Kev Hooper was Right' (Hooper was the opposition police spokesman who first alleged police corruption in 1977). He also unsuccessfully sued Sturgess, Attorney-General Nev Harper and detective Robert Cassidy for false imprisonment, malicious process, malicious prosecution and trespass.

Right to Life and its energetic president, Margaret Tighe, always exerted the most influence in Victoria, where its efforts were complemented from 1979 by Women Who Want to be Women, a broader conservative alliance run by mother of eight Babette Francis. Babette was married to Caulfield MLA Charles, and for a time the groups coveted direct political influence. Ila Vanrenen recalls the greeting of one delegate at a stormy meeting of the Liberal state council which defeated a motion that abortion was a matter for the individuals concerned: 'Hello Ila, you little murderer'. When Charles Hider decided to leave Monash in the upper house for Glenhuntly in the lower house in March 1979, he faced a concerted disinformation campaign: 'Don't Elect This Murderer' read the Right to Life how-to-vote card, tastefully covered in foetuses. Emboldened by success, Right to Life made an expensive attempt to run a candidate in Monbulk two years later, but the effort came to nought when Wainer himself ran at the last moment, attracting 11 per cent of the vote. The abortion debate was longer merely about ideas; it involved preventing the spread of the ideas of others.

~

Victorian lawmen implicated in the Kaye Inquiry slipped into ignominy. The trial of Matthews, Ford, Jacobson and Adam before Justice Starke in March and April 1971 traversed familiar terrain, albeit that the defendants looked rather less defiant than hitherto. Ford was still almost phosphorescent with anger. When Whitton came to watch a day of proceedings, the detective fixed him with a glare. Whitton began counting in his head, slowly—he reached fifteen before Ford finally looked away. But Adam, a florid, seedy 140 kilograms, was a far cry from 'Thumper', scourge of the cornered crook. Perhaps it is why the jury accepted such exchanges in the trial as:

> Norman O'Bryan [prosecutor]: Mr Adam, I understand that you have a nickname.
> Adam: Yes, I do.
> O'Bryan: Perhaps you'd like to share that nickname with the court?
> Adam: Honest Fred.

Adam went free, although he lived only another year; the rest were jailed. The conclusion satisfied nobody. Matthews, Ford and Jacobson were punished not so much because they were corrupt but because they had failed to deliver and been turned on by dissatisfied customers. Those more reliably corrupt, as it were, escaped. 'I honestly don't believe we knew a lot', admits Bruce Hanford. 'And the cops the system gave up…well, I think there were better cases for corruption against others. They certainly weren't the crookedest cops in the Victorian police.' Some now saw the police as scapegoats for political inaction, and even corruption higher up. One juror, Kew councillor Dorothy Buchanan, shared candid views with *Truth*:

> You see, nothing is in a separate compartment; it is all one big mess, you see. And X is right in the middle of it, right up to his dirty neck, and he has got so much to hide and of course to pay back by protection of these policemen that are doing the wrong thing by the community, you see, so it is a case of nothing for nothing.

The clear inference is that 'X' was Buchanan's local member, Rylah, against whom she had run as an independent in the same election as Wainer had represented the Progressive Reform Party. Rylah had just foreshadowed retirement from politics, and detractors were queuing to condemn him. Buchanan's interview became a ground for unavailing appeals by Ford and Matthews to the full court, followed by unsuccessful appeals for clemency to Attorney-General George Reid.

Jacobson was released after thirteen months from Ararat Jail, with remissions for behaving as a 'model prisoner'; Matthews and Ford emerged from D Division at Pentridge in August 1973 amid the glare of television cameras. Matthews went on to an improbable second career as consumer affairs writer for *Melbourne Observer*. Ford faded from view, still wondering how he had ended up on the wrong side of law he had dedicated himself body and soul to protecting: 'I know I should have been stronger. Then things could have been different'. And, though cleared of wrongdoing, mud stuck to The Dutchman, his dreams of higher office thwarted. 'Yes, the inquiry did hurt my career', Frank Holland complained on retiring in May 1975. 'For a start [chief commissioner] Noel Wilby told me straight out that he would not make me chief of CIB because of the fact I had been mentioned in the inquiry...Yes, it *did* hurt, I don't mind telling you.'

Yet, if investigations of police corruption scarcely delved deep enough, they went far further than those into medical corruption. It's arguable that the behaviour of doctors, in their rapacity and recklessness, was every bit as unconscionable as those of law enforcement officers. While the Australian Medical Association did the littlest possible, a cohort of medically qualified abortionists, unsupervised and unregulated, cornered a hugely lucrative market. Illegality served not the ends of morality but the needs of greed: as Wainer observed acidly, nobody ever met a poor abortionist. There are several possible explanations for the AMA's indifference, most damning of which is that everyone benefited: a sizeable proportion of Victorian GPs referred patients to abortionists in return for commissions. Assuming conservatively that about half the abortions in Victoria were the result of referrals and there was an average kickback of 20 per cent, GPs in the days of abortion's illegality were trousering between $1.5 million and $2.5 million annually for services rendered, at a time when their average earnings were about $11 000. Policemen's wads of $10 notes pale by comparison.

By his works in the late 1960s and early 1970s, Bertram Wainer won iconic status. He was thought headstrong, erratic, egotistical and self-serving—not without justification at times. But some of these same characteristics made him the kind of leader around whom people rallied. Political establishments were then less yielding, less diverse, less heedful of complaint. Wainer was a man of his time, a crash through or crash leader, whose very intractability was what made him effective.

Nonetheless, on his own medical establishment, Wainer was in hindsight rather gentle—perhaps rather too implicated. As he told Bert Vanrenen: 'We *all* do it'. His emphasis was on the 'all' but might well have fallen on the 'it'—that is, refer patients to doctors distinguished mainly by avarice and preparedness to break the law. What proportion of GPs checked that the abortion providers they served were competent and affordable? How many were influenced in their decision making by the size of the commission on offer? In *It Isn't Nice*, such questions went not just unanswered, but unaddressed.

Wainer's Fertility Control Clinic steadily became part of the landscape, distinguishable by the knot of protesters at its entrance, and the size of its mailbag. The Wainer papers are rich in testimonials, usually brief, mainly heartfelt: 'Although you won't remember me, I certainly will never forget your clinic for its warmth and understanding shown to me when I needed it most'. These are mixed with Right to Life agitprop, such as: 'Do you realize Satan has used you? Abortion is the abomination spoken of by the prophet Daniel'. Any veneer of civility washes off quickly: 'Thank you for your letter of the 17th of September. Its tone certainly assisted me in understanding a little of what makes a murderer!' The murderer by which the clinic is known, however, is Peter Knight, who arrived in July 2001 intending to destroy the building, and who shot security guard Steve Rogers before being overpowered—a hint of the pressures faced by American doctors who routinely arrive for work in bulletproof vests.

Wainer continued hankering for action, returning to the role of anti-corruption crusader as chief informant of the *Board of Inquiry Into Allegations Against Members of the Victorian Police Force* that Barry Beach QC was appointed to lead in March 1975. It was a costly business, again to the police's reputation, and again to Wainer's pocket, especially an ill-advised defamation suit against Police Association secretary Tom Rippon over remarks in an interview on *A Current Affair* in October 1976. By the time the suing was done in June 1979, Wainer faced a $51 436 legal bill from Haines, Blaikie & Polites, which he furiously and unavailingly disputed. Wainer died in January 1987, a week after his fifty-ninth birthday, but having packed enough living in for two lifetimes—a commanding, confronting, forthright and flawed figure around whom something always seemed about to happen when it wasn't already happening.

~

So it came to pass that abortion obtained de jure legality in Australia, even if, in the country's three most populous states, it remains a crime—that is to say, part of the relevant *Crimes Act*. Some of the law concerned is of decidedly recent vintage: legislation has come to Western Australia, Tasmania and the ACT only in the last decade. And, where reform began, in Victoria, it was not so much a step along the path of unstoppable progress as a collective stumble involving some with the best intentions and some with the worst, which the common law rather nimbly accommodated. Soon enough, those individuals went their separate ways, as if to emphasise the improbability of their initial alliances. Andrew Fraser remembers dining one night at Melbourne's Flower Drum with Belle Moran's boys Lewis and 'Tuppence' when Charlie Wyatt poked his head around the door. The Morans excused themselves, pursued their mother's former lover into the lane outside and beat him senseless. Yet, had it not been for Wyatt's defection to Wainer's cause, there might never have been the opportunity to demonstrate that bad laws make bad police.

The events of 1969 and 1970, too, slipped swiftly into history, allowing a generation to take for granted the accessibility of safe, legal abortion—but then, it is not uncommon for Australians to enjoy liberties they barely understand. This permitted a neglect of the story's lessons, in particular that the illegality of a good or service bound to be sought anyway usually means super profits for providers and avoidable suffering for consumers—something evinced daily in the 'war on drugs'. It has also let elected officialdom off the hook for decades since. It is staggering that laws with such widespread application—two in three Australian pregnancies are unplanned; one in three Australian women will have an abortion in their lifetime—have consumed so little legislative energy.

The proof of the Menhennitt Ruling has been in its longevity, but there are arguments for its renewal. Just as the old *Offences Against the Person Act* was devised in the pre-asepsis age when the 'procuring of a miscarriage' seriously endangered a mother's health, and was arguably made redundant by subsequent radical improvement in infection control, so too does the Menhennitt Ruling belong to a different era of foetal viability—and, indeed, of feminist consciousness. In so ruling, for example, Menhennitt accorded the doctor a primacy in decisions relating to abortion that no longer applies, and has consolidated bureaucratic influence. Dr Lachlan de Crespigny and ethics professor Julian Savulescu note: 'Abortion is one of the few medical interventions in which the doctor–patient relationship is regularly overridden by uninvolved third parties'.

So the campaign for 'abortion on request' or 'abortion on demand' continues, if neither phrase seems quite apposite. 'Abortion on request' still submits the woman to authority, furtively whispering: 'Please sir, may I have an abortion'. 'Abortion on demand' has an incongruously bullying edge. Sue Ingleton jokes: 'It's as though women walk in, bang their fist on a counter and say: "I demand my abortion!"' Likewise, as Germaine Greer observes, to describe abortion as a 'right' that was 'won' scarcely fits abortion's usual circumstances.

> What women 'won' was the 'right' to undergo invasive procedures in order to terminate unwanted pregnancies, unwanted not just by them but by their parents, their sexual partners, the governments who would not support mothers, the employers who would not employ mothers, the landlords who would not accept tenants with children, the schools that would not accept students with children. Historically the only thing pro-abortion agitation achieved was to make an illiberal establishment look far more feminist than it was.

The '*only* thing'? Greer's is a useful antidote to triumphalism but only a partial reading. What the legalising of abortion did was make rather less legally intimidating and somewhat less medically dangerous what remains a decision of often utmost difficulty—but that is not a negligible development. Consider Beth Wilson. Victoria's health services commissioner has a lifetime of tireless work for the community behind her, a life inflected by legalised abortion and Bert Wainer's clinic, of which she was an early patient. She very honestly relates a story in which no streets were skipped down.

> I left home at fifteen because my mum was what in the 1950s they called a 'deserted wife'. I was tired of walking round with huge holes in my shoes, so I worked in shops and factories, anything I could find. Then at twenty-one I went back to doing Higher School Certificate four nights a week while I worked in a frozen foods factory…

> Just a couple of weeks before the exam the girl on the night shift had a miscarriage. So I said: 'I'll do the double shift providing I can study at work.' So I'd be going out checking the level of chemicals in the dried peas, then racing back to study a bit more of the *Web of Life* which was our biology textbook. I was leaving work at midnight and coming back at 7am. Because I *dreamed* of going to university. I used to go past Monash and think: 'If only I could get in there. Even just for a year. It would be fantastic.' And when I passed my exams I took law because it was the longest possible course.

Wilson was ecstatic. Education would free her from the grind of menial labour, and spare her the ordeals her mother had faced. Then, in her third year, she found herself pregnant. She was devastated: all that hard work was in jeopardy. So was her relationship.

> I was with a partner who had been married, who had children but didn't want more. So I was utterly, utterly miserable. Because I *did* love that child. I *did* have those feelings that you get when you're pregnant. It wasn't at all what I'd expected. It was very emotional.
>
> I remember the day that I went to the clinic, someone was holding this little baby. I was looking at it, going: 'Oh my God, what a beautiful baby. *Look* at this beautiful baby. I've never *seen* such a beautiful baby.' This baby, at the very instant I was about to get rid of mine, took on these God-like characteristics.

Wilson struggled to surmount the experience. She developed a persona for the aborted foetus, calling it 'Sarah', and marking what would have been its birthday. Her relationship never recovered: 'From a woman's point of view, if you feel like the man you're making love with doesn't want you to bear his child, it's confronting and damaging to a relationship. When you're young you're romantic. Thank goodness'. She also found that this reaction isolated her from other feminists.

> A lot of feminists hated you for saying you had a negative experience of termination. They'd fought so hard to promote the woman's right to abortion, you were letting the team down if you said it had been hard. I remember being really told off by women who [had] gone in and taken abortion in their stride—y'know, ra-ra-ra. It wasn't like that for me.

But in separating a bad choice from a worse one, Wilson has never thought she got it wrong. Part of loving 'Sarah' was acknowledging the poor quality of life Wilson would have offered.

> The choice for me was between something that I had worked really hard my whole life for or losing it all to be a single mum for which I was too young, and didn't have the emotional or the financial support. So I was exceedingly grateful that Bert Wainer's clinic was there, and that it didn't have to be illegal as well, which would have added another layer of awfulness to the whole thing.

There were not quite five years between the abortions of Carolyn Jamieson and of Beth Wilson, yet they are separated by gulfs not just of outcome but of awareness and experience.

Acknowledgements

This book began as an article in *The Monthly* that would not stop growing, on a subject of which I had not previously even fantasised of writing. I owe my first thanks, therefore, to the magazine's editor, Sally Warhaft, who did not let the improbability of the idea stand in its way, and its proprietor, Morry Schwartz, a generous impresario.

Writing nonfiction, you soon grow to value generosity. There's not much in it for people to talk to or otherwise help you. You take advantage of their patience and understanding—and hope it's not too obvious. The following put up with long and, in many cases, multiple interviews for this book, and were very gracious about it: Peter Berman, Nicola Black, Brian Bourke, Dianne Bretherton, Candy Broad, Kevin Childs, Dr Ken Davidson, Beatrice Faust, Andrew Fraser, Justice Bill Gillard, Dr Robyn Gregory, Bob Haldane, Bruce Hanford, Gwen Harston, Corinne Heath nee Blackwell, Charles Hider, Sue Ingleton, Dr Eve Janover, Justice William Kaye, Justice Allan McDonald, Janice McIlree nee Wakely, Phil Opas QC, Dr Max Sizeland, John X Smith, Ralph Stavely, Peter Steedman, Bert and Ila Vanrenen, Dr Jo Wainer nee Richardson, Evan and Noela Whitton, Beth Wilson, Justice John Winneke, Dr Nicole Woodrow and Justice Sir John Young. SEK Hulme QC and Justice Michael Kirby were kind enough also to provide written memoirs of Cliff Menhennitt. Thanks, too, to Justice Elizabeth Hollingworth for suggesting them both.

Jo Wainer paid me the great compliment of permitting my access to the Wainer papers, which are deposited at the State Library of Victoria, having been lovingly catalogued by Robyn Gregory. Robyn also shared with me both the fruits and the shoots of her PhD research, which were altogether invaluable, and once we started yarning about our shared interest we became quite difficult to stop.

Much of the material for this book lay well off the beaten track, and certainly very well off the googled one. The Vanrenens, Ila and Bert, spared no effort in helping me, delving ever deeper into their garage to disinter long-lost files. Di Bretherton was kind enough to muster a big collection of correspondence and mementos of her father, Rodney, as was Helen Morris to lend me the unpublished two-volume autobiography of her father, Cedric Ralph. Janice McIlree shared relics and photographs of her relationship with Ken Davidson. I'm sure that Bruce Gardner at the Office of Public Prosecutions will rest content if he never hears my voice again, but I'm grateful for his assistance in accessing the boxes and boxes of court files I sought. Thanks also to Joe Saltalamacchia, prothonotary of the Supreme Court, and Ross Nankivell, senior legal officer at the Victorian Bar Council. For kindnesses too various to mention, thanks to Juliette Brodsky, Mark Finnane, Helen Garner, Madonna Grehan, Philippa Hawker, Noreen Megay, Deborah Robertson, Michelle Schwarz, Monique Schwarz and Terri-ann White.

The librarians and archivists who make research possible seldom go explicitly recognised, so I'd like to mention a few whose care and zeal was noted and appreciated: Lois McEvey, Paul Dee and David Flegg at the State Library of Victoria; Darren Watson and Laura Shannon at the National Archives of Australia; Caroline Oxley and Terry Claven at the Victorian Police Museum; Sue Fairbanks at University of Melbourne Archives; Patrick Condron at the Brownless Medical Library; James Butler at the Supreme Court Library; Anne-Marie Van de Ven at the Powerhouse Museum; and all the staff at the Registry of Births, Deaths and Marriages, and at the Public Records Office Victoria—except, perhaps, the surly and officious security guard at the latter's front desk.

It's been a pleasure to bring this book to fruition at Melbourne University Publishing. Foong Ling Kong was everything I could have hoped for in a commissioning editor—smart, dedicated, flexible, optimistic and honourable—and Paul Smitz gave the text attentive and effective treatment. Another MUP author, Pamela Bone, was a great friend to this book, as indeed she was to me for many years. She responded to an early draft with all the warmth and enthusiasm she showed everyone who knew her well. I miss her very much and salute her indomitable memory.

Inevitably, no-one had more to tolerate than my girlfriend, Charlotte Barker, who never wearied of discussing the subject, never complained of the time and energy expended in its pursuit, and never wavered in her belief in...well, me. When the going got grumpy, she was simply more patient and kind. As she is mine, Charlotte was this book's first and best friend; I dedicate it to her with deepest love and gratitude.

Bibliography

Papers (State Library of Victoria)

Bertram Barney Wainer (1928–87)

Papers (University of Melbourne Archives)

Records of the Progressive Reform Party (1970–71)

Papers (Private)

Artefacts and correspondence of Rodney Bretherton (held by Dianne Bretherton)

Clippings and correspondence related to *the Queen v Vanrenen* (held by Bert and Ila Vanrenen)

Reports

Interim Report on the Decline of the Birth Rate, National Health and Medical Research Council, Eighteenth Session, Canberra, 22–24 November 1944.

'Past Patterns, Future Directions': Victoria Police and the Problem of Corruption and Serious Misconduct, Office of Police Integrity, Government Printer, Melbourne, 2007.

Report of the Board of Inquiry into Allegations against Members of the Victoria Police Force, Government Printer, Melbourne, 1976.

Report of the Board of Inquiry into Allegations of Corruption in the Police Force in connection with Illegal Abortion Practices in the State of Victoria, Government Printer, Melbourne, 1971.

Report of the Royal Commissioner Appointed to Inquire into Off-the-Course Betting Together with Minutes of Evidence, Government Printer, Melbourne, 1959.

Report on the Victorian Police Force, Government Printer, Melbourne, 1971.

Royal Commission into the Decline in the Birth-Rate and Increased Mortality of Infants, Government Printer, Sydney, 1904.

Royal Commission on Human Relationships, Government Printer, Canberra, 1977.

Theses

Gregory, Dr Robyn V, Corrupt Cops, Crooked Docs, Prevaricating Pollies and 'Mad Radicals': A History of Abortion Law Reform in Victoria, 1959–1974, Thesis Collection, RMIT University Library, Melbourne, 2005.

Official Series

Victorian Law Reports
Victorian Parliamentary Debates

Court Records (National Archives)

Transcript of Evidence before Registrar in Bankruptcy of Stanley Charles Wyatt, 1963–75.
Stanley Charles Wyatt v The Queen, High Court of Australia, 1972.

Court Records (Office of Public Prosecution)

The Queen v Bayliss & Sizeland
The Queen v Bretherton & Dixon
The Queen v Crombie
The Queen v Davidson
The Queen v Fenton Bowen & Hickey
The Queen v Flynn
The Queen v Heath, Buchanan, Heales, Manser, Stuchberry & Grima
The Queen v Troup, Berman & Young
The Queen v Vanrenen

Police Service Records (Victorian Police Museum)

Frederick John Adam
Kevin John Carton
Jack Ralph Ford
Francis Gerald Holland
Martin Robert Jacobson
John Edward Matthews
William Wall Warner Mooney
Noel Edmund Joseph Murphy
Frederick Wenzel Russell
Gordon Albert Timmins
Stanley Charles Wyatt

Inquests (Victorian Public Records Office)

Mabel Ambrose
Olive Babaud

Zelma Bestwick
May Bourke
Norman Bradshaw
Elizabeth Bren
Mary Brown
Marla Buckstein
Sandra May Chamberlain
Daphne Clark
Bertha Coughlan
Ada Criutchett
Alice Dicker
Mary Douthat
Irene Fahey
Jane Flinn
Victor Grimshaw
Maria Gyemant
Janie Harrington
Mabel Hodgkinson
Kathleen Hudson
Carolyn Jamieson
Edith Kohlman
Dominique Kristaly
Vera Madden
Jane Mateer
Beryl Moreno
Hazel Morrell
Margaret Sarah Mould
Alberta Neal
Ada O'Neil
Jane O'Neill
Eva Pitt
Margaret Priest
Doris Sanderson
Vija Sprogis
Jean Taylor
Stella Tennant
Beryl Wallace

Books

Allen, Judith, *Sex & Secrets: Crimes Involving Australian Women Since 1880*, Oxford University Press, Melbourne, 1990.
Atwood, Margaret, *Surfacing*, Virago, London, 1994.

Baird, Barbara, *'I Had One Too...': An Oral History of Abortion in South Australia before 1970*, Women's Studies Unit, Flinders University, Bedford Park, 1990.
Barth, John, *The End of the Road*, Bantam Books, New York, 1983.
Beaney, James, *Dr. Beaney's Vindication : With Reflections on the Inquest Held upon the Body of Mary Lewis*, W. B. Stephens, Melbourne, 1866.
Bennett, John, *Abortion Law Reform*, Civil Liberties Publication, South Yarra, 1968.
Berman, Peggy with Kevin Childs, *Why Isn't She Dead!*, Gold Star Publications, Melbourne, 1972.
Blainey, Geoffrey, *Jumping over the Wheel*, Allen & Unwin, Melbourne, 1993.
Bourne, Aleck, *A Doctor's Creed: The Memoirs of a Gynaecologist*, Victor Gollancz, London, 1963.
Bowman, Margaret and Michelle Grattan, *Reformers: Shaping Australian Society from the 60s to the 80s*, Collins Dove, Burwood, 1989.
Brennan, TC, *The Gun Alley Tragedy*, Gordon & Gotch, Melbourne, 1922.
Bretherton, Rodney, *Abortion RU486: Anecdotes of Anguish and Hope*, self-published, Daylesford, 1997.
Briggs, Asa, *Victorian Cities*, Penguin, Harmondsworth, 1968.
'Caddie', *The Autobiography of a Sydney Barmaid*, Constable, London, 1953.
Calwell, Arthur, *Be Just and Fear Not*, O'Neil in association with Rigby, Hawthorn, 1972.
Cannold, Leslie, *The Abortion Myth: Feminism, Morality and the Hard Choices Women Make*, Allen & Unwin, St Leonards, 1998.
Cannon, Michael, *The Land Boomers*, Melbourne University Press, Carlton South, 1966.
Carr, Thomas, *Infanticide: Morality of Medical Practice*, republished from *Austral Light*, Melbourne, 1900.
Carter, Isabel, *Joan Rosanove QC: Woman in a Wig*, Lansdowne, Melbourne, 1970.
Coleman, Peter, *Obscenity, Blasphemy and Sedition: 100 Years of Censorship in Australia*, Angus & Robertson, Sydney, 1974.
Cusack, Dymphna, *Jungfrau*, The Bulletin, Sydney, 1936.
Dark, Eleanor, *Waterway*, Collins, London, 1938.
Davison, Graeme (ed.), *The Outcasts of Melbourne*, Allen & Unwin, Melbourne, 1985.
Devanny, Jean, *Dawn Beloved*, Macaulay, New York, 1928.
——*Riven*, Macaulay, New York, 1930.
——*The Virtuous Courtesan*, Macaulay, New York, 1935.
Didion, Joan, *Play It as It Lays*, Weidenfield and Nicholson, London, 1971.

Dower, Alan, *Crime Chemist*, Long, London [1965].
——*Deadline*, Hutchinson, Melbourne, 1979.
Drysdale, George, *The Elements of Social Science, or, Physical, Sexual, and Natural Religion / by a Graduate of Medicine*, E. Truelove, London, 1869.
Ferrier, Carole, *Jean Devanny: Romantic Revolutionary*, Melbourne University Press, Carlton, 1999.
Ferris, Paul, *The Nameless: Abortion in Britain Today*, Penguin, Harmondsworth, 1967.
Finch, Lynette, *The Classing Gaze: Sexuality, Class and Surveillance*, Allen & Unwin, St Leonards, 1993.
Finnane, Mark, *J. V. Barry: A Life*, UNSW Press, Sydney, 2007.
Fraser, Andrew, *Court in the Middle*, Hardie Grant, Melbourne, 2007.
Frydman, Gloria, *Protestors*, Collins Dove, Melbourne, 1987.
Fryer, Peter, *The Birth Controllers*, Secker & Warburg, London [1965].
Galbally, Frank, *Galbally!: The Autobiography of Australia's Top Criminal Lawyer*, Penguin, Ringwood, 1990.
Galbally, Frank with the assistance of Richard Shears and Isobelle Gidley, *Galbally for the Defence*, Viking, Ringwood, 1993.
Grimshaw, Patricia and Lynne Strahan, *The Half-Open Door: Sixteen Modern Australian Women Look at Professional Life and Achievement*, Hale & Iremonger, Sydney, 1982.
Grover, Monty, *Hold Page One: Memoirs of Montagu Grover, Editor*, Loch Haven Books, Main Ridge, 1993.
Haire, Norman, *Birth Control Methods (Contraception, Abortion, Sterilisation)*, G. Allen & Unwin, London, 1936.
——*Everyday Sex Problems*, F. Muller, London, 1948.
Haldane, Robert, *The People's Force: A History of the Victorian Police*, Melbourne University Press, Melbourne, 1995.
Hall, Ruth, *Dear Dr Stopes: Sex in the 1920s*, Deutsch, London, 1978.
Harwood, Gwen, *Collected Poems 1943–1995*, UQP, Brisbane, 2003.
Hickie, David, *The Prince and the Premier*, Angus & Robertson, London, 1985.
Hicks, Neville, *'This Sin & Scandal': Australia's Population Debate, 1891–1911*, Australian National University Press, Canberra, 1978.
Hurst, John, *The Walkley Awards: Australia's Best Journalists in Action*, John Kerr Pty Ltd, Richmond, 1988.
Irving, John, *The Cider House Rules*, Ballatine Books, New York, 1993.
Johnston, Marjorie with John Wippell, *Ansell: Portrait of an International Company*, Campbell Public Relations, Jolimont, 1990.
Knowlton, Charles, *The Fruits of Philosophy: An Essay on the Population Question*, Freethought Publishing Company, London, 1877.

Lake, Marilyn, *Getting Equal: The History of Australian Feminism*, Allen & Unwin, Sydney, 1978.
Latch, Brian with Bill Hitchings, *Mr X: Police Informer*, Dingo, Melbourne, 1975.
Loewenstein, Wendy, *Weevils in the Flour: An Oral Record of the 1930s Depression in Australia*, Hyland House, Melbourne, 1978.
Marshall, Audrey and Margaret McDonald, *The Many-Sided Triangle: Adoption in Australia*, Melbourne University Press, Melbourne, 2001.
Matthews, Jill Julius, *Good and Mad Women: The Historical Construction of Femininity in Twentieth-Century Australia*, Allen and Unwin, Sydney, 1984.
McCalman, Janet, *Sex and Suffering: Women's Health and a Women's Hospital*, Melbourne University Press, Melbourne, 1998.
——*Struggletown: Public and Private Life in Richmond 1900–1965*, Griffin Press, Melbourne, 1984.
McMichael, Tony (ed.), *Abortion, the Unenforceable Law: The Reality of Unwanted Pregnancy and Abortion in Australia*, Abortion Law Reform Association of Victoria, Carlton, 1972.
Moran, Herbert, *Viewless Winds: Being the Memoirs and Digressions of a Surgeon*, Peter Davies, London, 1939.
Morgan, Kevin, *Gun Alley: Murder, Lies and Failure of Justice*, Simon & Schuster, Pymble, 2005.
Murray, Robert, *The Split: Australian Labor in the 1950s*, F. W. Cheshire, Melbourne, 1970.
Park, Ruth, *Fishing in the Styx*, Penguin, Ringwood, 1994.
——*The Harp in the South*, Angus & Robertson, Sydney, 1948.
Pearl, Cyril, *The Wild Men of Sydney*, W. H. Allen, Sydney, 1958.
Pensabene, Tony, *The Rise of the Medical Practitioner in Victoria*, Australian National University Press, Canberra, 1981.
Piddington, Marion, *Tell Them! or the Second Stage of Mothercraft*, self-published, Sydney, 1925.
Prichard, Katherine Susannah, *Intimate Strangers*, Angus & Robertson, Sydney, 1937.
——*Winged Seeds*, Australasian Pub. Co. in association with Jonathan Cape, Sydney, 1950.
Ralph, Cedric, *Memoirs: The Pastime of Old Age*, 2 vols, self-published, Melbourne, 1993.
Reagan, Leslie, *When Abortion Was a Crime*, University of California Press, Berkeley, 1997.
Reeves, CE, *The Queen v. Beaney: Extraordinary Charge of Murder against a Medical Man, in Consequence of a Diseased Womb Being Ruptured after Death*, W. B. Stephens, Melbourne, 1866.

Reiger, Kerreen, *The Disenchantment of the Home: Modernizing the Australian Family 1880–1940*, Oxford University Press, Melbourne, 1985.
Richards, Michael, *The Hanged Man*, Scribe Publications, Carlton North, 2002.
Rout, Ettie, *Safe Marriage: A Return to Sanity*, William Heinemann, London, 1922.
Russell, Edna, *Bricks or Spirits? The Queen Victoria Hospital*, Australian Scholarly Publishing, Melbourne, 1997.
Ryan, Edna and Anne Conlon, *Gentle Invaders: Australian Women at Work 1788–1974*, Thomas Nelson, Sydney, 1975.
Siedlecky, Stefania and Diana Wyndham, *Populate and Perish: Australian Women's Fight for Birth Control*, Allen & Unwin, Sydney, 1990.
Stopes, Marie, *Married Love: A New Contribution to the Solution of Sex Difficulties*, A. C. Fifield, London, 1918.
Strahan, Lynne, *A Bay To Look On: A History of the Williamstown Hospital*, Williamstown Hospital, Williamstown, 1991.
Summers, Anne, *Damned Whores and God's Police: The Colonisation of Women in Australia*, Penguin, Ringwood, 1975.
——*Ducks on the Pond: An Autobiography 1945–1976*, Penguin, Melbourne, 2000.
Swain, Shurlee and Renate Howe, *Single Mothers and Their Children: Disposal, Punishment and Survival in Australia*, Cambridge University Press, Melbourne, 1995.
Tennant, Kylie, *Ride on Stranger*, Sirius, Sydney, 1945.
——*The Joyful Condemned*, Macmillan, London, 1953.
——*Tiburon*, The Bulletin, Sydney, 1935.
Tingwell, Charles and Peter Wilmoth, *Bud: A Life*, Pan MacMillan, Sydney, 2004.
Wainer, Bertram, *It Isn't Nice*, Alpha Books, Sydney, 1972.
Wainer, Jo (ed.), *Lost: Illegal Abortion Stories*, Melbourne University Publishing, 2006.
Wallace, VH, *The Wallace Story*, self-published, Hughesdale, 1973.
Walter, James and Margaret MacLeod, *The Citizens' Bargain: A Documentary History of Australian Views*, UNSW Press, Sydney, 2002.
White, Terri-ann and Linda Savage Davis, *Stories from Our Lives: Women's Experiences of Abortion*, Bequest of Megan Sassi/Abortion Law Reform Association (WA), Perth, 1994.
Whitton, Evan, *Amazing Scenes: Adventures of a Reptile of the Press*, Fairfax Library, Sydney, 1987.
Wilson, Rhonda, *Good Talk: The Extraordinary Lives of Ten Ordinary Australian Women*, McPhee Gribble, Fitzroy, 1984.

Wollstonecraft, Mary, *Maria or the Wrongs of Woman*, Norton, New York, 1975.
Wyles, Lilian, *A Woman at Scotland Yard: Reflections on the Struggles and Achievements of Thirty Years in the Metropolitan Police*, Faber, London [1952].
Yates, Richard, *Revolutionary Road*, Little Brown, London, 1961.

Journal Articles

Barry, J, 'The Law of Therapeutic Abortion', *Proceedings of the Medico-Legal Society of Victoria*, vol. 3, 1938, pp. 119–22.
Bretherton, Rodney, 'The Case for Abortion Law Reform', *Medical Journal of Australia*, vol. 2, no. 17, 25 October 1969, pp. 860–2.
Carthew, Zoe, '"She Had Not a Baby Face": The Death of Bertha Coughlan', *Provenance: The Journal of Public Record Office*, no. 5, September 2006.
Cica, Natasha, 'Abortion Law in Australia', Australian Parliamentary Library Research Paper, 1998.
de Crespigny, Lachlan J and Julian Savulescu, 'Abortion: Time to Clarify Australia's Confusing Laws', *Medical Journal of Australia*, vol. 181, 2004, pp. 201–3.
Faust, Beatrice, 'Abortion, Corruption, Doctors!', submission to Royal Commission on Human Relationships, 1975 (revised 2004–06).
Finch, Lynette and J Stratton, 'The Australian Working Class and the Practice of Abortion, 1880–1939', *Journal of Australian Studies*, no. 23, November 1988, pp. 45–64.
Hill, Arthur, 'Why Be Morbid? Paths of Progress in the Control of Obstetric Infection, 1931 to 1960', *Medical Journal of Australia*, 25 January 1964, p. 101.
Moore, Nicole, 'The Politics of Cliche: Sex, Class, and Abortion in Australian Realism', *MFS Modern Fiction Studies*, vol. 47, no. 1, Spring 2001, pp. 69–91.
Smyth, Brettena, 'Limitation of Offspring: Being the Substance of a Lecture Delivered in the North Melbourne Town Hall, and Elsewhere, to Large Audiences of Women Only', Melbourne, 1893.
Spencer, G, 'Pre-marital Pregnancies and Ex-Nuptial Births in Australia 1911–1966: A Comment', *Australian and New Zealand Journal of Sociology*, no. 5, October 1969, pp. 121–7.
Wainer, Jo and Bertram Wainer, 'Pathways to Abortion', Department of Sociology, La Trobe University, 1975.
Wood, Carl, N Shanmugan and E Meredith, 'The Risk of Pre-Marital Conception', *Medical Journal of Australia*, 2 August 1969, pp. 228–32.

Woodrow, Nicole, 'Termination Review Committees: Are They Necessary?', *Medical Journal of Australia*, vol. 179, 2003, pp. 92–4.

Newspapers and Periodicals

The Age, *The Argus*, *Australasian Medical Gazette*, *Australian Medical Journal*, *The Bulletin*, *The Courier-Mail*, *The Digger*, *The Herald*, *The Lancet*, *Medical Journal of Australia*, *Police Life*, *Smith's Weekly*, *The Sun*, *Sydney Morning Herald*, *Truth*

General Reference Works

500 Victorians
Australian Dictionary of Biography
Sands & McDougall directories (Melbourne)
Telephone directories (Melbourne)
Who's Who in Australia

Video Recordings

Abortion, Corruption and Cops: The Bertram Wainer Story, Film Australia Interest Program in association with John Moore Productions, Lindfield, 2005.

Index